THE NEW GOTHIC

EDITED BY BRADFORD MORROW AND PATRICK MCGRATH

"Eeriness abounds." —Washington Post Book World

THE NEW GOTHIC

EDITED BY BRADFORD MORROW AND PATRICK McGRATH

Today's most electrifying writers reanimate—and reinvent—the genre of Mary Shelley and Edgar Allan Poe.

Stories by: Kathy Acker • Martin Amis • Scott Bradfield • Angela Carter • Robert Coover • Janice Galloway • John Hawkes • Jamaica Kincaid • Patrick McGrath • Bradford Morrow • Yannick Murphy • Joyce Carol Oates • Ruth Rendell • Anne Rice • Peter Straub • Emma Tennant • Lynne Tillman • William T. Vollmann • Paul West • John Edgar Wideman • Jeanette Winterson

"Eeriness abounds."—*The Washington Post Book World*

"A welcome collection. Fans of more traditional supernatural thrills can rest assured that the walking dead are still among us." —*The New York Times Book Review**

NOW IN PAPERBACK ❖ VINTAGE BOOKS

CONJUNCTIONS

Bi-Annual Volumes of New Writing

Edited by
Bradford Morrow

Contributing Editors
Walter Abish
John Ashbery
Mei-mei Berssenbrugge
Guy Davenport
Elizabeth Frank
William H. Gass
Susan Howe
Kenneth Irby
Robert Kelly
Ann Lauterbach
Patrick McGrath
Nathaniel Tarn
Quincy Troupe
John Edgar Wideman

Bard College   *distributed by Random House, Inc.*

EDITOR: Bradford Morrow
MANAGING EDITOR: Dale Cotton
SENIOR EDITORS: Susan Bell, Martine Bellen, Karen Kelly,
    Kate Norment
ART EDITOR: Anthony McCall
ASSOCIATE EDITOR: Eric Darton
EDITORIAL ASSISTANTS: Alex London, Jennette Montalvo

CONJUNCTIONS is published in the Spring and Fall of each year by
Bard College, Annandale-on-Hudson, NY 12504. This issue is made
possible in part with the generous funding of the Lannan Foundation
and the New York State Council on the Arts.

Editorial communications should be sent to 33 West 9th Street, New
York, NY 10011. Unsolicited manuscripts cannot be returned unless
accompanied by a stamped, self-addressed envelope.

Distributed by Random House.

Cover art: "Rose," 1992, by Donald Baechler. Courtesy of the artist.
Cover design by Anthony McCall Associates, New York

SUBSCRIPTIONS. Send subscription order to CONJUNCTIONS, Bard
College, Annandale-on-Hudson, NY 12504. Single year (two volumes):
$18.00 for individuals; $25.00 for institutions and overseas. Two years
(four volumes): $32.00 for individuals; $45.00 for institutions and
overseas. Patron subscription (lifetime): $500.00. Overseas subscribers
please make payment by International Money Order. Back issues
available at $10.00 per copy.

Reproduction of John Adams score © 1991 by Hendon Music, Inc., a
Boosey & Hawkes Company.

Printers: Edwards Brothers.
Typesetter: Bill White, Typeworks.

ISSN 0278-2324
ISBN 0-679-74399-5

Manufactured in the United States of America.

TABLE OF CONTENTS

GUEST EDITOR'S NOTE

A BOOK BEFORE Satan's moment of triumph in *Paradise Lost*, with the terms of Eden set and the story of creation rehearsed, the angel Raphael cautions an overly curious Adam, who has asked about the spheres: "Be lowly wise:/ Think only what concerns thee and thy being;/ Dream not of other worlds, what creatures there/ Live, in what state, condition, or degree. . . ." Then, "cleared of doubt . . . and freed of intricacies," Adam returns for a time to his bower, the angel ascends and, with Miltonic inversion, advice filters in from paradise, through a messenger whose name hints at both the prospect of healing (*rapha-el* — God heals) and the early history of his health (*rapha'im* — Hades or Shades).

The authors of the work gathered here under the broad rubric of Other Worlds have each, with Eve, resisted such a message, choosing instead to explore the ironic particulars of its transmission. That exploration has led to a variety of approaches stylistically, and to distinctions of inquiry along horizontal and vertical axes. Some of the contributors are inclined to a religion of descent, and invert their cathedrals; others direct their spikes laterally, looking at love and related exactions; still others track the progress of spirit in its vault. Genres range from lyric and polemic to elegy, exegesis and spoof. The only thing the writing has in common, as I've seen it, is an emphasis on the important recognition of borders and a desire to approach, respect or cross them — theme enough for a confusing cultural moment, in which so many fertile minds seem neutralized.

Assembling this issue, I looked for work that moved *through* such confusion. The result is topical in that many of the pieces address contemporary phenomena such as homelessness, religious revival, the Gulf War, Columbus and the New World, "disconnection," reaction and experimentation in the arts, shifting political and sexual boundaries — in short, the lines behind which we sense each other daily or don't. From the start, however, I was drawn less to subject matter than to the compelling qualities of a writer's structural instinct, and in this light I factored in both chance-submission and Milton's notion that Earth, too, was an Other World in the mind of its maker.

More than perfunctory thanks are due to the following people for the help they offered as I collected material for this anthology: George Angel, Susan Bell, Lee Ann Brown, Elaine Lustig Cohen, Raymond Foye, Forrest Gander, Mirene Ghossein, Peter Gizzi, Eli Gottlieb, Adina Hoffman, Brian Kiteley, Robin Robertson, David Stern, Lewis Warsh, Eliot Weinberger, the CONJUNCTIONS staff, and especially Brad Morrow, who first raised the idea of this issue, then generously gave of his sabbatical time and his spirit.

— Peter Cole
October 4, 1992
San Francisco

From Perduta Gente
Peter Reading

— *Talk Terms Today*
OR REGRET IT FOR THE REST
OF YOUR LIFE

Now we arrive at the front of the ruin;
   here are there moanings,
shrieks, lamentations and dole,
here is there naught that illumes.
Mucky Preece lives in a pigsty beside the
   derelict L Barn,
   tetrous, pediculous, skint,
   swilling rough cider and Blue.
Now lie we sullenly here in the black mire —
   this hymn they gurgle,
being unable to speak.
Here they blaspheme Divine Power.
Money no object to buyer of L-shaped
   picturesque old barn
   seeking the quiet country life
(two hundred and twenty-two grand,
Property Pages last night —
with which Mucky Preece is involved,
scraping the squit from his arse).

———————

9

101

terribly sick with her meths, but
she kept on and on vomiting through
the night, but with nothing left to
sick up (the front of her scraggy
overcoat covered in the methsey,
vegetable - soupy slime — the
stench abominable) so that
between honks she screamed hor-
ribly. The only sleep we got was
after one of the old hands dragged
her off, still screaming, and dumped
her in the alley round the corner
where the dustbins are.
Today is _Monday_: in St. Batolph's
crypt they give out free clothes to us

Don't think it couldn't be you —
bankrupted, batty, bereft,
huddle of papers and rags in a cardboard
    spin-drier carton,
bottle-bank cocktails and Snow soporifics,
    meths analgesics,
beg-bucket rattler, no-hope no-homer,
    squatter in rat-pits,
busker in underground bogs
(plangent the harp-twang, the *Hwaet!*
Haggard, the youthful and handsome whom I
    loved in my nonage;
vanished, the vigor I valued;
roof-tree and cooking-hearth, sacked).
Bankrupted, batty, bereft —
don't think it couldn't be you.

———————

Worse than the Shakes is the Horrors — the rats and
    echoing voices . . .

    echoing voices
under the flyover, rubble and streets of
    boarded-up derries —
No Go for ambulance, fire-brigade, milkman,
    Post Office, Old Bill . . .

    when they demolished his sty
Mucky Preece, alias Tucker,
tramped from the sticks to the Borough —
his mother was only a gippo,
his only possession a bucket . . .

sometimes it seems like a terrible dream, in
which we are crouching
gagged, disregarded, unsought
in dosshouses, derries and spikes,
and from which we shall awake,

mostly it seems, though, we won't.

––––––––––

How doeth the citie sit solitarie that
was full of people?
She that was great among nations hath no
comforter, all her
friends haue dealt treacherously.

Something is in the air, more and more nutters,
alcos and dossers,
dole diuturnal.

Sometimes it seems like a terrible dream from
which we'll awaken;
but mostly it seems that we won't.

Let us descend, though, through urinous subways to
miseries greater,
al doloroso ospizio, where the
newly tormented
sample new torments.

Woe vnto them that decree
vnrighteous decrees and that turn
the needy from iustice and robbe
the rights from the poore of my people.

What will ye doe with yr wealth
in the day of the storme which shall come
from afarre, when all that remaines
is to crouch with those ye haue oppressed?

––––––––––

Week of continuous Blue,
total amnesia, no recollection of
        date or condition,
    skipper or kiphouse or spike,
    contusion and blood on the scalp,
    spew, epilation, the squits,
sight as through flawed glass, misted, contorted,
        nuns from St Mungo's
    doling out dry bread and soup,
    Mucky Preece skinning a cat
    (bashed-in its head with a brick)
    to add to the vegetal stew
    bubbling up in the bucket,
swayingly unzips and waggles his penis,
        smirched with the cat's gore,
    urinates into the face of a Blessed
        Sister of Mercy.

    [And don't think it couldn't be *you*:
grievously wounded veteran of the
        Battle of Bottle,
    jobless, bereft of home, skint,
down in the cold uriniferous subway
        spattered with drooled spawl,
lying in layers of newspaper ironies —
        Property Prices,
smug To the Editor platitudes on The
        Vagrancy Issue,
        ads for Gonzalez Byass;
dosser with Top Man carrier-bag, en-
        swathed in an *FT*;
Gizzera quiddora fiftyfer fuggsay,
        bankrupted, I been,
    fugginwell bankrupted, me;
    dolent, the wail from the Tube;
    and don't think it couldn't be *you*.]

Legions of comatose owners of nothing
　　under the concrete
arches are juddered awake,
impotent, dolent, bereft —

radioactive spent rods,
bound for reprocessing from the reactors,
　　carried in finned flasks,
rumble by railway by night through a city
　　hugely unconscious.
Nothing can ever be done;
things are intractably thus;
knowing the bite of grief, all will be brought to
　　destiny's issue;
those having precognition suffer
　　sorrow beforehand.

Grief-bitten impotent owners of nothing,
　　holding opinions
gagged, disregarded, unsought.

———————

Carrying on as though nothing is wrong is
　　what we are good at:
incontrovertible end;
shrieks, lamentations and dole;
lost livers, roof-trees and hearths;
on the waste ground at the back of the factory
　　there's a crone scumbag
that kips in a big cardboard box,
etiolated and crushed;
those having precognition suffer
　　madness beforehand
(**Efforts are now being made to encase in
　　concrete the . . .**); meanwhile,
here is a factory daily producing
　　thousands of badges
emblazoned with **Have a Nice Day.**

On Saving History
Fanny Howe

About saving history, Karl Rahner wrote:
"This concept is based on the theological assumption
that people have to hope for and accept grace
within history and that grace itself
is historical, and that history itself
— with all it involves — like the unity of humanity —
is grace."

Out of this concept, then, comes another:
that there is a secondary history — a record
of those exceptional revelation experiences that happen
both collectively and individually
to people throughout time.

The concept of saving history remains undeveloped
in developed Catholic theology
and is most discussed in underdeveloped countries
as an aspect of "liberation theology."

Meantime, profane history is the one
that is taught and written about; it is experienced
as palpable, visible, measurable, and hostile.

Saving history makes no distinction between nature
and numinous. One famous instance
in saving — or salvation — history is the encounter
between Moses and Yahweh.
Another is the chariot vision of Ezekiel.
And a third is the Annunciation, when the angel
appeared to Mary and she responded, "Let it be."
All of these events occurred without witnesses,
but two of them at least
are believed to belong in ordinary time.

Many people have doubted Mary's story
about the angel, just as the apostles denounced
and doubted Mary Magdalene when she announced
that she had just encountered Jesus
at the mouth of his tomb.
Experiences of a mystical, or salvific, nature,
when they occur to women solitaries,
need to be written down to be believed —
as they so often were, in Medieval cloisters.

Invisibility is a frequent feature
in the revelation experience. Either one person alone
is a witness — or a group of people who are considered
worthless — children, lunatics — have it.
But even conceptually
invisibility is critical to the experience
of revelation.

What we want to protect, from one day to the next,
is the site of the invisible: the defunct body.
Where liberation theology takes form
is where people are so reduced by the force
of others more fortunate than themselves
that they know that they are like chattel
or cattle in terms of their worth.

No amount of tender rhetoric — "We are all human" —
can keep them safe
from the determinations of the powerful.
What defense can a person
put up against the tyranny of reason?
Only one: saving history which is hidden.

Invisibility has something in common with interiority,
when perspectives are moved around.
My interior life (the secret dreams and ideas
that root around the edges of my skin)
is visible to me.
It is illuminated — a mirror of the world
I can gaze into, with my eyes closed.
But your interior life is invisible to me.
What I see, and measure of you is gesture.

Why not kill what I can evaluate?
Invisible history answers this difficult question
by giving a response outside the realm
of the reasonable. If you kill
what you can measure, then you are also killing
something you have in common with your victim:
transparent visions.

Profane history has never been able to answer the question:
Why not kill?
Because within the parameters of reason and materiality
there is always a way to justify murder.
The only escape from the problem
is to escape from the parameters that evaluate
life on earth economically
and to construct a secondary history, a common area
that has no boundaries.

This area is a given.
But like the world history of resistance
movements, it isn't acknowledged in the core curriculum.
Those who do acknowledge it wholeheartedly
tend to live in underdeveloped countries
where they are treated as tools, or scum.
Or else they are women (mothers, solitaries, religious)
who are unable to collaborate
with those who are comfortable inside
the parameters of reason and materiality.

All of these people have a way
of mucking up the plans of the forceful. They
are viewed as problematic, if not disposable,
because they don't grasp the necessity of numbering
the visible. (But they keep being born.)

In the literature to date
on liberation theology, there is a place
for saving history. It shares with profane history
an apocalyptic vision of humanity
and only there (at the end) do the two perspectives
merge like parallel lines

in infinity. Until then there is this experience
of unreconcilable activity —
between an interior life which is invisible,
and a visible life which is extinguishable.
It would be good to know them
as one and the same.

From Out With The Stars
James Purdy

HAROLD RESZKE had almost blindingly blue eyes, a strong nose with flaring nostrils and a kind of cornsheaf of billowing yellow hair. His arms, always on the massive side, had become Herculean by reason of his using a crutch to hold up his considerable frame and weight. He smarted continually from his injury, for he had been somewhat of an athlete. He motioned Val to the piano stool as his only greeting.

Sitting stiffly before the keyboard, Val could hear dishes being moved about in the kitchen, and water running, then sighs and sniffles, followed by a kind of grumbling.

Harold rose with injured dignity from the chair beside the piano stool and banged closed the door from which the dishwashing sound had arisen.

"Now play me your latest song, will you please," Harold commanded.

Val plunged in. Harold closed his eyes, and his head moved dramatically in time with the music. Then all at once, he cried, "Stop there, Mr. Sturgis. What are you changing keys for and what is the meaning of this section?" He pointed bellicosely with his crutch to the keyboard.

"Ah," Val sighed, remembering what Abner had found at fault with his music.

"Aren't you saying too much, and have you not made a detour from your opening section, Mr. Sturgis?"

"Please call me Val."

"We will see," Harold said, and he began writing some notes down on a piece of music paper.

At that moment Laetitia entered, and stared lengthily at the newcomer. Val turned a languid look toward her, and nodded.

She wiped her sudsy hands on her apron, scowled and hurried from the room.

"Now, Mr. Sturgis," Harold was so majestic and handsome at that moment, Val lost all train of thought, but a blow from the

19

crutch on the floor by his leg brought him back to harmony and counterpoint.

"Sit over here," Harold Reszke ordered Val.

Val sat in a chair as far away from Harold as he could, for he remembered Abner's warning and the scowling look Laetitia Reszke had given him dampened his spirit.

"Well, what are you doing ten feet away, sir," the teacher raised his voice. "I want to go over your new song which Mr. Blossom sent me the other day. I've jotted down a few things here for us to go over together."

In his confused state Val could barely decipher what Harold had written down for him to read.

"This is a very beautiful passage here," Harold Reszke pointed to the second page of the score. "You've set this for soprano of course."

Val nodded. He could feel the teacher's breath touching his hair.

"I didn't mean to shout at you just a few minutes ago," Harold Reszke apologized. "Let me tell you sir, you do have talent, just as Mr. Blossom has testified. Maybe more even . . . But look here now."

The teacher inquired why Val had put such a long part for the piano at the end of the song.

"Would you consider abbreviating that section perhaps, or do you even want such a long piano finale there. Do you see what I mean?"

Val was aware then that the teacher had placed his large powerful left hand uncomfortably on Val's shoulder. Harold Reszke went on then pointing out here and there notes which he thought could be changed, or best omitted.

"You could very easily transpose this beautiful song for the male voice one day." Harold spoke throatily and his left hand with the wedding ring handed back the sheet music to the composer. Then moving violently in his chair Harold got out, "Will you work then, sir, on the changes I have suggested?"

Val nodded painfully, overcome with gratification. He had found someone who both encouraged him and yet held him to the only discipline he had ever known.

"Are you sure you heard what I just said to you?" Harold demanded in his booming voice.

Val nodded and choked out a "*yes.*"

As Val gathered up his sheet music he came then face to face with his teacher. All at once standing without his crutch the teacher by reason of his great height and the strength of his arms gave the impression he was towering above the younger man as if on some raised platform, such as one saw in music dramas.

Harold grasped Val by the shoulders, almost shaking him.

"Come tomorrow," the teacher said in a voice loud enough to be heard in the next room.

"Let me tell you again, Val," the teacher went on. "You have a real talent — a true gift. Nourish it, live by it — do you hear me?"

Motionless, unable to respond just then, Val could only look into the eyes of Reszke.

"Come tomorrow, and bring the corrections," Harold resumed his stern almost angry tone.

Babbling thanks, confounded by such praise and kindness, Val rushed out of the room.

In the hallway leading down to the front stairs, Val dropped all of his music. Hurriedly stooping down, hands trembling, he began trying to gather up the sheets of music in order to put them into his attaché case.

All at once he could hear Laetitia's voice raised in a kind of fury. "Do we have to have someone like that traipsing in here?" Harold Reszke's wife shouted. "Are we that hard up now? I might have known, any pupil of that old pederast Abner Blossom would be paying court to you! The minute my back is turned, and you are all by yourself!"

All at once Harold could be heard shouting wildly, and his shouts were followed by squeals and whines from Laetitia as Harold slapped her. Val crept on down the stairs. At the front door he paused. He was out of breath and so confused he hardly knew in what direction to turn to take the way back to Grove Street.

Going home Val began to come out of his conflicting feelings about his afternoon with Harold Reszke. All at once it became clear: he had found in this teacher someone who would both encourage him to compose and who would also correct his faults and discipline his talent. He felt a deep gratefulness to Abner Blossom for having introduced him to Harold, and the unpleasantness of Laetitia's outburst was forgotten. He could hardly wait now to share his good news with Hugh Medairy. Though Hugh was, he feared, a bit jealous of Val's burgeoning talent, he could always count on his roommate to share his happiness and good luck.

In his excitement at the door of the flat, he dropped his keys several times before he could put them in the lock. Opening the door at last he rushed in. He was about to call Hugh's name, but there was a kind of indefinable but palpable change in the room's atmosphere. There was even a different smell as if he had opened the door to someone else's apartment.

He put down his attaché case and his keys and stood looking about him.

"Ah, well," he spoke like someone explaining the change to another person.

All the valises, hatboxes, packages were gone. The apartment itself looked nearly vacant except for the upright piano.

Going toward the tiny kitchen, Val sat down heavily and loosened his tie. His feet hurt from the long walk and he removed his shoes.

Hugh had finally gone! A hurt like that from some sharp instrument against his chest drew a kind of faint sound from his tense mouth and jaw, a sound he had never heard himself make before. Yes, he had known of course that Hugh would leave, but he had never believed it until now. His oldest, most dependable friend had deserted him.

He felt at that moment he had no one in the world.

Then on the big deal table he caught sight of an envelope with his name in Hugh's handwriting. The envelope had not been sealed, and a note on expensive stationery fell out. Val read:

> I will never forget our years together, will never forget
> you, Val. I will always care. But my own unhappiness
> with you was beginning to make me lose my deep love
> and appreciation for you. Do you understand, dear friend.
> Call me at the following number and address.

The notepaper fell from Val's hands. Looking about he saw that it was past evening now, the deep night of the city was everywhere.

He did not bother to light the center light.

Lethargically he picked up the notepaper and stared at the message. His boyhood, perhaps his youth even, was over. They had come to the Great City, Hugh and he, to make their fortune. A choking sorrow and depression came over him.

Then he thought of Harold Reszke, as the only light at the moment in such sorrow.

Leaving the apartment he began walking toward West Street in the direction of the water. Some of the street lights had gone out, making the night truly oppressive and black. Before he knew it he was standing on the docks, which people in that neighborhood called Suicide Docks.

The thought of suicide was not new to Val. His and Hugh's life had been nearly unendurable at times, never easy. Then he thought of Harold Reszke's encouragement, and he thought also of Abner Blossom's kindness. He looked at the still, black water, then turning abruptly he made his way back to his empty flat.

From that day on, Val Sturgis did nothing but compose. Sometimes he stayed up all night, falling exhausted when the early morning light streamed into his Grove Street flat.

He put away the photo of Hugh Medairy, taken by Cyril Vane.

Every day except Sunday now he came to Harold's place and showed him his new songs. Harold would sit down at the grand piano and play them. Sometimes he would stare at Val in a kind of stunned wonderment.

"You wrote all these since you have been coming here?" Harold would always repeat this statement. Then he would smile slowly and shake his head.

Val wondered where Laetitia was now during their lessons, but had not the courage to inquire. His relationship with Harold was becoming strained, which reminded him of his last days with Hugh. He wondered what he would do if Harold would suddenly also close the door on him and there would be no more lessons and who knows perhaps he would write no more songs.

One day almost out of the blue while Harold was going over one of the songs he had written the day before, Val blurted out: "Do you know, sir, that Mr. Blossom is writing a full-length opera."

Harold put down the sheet music and looked at his pupil with a half-humorous, half-baffled expression.

"What is the subject — do you know?"

"The subject," Val spoke with embarrassment and a flush spread over his face. "I'll try to explain. . . . A while back I found a libretto. It had no clue on it as to its author or when it was written. It was in very bad condition. I read it with fascination. Then, absent-mindedly, one day I left it behind at Mr. Blossom's." Val stopped, fearing he was giving away a secret.

"Go on," Harold said, and rising, not bothering to use his crutch, he came over and sat beside the song composer.

"Mr. Blossom was even more taken with the libretto than I had been. He began then immediately writing his own libretto based on the one I had found."

23

"But what is the subject — I asked you," Harold evidenced impatience and growing irritation.

"I don't know I should tell you."

Harold made a sound of extreme displeasure and Val recalled the furious anger he had shown toward his wife on Val's first visit to the Reszkes'.

"It concerns the photographer Cyril Vane."

"Cyril Vane!" Harold gasped and his face took on an entirely different color and expression, the veins in his eyelids appeared flushed and his lips closed tightly about his teeth.

"How on earth did you ever hear of him?" Harold spoke softly now, perhaps trying to control his emotion.

"I was photographed by him," Val said.

Harold had gone rather pale in contrast with the flushed color of his face a few moments before. "Go on," he said in an almost inaudible tone.

"That's all there is to it; Mr. Blossom thought my roommate and I should have some good photos, so we went to Mr. Vane's studio."

"And your roommate has left you, I believe you told me last time."

Val nodded.

"I am surprised that Mr. Blossom would send a young man like you to meet Cyril Vane." Harold had regained his composure, but he had taken on a distant, formal, almost hostile calm.

"Anyhow you have your songs," Harold said at last. "Nothing, nobody should be able to take away your talent."

"Excuse me, Harold," Val began, still uneasy he had permission to call his teacher by his first name.

"Yes," Harold encouraged him when the song composer failed to go on with what he was saying.

"Did you also know Mr. Vane perhaps?"

Harold colored again.

"I met him in Paris years ago. Before I was married."

"And did he photograph you also?" Val spoke in a kind of whisper.

Harold nodded, and then rising, reaching awkwardly for his crutch, he sat down at the piano. He began playing Val's latest song. After he had finished, Harold turned to his pupil: "These last songs have something deeper in them, Val. You are growing right before my eyes! It's incredible! Do you realize what you are doing? Of course not! Listen, go home and write me something new, do you hear. Write another song."

Harold Reszke looked at the wall clock, indicating the lesson was over.

In saying goodbye today, Harold took Val's hand in his and pressed it painfully, holding it a long time.

"What does anything matter to a man who has your talent," the teacher said, bidding him a final goodbye.

In the days that followed, Val Sturgis did nothing but compose. Sitting at the piano he first of all played anything which came into his mind, and then when he had hit on something which he felt expressed everything he was feeling, everything perhaps which he had ever felt, he took out his music paper and frantically tried to put down all the notes which had been pouring out of him as he sat at his broken-down piano.

He wrote for hours, and then looking back on what he had written he went to a messenger service and had the new song sent at once to Harold Reszke.

The next day a similar thing had happened. Whether it was Hugh Mediary's having deserted him or Harold Reszke's amazing encouragement and kindness, he was in a kind of delirium of work, possessed of an energy which appeared to have no cessation.

During the early morning hours he played what he was feeling, letting his fingers find by themselves what his own words and heart did not dare tell. Then he would rush to his music paper and attempt to write down all he had heard come from the keys of his wretched piano.

Again he would take the manuscript and send it to Harold by messenger.

Worn out then he would lie down on an old mattress placed upon the floor and look up at the high ceiling. Then in utter exhaustion he would fall fast asleep and sleep on for twelve or fourteen hours.

One evening as Val was brooding and drinking cup after cup of the Arabian coffee sent him by Cyril Vane, he heard a very faint tapping at his door. Thinking it probably was the man who cleaned the halls occasionally, he paid no attention. The tapping became louder then and more insistent.

Dragging himself to the door, he asked in an irritable tone who it was.

Harold's voice replied.

25

Val flung open the door.

Harold came in without a word, and sat down at the piano.

He played a few chords and smiled.

"Did you read what I composed?" Val watched his visitor with growing uneasiness.

"So this is where you live, and have your being." Harold then brought out from his satchel the songs which Val had sent him by messenger.

Val stared at the manuscripts.

"Don't pretend you don't know what they are worth, Val," Harold spoke. "I played them myself on the piano. Played them is not the word I guess. Anyhow I have lived with them from the day they arrived. They are not only beautiful, Val, they are faultless."

"Faultless," Val repeated. He sat down beside his teacher.

"Do you have anything to drink?" Harold wondered. He wiped his forehead with a cloth he took from his hip pocket. "Managing this damned crutch up all those stairs," he muttered.

"I have some brandy, Harold."

"Brandy will be just the ticket."

Val brought out one of the bottles of French cognac which Cyril Vane had bestowed on him and two glasses.

"Ice?" Val tried to keep his voice from quavering.

"Don't bother." Harold opened the brandy bottle and poured the two glasses. "Val, listen to me. Listen carefully. Tell me, have I given you something?"

"Given me something." The composer looked away. "What a question." He drank hurriedly from his glass. "You've been my salvation after Hugh left. You've. . . ."

"I hoped you wrote these latest songs because of our — friendship."

"Friendship, Harold! I think you must be my Muse."

This remark appeared to trouble Harold Reszke. He poured himself another cognac.

"Val, play close mind now to what I am going to say. I am not your Muse. Maybe I awakened her perhaps. But you have your Muse. You don't need me, Val. You don't need anybody. Don't you understand? I believe maybe you don't. No matter. Val, you have your whole life and career stretching before you. You don't need me. Look what I am." He stared wildly at his crutch. "I might have been your Muse once in Paris, but there is such a thing as destiny."

"Thank God you liked the songs, Harold." Val felt a growing apprehension, and he made this remark only to prepare himself for what he felt was some fearful pronouncement from his teacher.

"*Like* is a pallid word for what I felt. You have brought back to me my own youth and hopes. When I played your songs I thought I had written them . . . in Paris. The truth is I will never write anything again."

Harold stood up shakily.

"Do you have any coffee?" the teacher wondered, and took up his crutch. "Make some, will you, while I use your WC."

Val stood for a while in a vortex of conflicting feelings. He knew something more was going to be said, something as shattering as Hugh Medairy's farewell note. Turning to his small stove, he put the water on to boil, and measured out the tablespoons of Arabian coffee. The brew was ready when Harold returned.

"No cream," the teacher spoke in his old severe tone.

They drank the black coffee for a lengthy while in silence, and Val rose at last and made another pot.

"What do you want to tell me, Harold?" Val said brokenly.

"I know you know, Val," Harold said. "Wait until you are married," he added.

"I will never be married, Harold. You must know that."

"No one knows that," Harold said. "How can I tell you?"

"Please just say it. You're hurting me too deeply in postponing your message."

"Message?" Harold scoffed. "See here, Val! I cannot go on being your teacher. Don't ask me why. Don't. . . ." Harold began to rise.

"Sit down," Val spoke in a manner and voice Harold had never observed before. "You don't need to tell me why but don't go. Wait until I have quieted down."

"Do you think if I didn't need this," Harold struck at his crutch, "do you think if I was what I was in Paris, I would be telling you I can't teach you any more? But you're not looking at the young composer Harold Reszke, the one both Cyril Vane and Abner Blossom were so taken with and whom Cyril Vane photographed. No, you're looking at somebody else, somebody I don't even know or care about."

"But you can't just end our friendship like this. I mean — "

"Friendship is a pretty poor word for it, Val."

"And I don't know what I'll do if you won't see me and hear my music."

"I've told you what it is, Val, but you don't understand. It's her, it's Laetitia. She's all I have and she won't let me share her love

27

with anyone else."

"But it's more than love, isn't it?"

"That makes it all the worse then."

But gradually, even as they spoke, Val Sturgis was retreating from his teacher. It seemed later to Val that he had moved into another room as the teacher was choking out his explanation, his apology, his farewell, his washing of his hands of him. Like Hugh Medairy he was vanishing before Val Sturgis' eyes, and Val Sturgis was already moving to a world Harold had once hoped to reach but had lost and then abandoned.

They embraced a long time at the door.

Coming back into the empty room, Val looked down at the sheets of music his teacher had brought to him.

"Everything in my life is a succession of goodbyes," Val said. He looked over at the piano. He picked up one of the imported bonbons from Mr. Vane and let it melt on his tongue.

Then he sat down at the piano and let his hands crash down on the keys. His head fell over his hands. He was too hurt to weep.

The River
Eliot Weinberger

HAVING DESTROYED the Indus valley cities of Harappa and Mo-henjo-daro, the tribes of warrior-shepherds we call the Aryans moved eastward into the Punjab and the foothills of the Himalayas. There, around 1500 B.C., in small villages — they hated cities — on the fertile banks of the Sarasvati River, the Aryan priests com-posed the sacred hymns, historical chronicles, mythological narra-tives and prescriptions for ritual now known as the Vedas.

In the early Vedas, the Sarasvati, not surprisingly, was the literal and figurative life-source of the people: mother, goddess, vehicle for trade, origin of gold, metaphor for blood, sap, milk and semen. Within 500 years, however, that fountain of life had dried up, com-pletely disappeared, and the Aryans migrated further east, to two other great rivers, the Yamuna and the Ganga (Ganges).

By 900 B.C. — the time of the later Vedas and the mythological treatises the *Brahmanas* — the vanished river had become both the lost river of memory and nostalgia, and a quite real, but now in-visible, body of water. The confluence of the three rivers — Ganga, Yamuna and Sarasvati, representing heaven, earth and the under-world — is still celebrated in Allahabad, where it is believed that the third river becomes visible to the enlightened.

Simultaneous to her geographical and mythological disappear-ance, Sarasvati, the river and the river goddess, had yet another transformation. She became, and remains today, the mother of poetry.

The modern has been the great age of an invented and generalized archaic, our poetry and all the arts filled with evocations and the bric-a-brac of ancient civilizations and the contemporary indige-nous peoples we consider as still living the ancient ways. The archaic has been our escape from the monstrosities of the century; in the words (and antique spelling) of Ezra Pound: "Only antient wisdom is/ solace to man's miseries." And more than solace: There has been a secret belief that if we could only untangle the mysteries

29

of what happened at the beginning — the origins of the universe, of mankind, of speech, of society, of cities — that if we could recover the beginning of the story, we could start it over again, correcting the evident mistakes that have brought us here.

Guy Davenport has written that "What was most modern in our times was what was most archaic." But more: What was most archaic was the longing for the archaic. For poetry — to speak only of poetry — regardless when, rises and has always risen from that vanished, sometimes banished river. At the most archaic (surviving) moment of every literature is a celebration of, or a nostalgia for, their own archaic.

In the beginning is the invention of the beginning. Every society has its epic, its "tale of the tribe," its invention of "us." In many ways, there is no "us" until "us" has created its own poetry. And it always begins at the beginning: the origin of the universe, followed in turn by an age of gods (now lost and usually lamented), the creation of man and the founding of one's own people, who are celebrated for their rites and accomplishments (ancient valorization for current practices), their legendary or historical heroes. There are descents to the kingdom of the dead to learn the wisdom of "our" departed. And, most important, there is the definition of "us" by contrast to the (usually subjugated) "others." That description of the "others" is, however propagandistic, the first ethnography, the admission of the alien into the discourse, the beginning of the continuing nourishing of a culture.

When a literature shifts from oral to written, from collective to individual and undated to dated authorship, this function shifts from a definition of a timeless "us" to a definition of "us in the present" — the way we live now — as imagined by its writer. And, in the parallelism that is the dominant form of nearly all early poetry, the present is always, as might be expected, yoked to the past. It is a present that is either wanting (we have lost the river) or, at best, unstable (we may have our river, but someday it too will be lost) — an instability that is implicit even in moments of glory.

Sarasvati, pure water. Sarasvati dressed in white, her faced rubbed white with sandalwood paste. The brightness of a thousand moons. Sarasvati astride her swan. Sarasvati who never marries. Sarasvati seated on a white lotus, floating above the mud of the world. Sarasvati, a blank page.

Small wonder that Pound's lines are themselves "antient wisdom." They come from his translation of the earliest surviving ethnopoetics anthology, the *Shih Ching*, the Book of Odes or Songs, and their guiding spirit, Confucius, is not only the most ancient (of whom we have records), but also the quintessential inventor of the archaic.

The 305 anonymous songs of the *Shih Ching* are a selection, reputedly made by Confucius himself, from a collection of over 3000. At the time the anthology was edited, around 500 B.C., these songs were already at least 300 to 700 years old. (They had originally been collected for the Chou emperors as a way for the central government to find out what the people were thinking.) As they were gathered from all over China, many of them had to be translated from their local dialects, or otherwise adjusted so that their melodies would fit the standard Chinese of the time.

The purpose of the *Shih Ching* is, in certain ways, similar to Johann Gottfried Herder's *Volkslieder* (1778) or Jerome Rothenberg's *Technicians of the Sacred* (1967) — to take two other famous anthologies of the "primitive." All three attempted a recovery of the wisdom of the "folk," the archaic "us," and both Rothenberg and Confucius — across their millennia — were presenting models *for use* of how poetry could be written. Furthermore, all three were self-consciously oppositional: Herder and Rothenberg to the prevailing classical canons (one in the service of German nationalism, the other to present an alternate lineage for modernism), Confucius and Herder to the decadence of the present. All three books were not anthologies in the original sense of the word — a gathering of the prettiest flowers in the field — but rather attempts to grasp and hold on to a small piece of that which was receding.

Once there were sounds that created the world, that could change the world. For some, the sounds were the names of gods. In the beginning was the Word, the Maya gods standing in the water, in darkness, Beckett characters talking the world into being. The Kabbalists claimed that the entire Torah was the name of God — who could say it all at once? The Vedas, similarly, are a transcription, a translation, a dilution of a single syllable that was elaborated by Viyasa, their mythical creator.

Prayer, chant, mantra, formula, poem: concentrated, rhythmical speech: Olson's "construct of energy." All attempt to recover that original force of sound. Metaphor: a circumvention of taboo

31

sounds, the only way to name the unnameable. God: the metaphor for God.

Confucius' anthology remained the central book of Chinese poetry for 2500 years, until the birth of the Republic in the beginning of this century. (It survived the book-burnings of the third century B.C. because it had been memorized by so many.) Not only as an image-bank and a catalogue of prosodic models, its intrinsic relation to the past itself dominated the poetry for those millennia.

For Confucius, a human ancestor is a divinity, and the past represents the achievement of a terrestrial order (reflective of the cosmic order) which has never again been accomplished, but *could be*. The past is a present absence, an object of desire. Moreover, it is an object of desire that is manifest in objects, remnants, relics. Chinese poetry, both early and late, is full of meditations on ruins. There are hundreds of poems about finding some artifact from the past, and thousands about remembering, and remembering those who, in history, are famous for remembering.

The Chinese poet, in his or her most typical persona, is alone somewhere in the Empire: in exile, on a government mission to the provinces, in religious seclusion, or — for a woman — at home, with her lover or husband away. It is a metaphor for the individual in the vastness of history. A product of separation, the Chinese poem was conceived as a fragment, a work that is permanently — like the final hexagram of the *I Ching* — "before completion." There are no Chinese epics — the closest it gets is the *T'ien wen*, a book of questions without answers — and the Chinese lyric always deliberately says less than it could. Even within the individual lines of the lyric fragment there are so-called "empty" (meaningless) words, through which the *ch'i* (the breath or the spirit) is meant to circulate through the poem, like wind in a ruins. And classical literary Chinese itself is so condensed that there are (particularly for Westerners) enormous gaps between the words — gaps that must be mentally filled, like broken pieces of cuneiform.

The English Romantics, following Volney, saw ruins as an allegorical emblem for the rise and fall of empires, the transience of human works and the permanence of nature. They, like the Chinese, saw ruins as a triumph of chaos over order, which, unlike the Chinese, they further extrapolated into a mind-heart dichotomy. The Imagists — with their preference, unlike the Renaissance, for an unrestored Hellenism — proclaimed the ruin and the fragment as proof of the endurance of art. The headless, armless Venus was still beautiful; a poem of only four surviving words ("Spring . . . / Too long . . . / Gongula . . . ") could still say it all. The Chinese imagined the fragment as a relic by which one mentally constructs the lost whole—the reader, as is now said, participating in the creation of the text. Like the moderns, they felt that the fragment was all that could be accomplished. Though their individual poems are not, like the moderns, assemblages of fragments, their language itself was.

Sarasvati, like all Hindu gods, has many names: Goddess of Speech, Living at the Front of the Tongue, She Who Lives on the Tongues of Poets, She Who Lives in Sound, The Power of Memory, The Power of Knowledge, She Whose Power is the Power of Intellect, She Who is the Power of Forming Ideas, She Who is Intelligence.

Memory, knowledge, intellect: There is a beautiful, if not be-lievable, theory of the origin of language advanced by certain paleolinguists. That language did not arise from the need to com-municate—"I'm hungry" or "Eat!" or "Look out!" or, the question that can't be answered, "Who's there?"—but rather from the need to think. Just as the visual system, from retina to cortex, produces a pictorial representation of the world, so language evolved to rep-resent that which could not be seen—beginning, for protection's sake, with cause and effect. The origin of language, then, becomes identical to the act of writing: it is how one discovers what one knows, and is only secondarily its record.

Since the middle of the eighteenth century what has changed in poetry is only that the manifestations, the emanations, of the ar-chaic and the "other" have multiplied along with the increasing archaeological and ethnographic information. For the last 250 years we have meditated more on exotic than local ruins. The earliest past with which we speak—and, like the telescopic memories of old people, it is always the earliest moment that seems most vivid—continues to be pushed back, now to the Paleolithic. Our "others" are no longer the subjugated neighbors, but a wide range of (equally subjugated) peoples—though the modern poet, unlike the poets from the archaic to the end of the European colonial em-pires, takes no pride in that subjugation, believing that the "other" is only another form of "us." Like everything else, it is a super-market of choices: ancient and foreign images, mythologies, rites, practices, philosophies, from which the individual discovers the ideas and objects of an idiosyncratic rapport: emblems of the universal human, an "us" to which one goes on pilgrimage to find the "I."

I thought, suddenly, of the mass animal sacrifices I had attended a few years before in a valley outside of Kathmandu. Hundreds of the faithful snaked in a single file over the hills: the men leading male kids on a tether; the women with roosters and plates heaped with yellow and red flowers, incense and clarified butter; the poorest among them holding a single egg dipped in blood. At the bottom of the ravine was an altar open on four sides, canopied by the hoods of four enormous gilt cobras. There a spring came out of the ground, and there too was the object of veneration: Kali, goddess of death and destruction, grinning, squatting on a prostrate corpse, with her legs spread and a skull cup between her thighs. One by one the priests decapitated the animals, splattered the blood on the image of the goddess, and carried the carcasses to the blood-red stream to be washed and cooked in huge simmering pots, the meat fed to the pilgrims.

As described thus far, it was a scene that the modern, urban connoisseur of the archaic has learned how to read. Birth and death and rebirth, cosmic time: Mother Earth (with her spring and open altar) turning into Mother Death (giving birth to a skull, demanding the blood of males) and back to Mother Earth again (the meat of the sacrifice nourishing the faithful). If Sarasvati is the continuing life of the mind, Kali is the eternal decay, death and rebirth of the body.

But what struck me most about the rite was its utter ordinariness. Here were not only peasants in traditional dress but also men in polyester suits. Teenagers carried boom-boxes, families were having boisterous picnics, small groups of men played cards. The mood was, above all, that of a Sunday outing.

The modern invention of the archaic has projected an aura of drama and solemnity onto traditional religious practice — a kind of mental Gothic cathedral for the forest where the rites are enacted and the myths told. And when the boom-boxes start appearing at the animal sacrifice, it is seen as a dilution of the past, a weakening of the faith.

Yet an essential quality of the archaic is precisely its lack of distinction between sacred and profane — its habitual daily commerce between the gods and the people. It is a sign of religious decadence when that exchange is relegated to a single hour of the week in a separate (and silent) house. To recover the ancient power of poetry, one must begin by recognizing that the ancient formulae, the sacred chants, were sounds that occurred — that still occur — amidst a general noise. To complain about the racket drowning out poetry is to imagine a past that never existed. Poetry is not a secret rite: it is a public act that is generally ignored. But if it were to disappear — and who knows, it has never happened — the worlds it organizes into speech might well vanish with it.

The invention of an archaic, the opening of the poem to the "other," is not merely the essential modernist enterprise; it is a primary activity of poetry itself. Metaphor: "to move from one place to another." The poem is not a vehicle, it is an act of transportation (if we can scrape away the fossil-fuel encrustations on that word). The poem, made of breath, blows us away — to everything that is not "us," to everything by which an "us" is created. Writer to reader, self to another self, living to the dead, city to another city, metropolis to nature, today to yesterday, this world to other worlds. Silence to sound to silence: the Hindu history of the universe. Louis Zukofsky — following Dante's belief that things move to recover what they lack, to correct a defect — writes: "Properly no verse should be called a poem if it does not convey the totality of perfect rest." But he's wrong: The condition a poem aspires to is not absolute stillness, the ataraxia of ascetics, but rather a state of perpetual motion. Art, said Louis Sullivan, does not fulfill desire, it creates desire. Stillness is death: the river turned to a pool. Robert Duncan, in his last poem:

> In the real I have always known myself
>   in this realm where no Wind   stirs
>   no Night
> turns in turn to Day,   the Pool of the motionless water,
>   the absolute Stillness.   In the World, death after death.
> In this realm,   no last thrall of Life stirs.
>   The imagination alone knows this condition.
> As if this were before the War, before
> What Is,   in the dark this state
> that knows nor sleep nor waking, nor dream
>   — an eternal arrest.

Eliot Weinberger

Our time is no longer a cycle or a linear progression but, like our myth of the creation of the universe, an omnidirectional "big bang." Bits of the past fly all around us; we ricochet off them as we hurtle with them into the nothing. (The projectivist poem, with its "field" composition, is a map of time.) And yet the poem remains, as it always has been, a hymn to, and a dream of, its vanished or invisible river, its lost or unexploded time. A poetry without its own archaic, that doesn't talk with the dead, that doesn't meditate on ruins, that doesn't know it is surrounded by others who contradict everything it says, that has no nostalgia — a poem, in other words, that is still, completed, in eternal arrest — can only exist at the end of Christian or Hindu or Confucian or Aztec time, when poetry will no longer be written. Beauty, said Breton — his "convulsive beauty" — arises from the tension between stillness and motion: a locomotive engine abandoned to the jungle, tangled with growth.

The only ending is a longing for ending. Edmund Spenser, a Christian and a self-conscious archaicist, abandons his epic with a truncated "unperfite" canto that yearns for completion:

> For all that moveth doth in change delight:
> But thence-forth all shall rest eternally
> With Him that is the God of Sabbaoth hight:
> O that great Sabbaoth God graunt me that Sabbaoths sight!

Even Dante, who was granted that sight, could only end his geometrically perfect poem lamenting the inadequacies of speech. For the vision of God erases memory — Dante compares it to a dream: its details lost, only some small sense of great passion remaining — and language without memory, an amnesiac poetry, cannot exist. His Paradise must remain a blank space, a silence, outlined by the poem: Its final metaphor is a geometer who cannot understand the circle he has drawn.

Spenser's best poem, "Prothalamion," celebrates an as-yet-unperformed marriage, like the couples in Bosch's garden, forever frozen in the moment before copulation, a poem that turns on an ironic refrain: "Sweete Themmes, runne softly, till I end my song." Ironic, for if the river ended when his song ended, if river and song ever ended, if we ever reached the future, we would reach the end.

Columbus
Friedrich Hölderlin

— *Translated by Richard Sieburth*

†HEAR THE WATCHMAN'S HORN AT
NIGHT
AFTER MIDNIGHT AROUND THE FIFTH HOUR

Thus Mohammed † Rinaldo,

Columbus

Barbarossa, qua free spirit

If there were a hero I wanted to be
            of a pastor or of a Hessian, (whose native
And could freely, *with the voice*   admit it   *speech*
                              Emperor Henry
It would then be a hero of the sea. *For to undertake action*
                    ( )
(Is) To (spoil) nothing, is the friendliest of all, that
                    But we are getting our dates
Among all
                    confused
                              Demetrius Polior-
            and order, absolutely
Familiar, temporary dwelling   *essential*
                                    cetes
            in order to learn and figures
                    Peter the Great
                    , parched beauty **(s) Henry's**
In the sand vessels ( ) burnt,
  Night and   **crossing of the Alps and that**
Out of fire, full of images, finely polished
                    with his own hands he gave the people

Friedrich Hölderlin

     food and drink & his son Con-
(Spyglass) telescope (higher law) higher edu- and it is necessary
      cation, in fact for **rad died**
To question the sky   *life*
          of poison
      Model of an innovator

      Of a reformer

      Conradin etc. .

But when you name them over

Anson and Gama *and buccaneers, and Aeneas*
And (Doria)?, Jason, Chiron's **all characteristic**
     rock caves and
The pupil in Magara's (grottoes) **of circumstances**
   shivering
In the rain of the grotto was taking shape
As on the (well-tempered) lyre a human image
From the impression of the forest, and the Templars,
       who (voyage) voyaged
     Buccaneers, voyages of discovery
To Jerusalem Bouillon, Rinaldo

Bougainville
 Their number is great   *as attempts to define the (orbis)*
        Hesperidean

 But they themselves are greater *orbis, (in contrast) as against the*

 And strike dumb   *the orbis of the ancients*

     the men

Nonetheless

Friedrich Hölderlin

And I want to go to Genoa

And inquire after the house of Columbus

Where he, *as if*

One were one of the gods
                    and a wondrous thing
Humankind, perhaps
        (seated)   *light*
In front of the granary, come from Sicily
Lived in his sweet youth   *but one turns back*

                    Essentially, like a

                    print-seller, standing there

                    displaying images of the
            Do you think   *lands*
                of the grandees (a) and sings
                        also
The splendors of the earth   [   ]

            But since you (ask)

    You ask me

As far as my heart

carries me, things will be fine

According to custom and art

                    as in the marketplace
        Columbus examines a map

39

Friedrich Hölderlin

But boarding the ship

ils crient rapport, il fermés maison

tu es un saisrien

while they were shouting

There was an impatient grumbling, *for*   *Manna and*

By a few paltry things   *bread from heaven*
The
As if thrown out of tune by the snow
earth   *It makes me bitter this*
The bell that   *lack of*
angry   *patience and kindness*
One rings   *my judge and guardian god*
and hastened   ([   ]) *with prophesying and*
For supper   */of prayer*
so that (it)   *great commotion, / with goodwill*
And they thought they were monks.
                                    For we are men
And one, an orator
Stepped forth   Yet out there, so that   *Plunge in O streams*
                                        (p) (ce)
and like a   we would leave   *Of love and*   **entiere personne content**
                        grace of God   **de son ame difficultes**
                                      connoissance
parson   the place, thus called   *and luck in his*
                                      rapport tire
in a blue   powerfully commanding   *to comprehend the powers,*
                                            O images
                        Of youth
jacket   the crew the voice of the seagod,   *as in Genoa, back then*
            so pure, by which   *The earthly kingdom, Greek,*
                                        imagined by a child
                        Powerfully under my eyes

40

Friedrich Hölderlin

Heroes recognize, whether they have
Lulled to sleep, fleeting
poppy spirit
gone right or wrong —
suddenly to me
Appeared

You are all this in your beauty

You are all this in your beauty apocalyptica

lui

moments tirees hautes sommeils the mariner
a les
Columbus aside   Hypostasization of the previous
pleures   **Naivete of scienc**
Passion for
And sighing together, at the hour
orbis
After the heat of day

They now saw,

For indeed there were many

lovely (cities) isles,

so that

With Lisbon

And Genoa divided;

For alone one can (not)

Friedrich Hölderlin

    Bear the wealth of the gods

    All alone; though

    the reins might be loosened

        by a demigod, but for the Highest

    It is hardly enough

    To act   where daylight shines

    And the moon, (therefore)

    therefore

    so

Ursprung der Loyoté

In fact (back then) often, when   Ευνομια, κασιγνηται τε, βα –

It gets too lonely   θρον πολιων, ασΦαλης δικα

(too lonely)   και ομοτροπος ειρανα, ταμιαι

For the gods, so that they   ανδρασι πλουτου, χρυσεαι

stick together alone   παιδες ευβουλου Θεμιτος

    or the earth; for (in pain) all too pure is

Friedrich Hölderlin

Either

But then

[ ] traces of ancient breeding

TRANSLATOR'S NOTE

This fragmentary Columbiad, first drafted at Nürtingen in 1801 and further elaborated at Homburg in 1805–06, may have been part of a cycle of poems dealing with the various heroes of the modern (or "Hesperidean") age. In a letter to Seckendorf of March 12, 1804, Hölderlin notes that he is currently very much occupied with myth, that is, with "the poetic aspect of history and the architectonics of heaven . . . and especially with national [myth] inasmuch as it differs from the Greek." The letter continues, "I have outlined the various destinies of heroes, knights, and princes, how they serve fate or act more or less ambiguously in relation to it."

As in Hölderlin's poem "Patmos," the voice and memory of the poet gradually modulate into those of the poem's hero. The central section of the poem is presumably spoken by Columbus himself, and appears to narrate the preparations for the expedition, the blessing of the ships, the squabbles among the crew, their greed for gain, etc. The French phrases that punctuate the text may be snippets overheard in the port of Bordeaux during Hölderlin's residence in that city; the French, at any rate, is pure Hölderlinian idiolect. The Greek at the end of the poem is from Pindar's Thirteenth Olympian: "Dika, unshakable foundation of cities,/ and Eirena, preserver of wealth:/ golden daughters of sagacious Themis./ They are eager to repel/ Hybris, brash-tongued mother of Koros./ Yet there is beauty/ to tell of here,/ and boldness moves me/ to tell it." (trans. Frank Nisetich)

My mapping of the poem is based on the transcription of the original manuscript provided in D.E. Sattler's 1975 *Einleitung* to the Frankfurt edition published by Roter Stern Verlag. Sattler distinguishes the various drafts (or "phases") of the poem by different styles of type in order to display the palimpsest-like quality of Hölderlin's late manuscripts. In this printing, the various temporal strata of the text are indicated in chronological order by: regular roman type, *italic type*, **bold type**, ***bold italics*** and CAPITALS.

—R.S.

Conrad and Lowry in Mexico
Ewa Kuryluk

RAISING HIS EYES to Popocatepetl, looming above them, Lowry remarks to Ernestine: Isn't our volcano a Moby Dick?
It has the air of beckoning us on, as it twitches from one side of the horizon to the other. Does it signal disaster?
The disaster is already at our side. It has just arrived from Acapulco, concentrates on you, Ernestine, and carries a Polish-English name: Korzeniowski — Conrad Joseph. We, the Lowrys plus disaster, sit on the terrace of a café, across from a drunken *pelado*, a serene little thief. I find myself in the right alcoholic equilibrium, oscillating between a state of subconsciousness and a state of surconsciousness. Hardly aware of what's going on, I, nevertheless, control events, although so far there are no events. I declare this country a land of nonevents, and watch Conrad pouring coffee into your cup, Ernestine, bending over you more than he should. This is a place of disastrous nonevents, of unsuccessful politicians and penniless writers. I wonder, Korzeniowski, what's the purpose of your coming here?
A crowded bus arrives from around the corner and an accident occurs. A peon is gravely injured. When his sombrero is lifted, a bloody mess appears where his face had been. Conrad jumps up and wants to offer first aid. Lowry stops him, saying: It's against the local law to touch the victim. It's a country of death and he's meant to die. The *policia de seguridad* will be here in no time. If you help him, they'll arrest you, something I would welcome. Therefore I just want to warn you. It's better to jump into the Popocatepetl than to be thrown into a Mexican jail, black as the lava of legendary nonevents. So I suggest you keep drinking and blinking at our best friend, the white killer whale. Instead of playing the samaritan, just tell me: what's the purpose of your dandy visit, Korzeniowski? I hope it's not us, since we're about to go go go. Tomorrow we head for Vancouver, that Salome of a city where my sweetie is supposed to dance the symphony of the seven veils — composed by Hugo Hitler, with a libretto by Musa Lini — and earn

44

us a fortune. My plump pudding, she'll buy me that villa of an island entitled l'Isola d'Archangel Gabriel. Don't interrupt me, dolly, or otherwise I'll forget the sonnet I composed for our *sehr verehrter Herr Doktor* Korzeniowski, my old pussy dog or, if you prefer, *polski pies.* Where was I? Oh, yes, that prepaid and pre-mailed paradise overshadowed by the pinions of my vulnerable wife Angelica d'Angèle we desire to acquire. That piece of poetry and fiction and belles lettres and essay in one. *N'est pas, mon ange? Mój aniel.*

No, *mon cher collègue,* I'm not *alcoolique.* Molly Moll, ignore what K says, and shut up yourself. I like you best silent as a carp *à la polonaise,* and that's what our distinguished guest fancies as well. Isn't that so, *mon auteur polo-anglais?*

Don't cry, cookie, don't mourn the bad bad bobby-boy of your husband, unless you want to perform the role I adore: Lady Xantippe in *The Dead Drunkard of Novogorod,* or is it *Malcolmovitch, the Vampire of Dnepropavlovsk?* No, that's not what you want? You wish to complain about the brute Lowrowski, spending his dolly's dollars on boozy booze, to Jossif Jossifovitch Konradowskij? Do tell him the truth! Penniless, broke, bathing in booze, I do spend your bucks on cheap whores and don't even enjoy it, while you howl at home. Go ahead, K, exude pure gold. She'll collect it between her thighs. Danae sweetheart, catch all our dear C ejaculates in Mexico. He, after all, is neither broke nor a Brutus. To the contrary, ours is the pleasure to sit at the table with the very best-selling *Pan Cogito Koryto.* Your anthem, *vive l'Angleterre. Ecrire c'est mourir un peu pour mon pays polonais,* extracts a Yang-tse out of my bladder.

I beg your pardon, sir. Your name isn't *Korytowski?* No roots in *koryto,* the till you have your snout in? No? You swear to God? Why, then, does your pen drip with porcine ink? Oh, come on! Admit that you're a hero. Haven't you fought your way to the feeding trough? Don't go away, cookie! No, I don't insult our Anglo-Pole, I'm absolutely unaware of harming him. I just want to know: how do you make it? That way, sweetie, we can try to barge in as well, instead of waltzing through the night with *Jean Bautista decolté.*

You want to go? But where to, dearest Ernestine? To Cyprus, Cythera? Maybe you want to join us, Joe? I, my delicious wife, and you, Konrad Patriote, we would make a superb triangle — drunk, romantic, and satanically angelic. Shall we embark for Madagascar, the New Palestine? Take a scooter to Panama? The Transsiberian to Vancouver? A yellow submarine to Zakopane?

No? You don't want to come? Damn it, Conrad, nothing works out. You're right, sweetie, all coincidence is fucked up. Look at her, Joseph, a pretty one, she has come here because of me, a *cochon de mal* she loves so much. Why can't she stop fondling my ass? Why do I have to abuse her all the time? I'm not even intoxicated with her charm, as are you, Korzeniowski, the *prince charmant* whose peripathetic eyes peregrinate between my wife's front door and her rear one.

Tomorrow, first thing in the morning, I want to read you, Prof. Cock, a novella I'm expanding into a novel-in-progress. Since I have enrolled in your writing workshop, it progresses so well that I should be able to finish it after my death, perhaps while traveling first class by the October ferry to Gabriola, the isle of the dead world literature. My stuff is awfully good, almost as good as Pearl Buck's, whose crap my bingo spouse takes in and excretes *en passant*. Oh, don't cry, Ernestine. I'm a drunk old fart, envious, without talent, neither a Conrad nor a Melville, although I too love the sea, especially the mystic waves of Bloody Mary and gin. I too would like to be rewarded with a Nobel's dynamite, enjoy publicity and big bucks, play the noblesse oblige of a well-to-do guy, day and night pay compliments to my sweetheart. Unfortunately, noble committees don't go for drunks.

When I hurt you, Ernestine, it's like cutting into my own flesh. You saw the blood under the sombrero? You saw the police mugs? It's all such a *Scheisshaus*, and I'm a big *Scheisser* whom God presented with the gift to narrate a disaster. An alcoholic who bullies his angel of a spouse, I'm nevertheless capable of spelling shit out. Screwing it in and out, I release the real thing, the odor we shall smell on the day of our last judgment.

Isn't she a Fra Angelica, Conrad? The way she bears with me. Convince Ernestine that she's an angel, Joseph, tell her that in my name. She needs to be reassured, or else she'll go down the drain, like myself. Bend over her, Conrad. Pee coffee into her teacup. Be kind to this sweet-sour puppy of mine. Let her share with you the *sauerkraut* of her life with me, the unsuccessful scum. I too scuba dived in the sea, but compared to your nautical sensibility mine is a big minus. No Copernicus, no King Sobieski behind me. Besides, I'm as fluent in English as you are in Polish — a plain disadvantage. But how did you dare to run away from your mom's po-la-ca right into the Anglo-ass of my legal spouse?

No, dolly, I don't insult our guest. I just spill out some questions and, exceptionally, reasonable ones. Why did you sack, my lad, your parents' rural pol-pot for the sake of the urban Mr. Shake and Mrs. Spare? Believe me, Jan Kott was mistaken, they aren't our contemporaries. Come on, Korytowski, confess: What made you desert *maman*?

Dead drunk, his teeth chattering, Malcolm Lowry meets a sober Conrad dressed in a fancy flannel suit. Dr. Conrad, I presume, says Malcolm, and has a big sip of gin. Are you in business? Joseph inquires. Certainly, replies Lowry. I had a novel rejected by fifty-five publishers, lost my only disk with another one. To fulfill my felicity, a donkey from *New American Lit* accused me of plagiarizing the Nigger of your *Narcissus*. I wait for my wife, the apple of your eye. She's due in a minute and I hope to be able to stand up and kiss her on the right spot, though I doubt I can find it. It's tough to have a wife.

It's tough not having one.

Is that so? What's up?

Shanghai.

The only place they have decent bars and girls, let me tell you before she arrives. The woman who isn't really my wife, but to whom I consider proposing tonight. Not a good idea? You're probably right. But here she comes. A beauty? Yes, she looks fine. Maybe slightly too fine, and too difficult.

And, indeed, she came in, Conrad notes in the evening, beaming with ostentatious charm. A stout piece of a woman, ready to plough the literary Lowry marsh, a suggestive, rustic, and homely nature. I immediately identify her as a vessel for male longings, a bosomy boat with glazed cabins and windows protected by tiny white curtains. A robust round arm. A watering pot. Bowing her sleek head of a maiden, she pronounces her name with pride: Ernestine, making clear that with her fair skin, hair, eyes and little knobby nose, she knows nothing of the wicked sea and the corrupt world. Pretty, touching, vulnerable, thoroughly feminine, she walks into the bar and all men's eyes focus on her. She addresses Lowry as sweetheart. She calls me a dear friend. Her teeth are white and smooth. Her tongue — an advertisement of perfect pink. She wears a blue dress with white polka dots, and white high-heeled shoes. In her large and comely face lips are outlined with crimson lipstick. She

47

has a good complexion and the paleness of her skin reminds me of the white, empty candor of a statue. The simplicity of her apparel, the opulence of her form, her imposing stature, and the extraordinary sense of vigorous life that seems to emanate from her like perfume exhaled by a flower, make her beautiful with a beauty of a rustic and Olympic order. I imagine her reaching up to clotheslines with both arms raised high above her head. And this causes me to fall to musing in a strain of pagan piety.

While Conrad continues writing, Lowry fails in one attempt after another to lay his future wife. No way. He fancies a bottle, not a female.

Projecting the image of the future Mrs. Lowry onto the formidable Mrs. Hermann of his *Nigger and Narcissus*, Conrad masturbates that night and wakes up to a creative morning. When Malcolm wakes up, he finds at his side a creature dissolved in misery. She wept all night and is asleep now, her red and swollen face buried between the pillows.

Ernestine is earth, young and fresh, as on the first day of creation, writes Joseph. Meanwhile Malcolm contemplates his bride with fear, gets up and proceeds to the kitchen to fix himself a drink.

A virginal planet, Conrad mimics himself, undisturbed by a vision of a future teeming with monstrous forms of life, clamorous with the cruel battles of hunger and thought. Ernestine — a modest, silent presence.

I draw no great comfort from her company, Lowry remarks to himself. Just the opposite: I draw comfort from her absence. Having established this, he returns to the bedroom, absentmindedly fondles Ernestine's big tits, and when she opens her eyes, proposes to her. She accepts and goes to the kitchen to prepare breakfast.

I wouldn't mind embarking with Ernestine on a long sea passage, muses Joseph in the evening. To Uruguay, for instance. We would arrive there in early October, when lemon trees blossom and give off heavenly smells. We could walk hand in hand along the shore, rent bikes, and ride on the pink roads, lie in the warm red sand, make love in a cheap hotel in Montevideo and eat enormous, inexpensive steaks in Carmelos. I would spray seed into her sad tropics and play my favorite game, the *post-coitum-animal-triste*. But do I really want to sleep with this girl for the rest of my life? To produce offspring? Take care of some drug addict of a son? In the long run I couldn't draw comfort from Ernestine's company, Conrad scribbles on the edge of a newspaper. Then he takes out his stationery and composes a letter to Lowry:

> Dear Friend: I encourage you with all my heart to marry Ernestine, a wonderful piece of femininity, to be treasured and guarded. My departure for Shanghai is imminent, and so I take farewell of both of you. Sincerely, J.C.

That night Malcolm succeeds in getting an erection. Once. His effort at ejaculation remains, however, only an effort. But he's pleased with himself, less drunk than usual, and writes:

Mom, kiss me good night, says Aeneas to Venus before the decisive battle. Next day corpses litter streets, his saffron dress edged with acanthus is torn, and Peter Brook's *Mahabarata*, performed at the BAM, makes the point that in the age of relativity time is a snowball, a hot-air balloon, a harbor where sails are pulled down, a missile inspected on site.

We head toward the land and the land dissolves. Like the curve of a bow the port disappears in the waves. Cliffs of the east meet the waters of the west. Manhattan's towers bow to Moscow's golden onions. Good omens abound, as do bad ones. Both hemispheres forget the Afghan holocaust and admire two horses grazing in a meadow. One is tattooed between his ears with a red star, the other wears starry stockings and striped shoes. Oh, what a wonderful view! Recently they got hemorrhoids from drinking blood. Recently they fed on grass. God bless them, the harmless creatures! Earth and oceans, support them! Winds and storms, help them forget that Troy was razed to the ground. The Trojan horse is such a dandy animal, its belly filled with the promise of peace.

But why is Aeneas's fleet holding a sure course over the sea, cutting through the waters that darken under the wind? Why is Venus driven by worry, pouring out complaints? Not satisfied with bones and ashes, Miss Universe requests a flood to sweep Troy away. Gods grant her request. Once the apocalypse is over, funeral games are organized for Anchises, Venus's dead lover.

But who cares anyhow? The world is a cage of wonders. Cancer genes yield practical applications. Oncogenes are believed to trigger cancers through different mechanisms, and clever strategies show promise against common colds. Everything happens at once. Reactors are built in space. Schoolchildren from Mississippi meet their schoolmates from Vitebsk to organize a Chagall show in Pennsylvania.

Useful medical applications begin to emerge. Cancer is the

answer to the question of metaphor, and so is AIDS. Tunnels can shelter us from nuclear waste. Tunneling efforts are scheduled to begin December 24, and giant tunneling machines are being specially designed to fit the geology of our planet. Nearly two zillion zillions will be required to tunnel us under. But tunneling represents the priority of our age, and the Grump Transtunnel Corporation is expected to do a good job. It will take them thirty-three years to complete the project. In the process eighty-eight zillion cubic meters of soil, enough to rebuild three hundred great pyramids of Egypt, will be hauled to the surface. The project is headed by the distinguished terra-engineer Faustophilos, and the consortium plans a crucial twenty-zillion stock offering in November.

It's September, and Underwood, my roommate, revels at my side. An alcoholic, he creeps slowly through the enchanted nightwood of the mutual text that writes down the two of us. Psyche and Techne embrace, as things wander in and out of our twin machine-minds.

In Milan short skirts inspire inventive spring openings. It's a wonderfully brave world: spring occurs in October, the fall fashion shows are fixed for February. When the earth is frozen, print dresses with shirred bodices and the over-the-knee stockings and soft silk blouses with tapered trousers gathered at the waist appear in collections that could have been put together by committees on cultural thought. An important innovation is shorts, which are skintight in stretch fabrics and paired with a low-neck camisole and a long jacket, or tailored and cuffed in linen or leather. Oh what a dazzling universe of wild colors and offbeat shapes, which take the rich by storm. Clothes are fitted so snugly, no bulge goes undefined. Short tight tops bare a sliver of flesh at the midriff. The newest creations fall from small natural shoulders and billow out around the hips, the shape reminding men of an upside-down flower. The sexy models on painterly cibachrome prints have blurred faces, the hair slicked back into knots and anchored by many silver-colored headbands, combs and barrettes, all worn at the same time. But the thighs are naked and invite my gaze and tail. Finally Ernestine is asleep and I can be by myself. Gin keeps me company and I savor the press-speak, which acquaints me with the world. *La Prensa* reopens in Nicaragua. A celebrated Chinese painter, who has immigrated to the United States, can't sell his work. He has enrolled in a multidisciplinary mental health program serving the homeless in Manhattan, and hopes for the best. I'm in love with Ernestine but neglect her. I don't want to hurt her but all the time I do.

Determination Suspension Diversion Digression Destruction
David Antin

in early august just after saddam hussein's iraqi army had overrun kuwait
i got a call from john hanhardt the film and video curator of the whitney museum
who wanted to know if i would do a performance in connection with an
exhibition he was putting on in november   the show called NON@#&?!SENSE
was going to concentrate on video film and radio works that interrupted
diverted destroyed and replaced conventional notions of representation and
narrative   and he wanted to include performance works as well   so i asked
him what other performers he was going to include   and he named connie
dejong stuart sherman and joan jonas   they were all artists i respected and
seemed to make sense in terms of the shows intentions   but why me?   john
said he thought my critical arguments and stories continually interrupted each
other to defeat the expectations of logic
                                     so i agreed   and some time in september
i had to give matthew his assistant a name for the piece   while saddam hussein
was pillaging kuwait and threatening saudi arabia   which our president had
announced he was determined to protect   with forces he had already dispatched
and was further determined to force him out of kuwait   by means that
were as yet in no way certain   so the name that i gave to the piece was

        determination   suspension   diversion
           digression   destruction

which i improvised at the whitney museum on november 27   or about six
weeks before the war began

1. determination

when you say that someone is determined its not immediately
clear   whether you mean he's constrained by something or
constraining something   when you think about it you say   a
straight line is determined   by two points   you dont say a
straight line determines two points   a straight line isnt
determined to go through two points   it is determined by two
points   then you say president bush is determined

51

David Antin

by which you
may mean he is determining a course of action   or that a course
of action is determining him

      we can say george bush is determined to get us into a war with
   iraq   of course we dont know that he's determined to get us
into a war with iraq   we may suppose he is only determined to
   get iraq out of kuwait   but we have a gut feeling about it he's
got a square jaw   narrow lips   a thin head   that looks like
theres not much sense in there   that is to say   he looks as if
he *has* thought   he looks like a man who could think   but
   not overmuch   he looks like someone with a narrow focus
                                                                    you
know how certain people with a narrow focus can fixate on
   individual things and see them clearly   but not much else
      george bush looks like he's fixated   but of course we hear
all of this from a distance   and the further away he is   the
easier it is for us to believe things about him   even though he's
like a star and you   never know what stars are like   you know
a star is far away you may even know how far away   but there
are so many things about them that you dont know   a star
   is like a divinity   we only see and hear of him through
television   where we know that he's been coached   and we
dont know what he really wants or   doesnt want   whether
   he's determined or determining   is he a particle in an
electromagnetic field   determined by its forces   or several
   electromagnetic fields   waltzing along towards some
predestined or randomized end   or is he such a field?

            imagine   one day   one day iraq suddenly appears
in kuwait   its strange it seemed such a surprise   though i'm
not sure its a surprise   i dont believe anything reported any
   more   but it seemed to be a surprise   to president bush and
his cabinet to congress   so we were all   surprised   and i
   knew about kuwait i knew kuwait had an emir and lots of oil and
   rich people in it   lots of rich people   and a royal family
and an elected parliament that not many people voted for   this
   parliament   which their emir had anyhow dissolved some
time ago

      it was not a large number of people who had the right to vote

52

in kuwait   somewhere i read it was something like a fifth?
   of the adult population   who had the right to vote on the
few things they were allowed to vote on   because kuwait was
not a parliamentary democracy   even when they had   a
parliament   because the parliament never had the right to do
   much of anything when they had one   the parliament that
the emir suspended when it threatened to do something   besides
approve whatever the emir wanted it to approve

         so i knew a few random things about kuwait   i knew it
   existed   which is probably more than most americans   and i
knew   it was next to saudi arabia   i knew it had lots of oil
      which was why it existed   and that it was supposed to have
had more cars per person than any other sheikdom in the middle
east   but beyond that   not much

         now suddenly iraq was over there in kuwait   I thought iraq
was busy   I thought they were busy theyd just had a war with
   iran   i thought what with killing each other in a cheerful way
   with the kurds and the shiites   there to be tortured or gassed
         and just having finished a war with iran   where theyd had
lots of fun killing each other over some mudflat in the persian
gulf or an oil well or two   theyd be too busy to get into another
   war just after   they finished the last one   we'd all seen
the terrible pictures of the dead and the wounded   in the
newspapers   and i figured theyd have to be too busy tending the
   wounded to go to war   and then suddenly there they were at
   war   theyd invaded kuwait and we were not ready for it

               then the clean-featured narrow-lipped determined
   president bush went on television and said how we were all
outraged   and said how this could not happen and should not
   happen   and that we would not let it happen   president bush
rushes onto tv to let everybody know that we are all outraged and
   that this is unacceptable   that saddam hussein must immediately
get out of kuwait   and   most importantly   he must not
   touch saudi arabia   and when you think of this you realize why
he must not touch saudi arabia   we all know this or we   think
   we do   im just rehearsing this to get together my sense of
what this determination means
                              saddam hussein must not touch

53

David Antin

saudi arabia because saudi arabia is our price fixer   without
saudi arabia we cant keep the price of oil down   or we might
find it difficult to keep it down   or maybe we merely cant be
confident that our oil interests will know in advance what the price
of oil will be   this is serious or seems serious   at least to
george bush   or at least we can imagine it is   so   weve
got to protect saudi arabia   so says president bush   but he
     also says we must protect the integrity of kuwait if saddam
hussein doesnt voluntarily get out   because it has a legitimate
government   which i'm not sure it has   but just what is
     our president going to do to protect this integrity?

          he begins by issuing stern warnings   iraq must get out
of kuwait   but what good is a warning without a threat   and
what good is a threat without a force to back it up   a credible
force   one you could believe in?   so it seems that the
president is going to send troops   to defend saudi arabia and
     persuade saddam hussein we mean business   it sounds good
          how good?   50000 troops good   its a small number
          its a small number if you think of the size   of iraqs army
          but 50000 troops will cost a lot of money   they have to
travel they need changes of underwear kleenex coughdrops   if
you have to move them you have to remember that each one weighs
     between   130 lbs and 230 lbs   though some of them will be
     women and theyre smaller   so lets say between 100 and 230
     lbs   but thats still a lot of gasoline   because you have to ship
them a long distance in large and inefficient vessels   and that
will use a lot of oil just at the time when there will be no oil
coming out of iraq or kuwait   because we will embargo it

               so oil prices will go up   which will make it more
expensive to ship all those people to the borders of kuwait
          kuwait is what?   something   like 8000 miles from new
york?   youre lucky if youre shipping them from new york   but
     what if youre shipping them from california   from pendleton or
ord?   thats a few thousand more miles?   but you're lucky
          you've got some ships in the indian ocean   a carrier in the
arabian sea   cruisers   in the mediterranean   its good to be
an imperial power   you have lots of divisions in germany that
     nobody needs   since the crumbling of the soviet empire in
     eastern europe   but you dont send them from germany   who

54

knows why?   maybe the local economies require them where
   they are   so you send them from north carolina and texas and
   california   and we hear about this and see selected pictures
of young men and women kissing their loved ones goodbye   on tv
   they show us lots of tearful farewells   or anxious conversations
by young men and young women worried how they will make their
   mortgage payments on army pay   so i figure president bush is
   determined to keep iraq out of saudi arabia

                                              sending a fleet with
50000 soldiers   thats determined

                                 but then he gets these 50000
   people in there and you know he's had second thoughts   saddam
hussein has 500000 soldiers some of whom are so far busy raping
   people in kuwait   what if he sends these people to rape people
in saudi arabia in spite of our naval vessels and their airplanes
and our 50000 soldiers?

                          they could rape the people who own the oil
   wells and still keep the wells pumping   then iraq would have
half of the world's oil reserve instead of 20% of it   half the oil
future of the world in their hands   which would allow them to
dominate opec and set the price of oil at their pleasure in the future
      if you accept this logic the situation is terrible   and we
   need a more credible deterrent because 50000 soldiers facing
   500000 is maybe not so credible   and we think the president
   is determined to be credible   and we supposed he was
determined to keep the iraqis out of saudi arabia   and maybe
   apply pressure to force them out of kuwait   but if saddam
hussein is determined   to stay in kuwait   there seems to be
no way that 50000 troops in saudi arabia would force him out
   which would require severe economic means   a strict
embargo or a blockade of iraq   and for this to be effective
would take a lot of time   which would mean money
      because every day we keep 50000 soldiers in saudi arabia
and a fleet around the coast of iraq would cost a lot of money
      and now george bush doesnt have lots of money   everybody
is worrying about the deficit in the american budget   which
every day is growing   the savings and loan disaster has cost us
hundreds of billions and could cost hundreds of billions more
      and now we hear that the banking industry is in trouble and
may also cost us billions   and nobody or   most importantly
none of george bush's friends wants to pay more taxes

David Antin

* * *

          so now george bush who started by being determined to
is being determined by   partly his desires and partly arithmetic
     and partly a kind of logic   because putting 50000 soldiers
in saudi arabia is somewhat   symbolic   50000 soldiers
     though a lot of people and quite expensive to maintain in the
saudi arabian desert   might not be too large a meal for a
determined iraqi army more than ten times its size to eat   it
     would be a heavy meal and expensive   the iraqi army would
surely have a tough fight   because of the aircraft carriers that
would come from the mediterranean and arabian seas   and their
     bombers would probably bomb the shit out of the iraqi army
     which would still vastly outnumber the american forces
     that might be overrun   after fighting heroically and killing
a very large number of people   and this might be militarily
satisfying but politically embarrassing for an american president
     yet if you assume that saddam hussein is a relatively
reasonable man   and you may not want to assume anything
of the sort   but it is the way of thinking that goes with the use
of symbolic deterrents   so you ought to assume it   or that his
     generals are relatively reasonable men   whom you might
expect to assume that a very large and powerful country that is
     willing to send 50000 soldiers 10000 miles to discourage a well
armed near eastern power from invading saudi arabia   would
be willing to send many many more if it had to   if its army was
in danger of being killed or captured or otherwise embarrassed
     because this is the principle of the reasonable deterrent
     50000 men and an embargo

          but then we start hearing new things on the radio and tv
     i hear new things on the radio   new disturbing things among
the things i know   saddam hussein is a bad man   he's quite
     willing to kill people   he has killed people before   this is
     not new   he's as bad as hitler   this is a little new   from
a government that has been supplying him with arms up to last week
or last year   "another hitler" seems a bit strong   but its
probably in there for the israeli lobby   then the most disturbing
     thing we hear is that he's a madman   this is a diagnosis that
comes from our president or from the people who work for our
president or who consult for people who work for our president
     and i'm not sure what this means   what does it mean to be

a madman in the politics of the middle east   is he madder than
assad in syria?   is he madder than king fahd or the emir of
kuwait   or yasir arafat   or shamir or sharon?   how do we
know?   how do we measure the madness of political enemies?
          do we give them a rorschach?   a t.a.t.?   in what way is
he mad?   in terms of american popular belief?   he does bad
and violent things   but lots of americans do bad and violent
things   the mafia does bad and violent things and nobody thinks
theyre mad   we just think theyre bad   maybe its just that he
does bad things in a way that americans dont expect   americans
dont expect american political leaders to do bad and violent things
to americans   at least they dont expect them to kill their
american political opponents   but this seems to be more
commonly expected in the middle east   so this seems to be a
difference of convention   so far as i can see saddam hussein
appears to be a bad man and a practical man   practical   within
the limits of his badness   and in this sense

          he had an economic dispute with kuwait   which because
he had a much larger and better equipped army   he felt he could
resolve with force   and seeing how easily he could resolve it
with force and without intervention   he simply decided to
carry   this application of force to its logical and practical
conclusion   the annexation of kuwait

          in principle this may have seemed practical and even logical
          even though it was mistaken   there was after all no power
in the middle east likely to come to the aid of kuwait   the israelis
were too far away and otherwise occupied   and the united
states was even further off and appeared uninterested   because
even if saddam took over kuwait and enriched iraq with kuwaits oil
reserve   what could he do with it but sell it?   no   he
must have thought that it would be illogical for the united states
to be seriously concerned   of course we would protest   we
would issue stern statements   but our ambassador to iraq had
already indicated that the dispute between iraq and kuwait was a
local affair   saddam hussein probably considered that it would
be illogical for the united states to intervene   that it would be
irrational to invoke economic sanctions   which would surely
result in oil price increases   that would conflict with the
interests of the industrial nations   and probably ruled out armed

intervention by the united states as so irrational as to be a form
of madness
                    so from this point of view   which of course i cant be
sure was the point of view of saddam hussein   though it seems
probable enough in terms of the way things worked out   saddam
hussein seems to be a bad and practical man who made the single
mistake of supposing that george bush was a rational and practical
man   and then made the worse mistake of continuing to believe
this while all the evidence was mounting to contradict it
      because it's beginning to appear that george bush may be an
irrational and impractical man   if you listen closely to the
statements our president keeps releasing
                                                      because now we are
hearing about a new order among the comity of nations   *a nation*
cannot behave the way iraq has behaved in the light of the new
relations among nations   which we may suppose means   in a
world where the soviet union is no longer a major player in
middle east power politics   *in the new world order a nation*
cannot be rewarded for aggression   if this means anything it
suggests that george bush   is determined to do more than keep
      saddam hussein from overrunning saudi arabia   it sounds like
he is determined to run him out of kuwait   and if he is
determined to do this quickly   it will not be patiently with an
      embargo and a credible but symbolic deterrent   and it will
require a much larger force
                                          one hundred and fifty thousand   two
hundred and fifty thousand   four hundred thousand men and
women   to deal with the half million soldiers saddam hussein
probably has in kuwait and the other quarter of a million he may
      have available just inside his borders   and then we wont be
able to stop there

                          if the american forces manage to drive the iraqi army out
of kuwait they cant simply roll up to the border and stop there
      if the american army drives the iraqi army back into iraq
      they cant just leave them there   theyll have to roll right
on into iraq   to basra or even baghdad   just to make sure
      they stay out of kuwait   and theyd probably start by driving
into iraq anyway   and this may explain the new stories weve
begun to hear on the radio and tv   saddam hussein may be close
to having a nuclear capability   he may be only a year or two away

from a nuclear device   this is not to say that he has an atomic
bomb   or a delivery system   but we are reminded that he has
chemical and biological weapons   that could conceivably be
deployed as warheads on his soviet built missiles   so there we
have it   more or less directly from our government   the
scenario of the madman with the atomic bomb

            faced with this threat our president can have no choice
but to destroy the iraqi nuclear capability and their arsenal of
biological and chemical weapons   this is the new determination

            in the beginning george bush was determined to protect
saudi arabia with a nominal force and to exercise economic pressure
to get saddam hussein out of kuwait   then perhaps because this
modest response could not be trusted to deter an irrational iraqi
leader   george bush was determined to defend saudi arabia and
drive saddam hussein out of kuwait   and then because the forces
required to do this would be very great   the cost significantly
greater   and the tactics much more aggressive   it now
appears that george bush is determined to crush the iraqi army
disarm the iraqi military machine   overthrow saddam
hussein and redesign the entire political situation in the
middle east

            we dont know that he is determined to do this   but it
certainly looks that way   in spite of the cost of establishing
this new order among nations the number of men and machines
he will have to deploy in the persian gulf   and the effort it will
take to get them there for the two or three months it may take to
overcome iraq   and the two or three years we may have to
maintain them there afterwards to ensure an acceptable
government in iraq   and how much will it cost?   20 billion
50 billion   or 100 billion   to maintain the comity of
nations?   and how much of it will be paid by our "allies"?

            of course if it costs us 100 billion   it may still be
less than a quarter of the price of our savings and loan disaster
which could cost us up to 500 billion   and the gulf crisis
has been such an absorbing diversion that maybe george bush
computed this all in advance   decided it was cheap at the price
and determined on this course from the beginning   its

David Antin

possible   but i am not completely convinced

          it seems just as possible   and maybe more likely that
once george bush determined to protect saudi arabia   from then
on he was determined by everything else

2. suspension

       my son just got out of ucla last year   actually a year ago
last january   where he studied political science   and what do
you do when youve studied political science in a college?
       college seems to develop you for a time   and then releases
you finally to make decisions about your life   its like a certain
kind of botanical organism   podlike   that releases spores into
the world   where it hopes that they take maybe   at least it
releases them   or they go away anyway   and maybe they take
    it takes in nearly grown children   and after a certain
period of time releases adults   and most of them came in
wanting to be adults   if they want anything at all   but they
usually stay children as long as they stay in college   to the
extent that the college keeps them feeling and looking like
children   because one of the things colleges do   like all
schools   is that they conspire to keep students feeling like
children   and this conspiracy is in part with the students
    who have been in schools most of their lives   and being
in school maintains a continuity with your childhood   you
know youre in school and you dont have to decide what to do with
your life   you may worry about it but you dont have to decide
    and when you get out of college you feel in a way   bereft
    not necessarily terrible   but bereft of your childhood
maybe   and you may feel great   but somehow youre suddenly
out there in the world   and it seems that theres now something
you have to decide   like what am i going to do with my life?

    you might have thought of that earlier and maybe you did
    but probably not consistently or very long   or even if you
did you never had to take your own advice and do anything about it
    and thats what creates the anxiety   the sense that now you
have to do something about it   i understand thats why most
young people in college dont want to think about it   i didnt

think about it very much either when i was in college and i dont
think too many people do   because theres not much you can
do about it till you get out

        so blaise studied political science while he was in college
        which means he was studying pretty much what he wanted
to study   taking courses in whatever interested him   19th
century russian literature or   chinese economics   weimar
culture the cold war the history of nigeria   which is what i
suppose a college is for   to present you with a chinese menu of
things to think about   unless you're in a training school that
turns you out to be a technician of such and such a type   capable
of doing a certain kind of job   and then youve had your training
and you go out and look for the job you were trained for
                                                        unless theres
a recession   when theres a recession maybe you do that for a
while   but if you dont find the kind of job you were trained for
        you worry   and maybe go back to graduate school or you
look for some other kind of job requiring your competence in
statistics or english composition or whatever the rest of your college
education fitted you for   or you may wind up driving a taxicab
        but blaise studied political science because he was the kind
of kid who used to read newspapers since he was nine or ten
        and he was used to listening to political arguments over the
dining room table just about all of his life   so he studied political
science because he was interested in politics the way he thought
        everybody was interested in politics   and he probably wanted
to win some of those arguments
                                so when he comes out of college
with a degree in political science it seems reasonable to suppose
that he'll look for some kind of job in politics   now what kind of
job can you get in politics with a bachelors degree in political
        science?   which ideally prepares you to get into a graduate school
of political science   that is a professional school that will try
to train you to write articles on political subjects in the learned
journals edited by the faculty members of similar schools or to
write books about politics that they will review   and if they
review them favorably will allow you to become a faculty member
of similar schools   and if they review them very favorably
        may classify you as an expert and enable you to become a
member of a political   think tank and perhaps a consultant to

practicing politicians on the area of your expertise   but blaise
is 23 years old and at this particular moment he doesnt want to
go to graduate school to learn how to write theoretical papers on
political subjects   he's 23 he's been in school for over 16 years
he's got a girlfriend who is 22   who has also just gotten out of
school last june   and they seem to be enjoying being together
    outside of the world of school they have an apartment in west
los angeles   theyre living together and she's been thinking about
going to study french culture in a graduate school in new york
where they probably dont write theoretical papers   but immerse
you in french language and culture with a view toward preparing
you for some kind of career in intercultural   relations with
france   a country with which she has had a long romance
        meanwhile she's got a job helping run the language labs at
ucla   which she doesnt like very much   but it lets her
stay in los angeles with blaise   who's got his job in politics
    he's a staff assistant to a liberal los angeles congressman
    its a nice job but a hard job   its the kind of job   that
only the young can do   its one tenth public relations and
nine tenths   trouble shooting   this congressman has a
    large district in west los angeles   where it seems everyone
has problems and wants their congressman to solve them
                                                    a santa
monica man in the hospital with cancer wants to get visas for
    his sons to come from the philippines to visit him before he dies
but the   immigration authorities are unsympathetic   an
engineer at lockheed has been transferred to a position where he
    needs security clearance but the government   drags its feet
        an enlisted woman from manhattan beach wants out of the
army because her superior officers are sexist   a man from
venice wants help because his navy son has been accused of
stealing and the navy is threatening a dishonorable discharge
        the city of inglewood wants more apartments in a h.u.d.
funded apartment complex set aside for its residents   el segundo
is troubled by noise from l.a.x. and is complaining about takeoff
patterns   a black principal is transferred out of a high school in
    torrance and there are charges of racism   the renters association
of santa monica wants a change in   pending housing legislation
    that was designed to protect them   but lets builders buy back
their buildings at prices that will allow them to turn handy
    profits in high priced real estate markets like los angeles

David Antin

san francisco and new york

      so what can blaise do about this?   sometimes a lot
sometimes not much and sometimes nothing at all   he gets
   security clearance for the engineer   gets the woman an
   honorable discharge   he's pretty good on visas   the airport
people have had enough bad publicity and will try to accommodate
el segundo on the takeoffs   blaise meets with the h.u.d. officials
   and the representatives of inglewood writes lots of letters but
   gets nowhere noticeable   but he gets his congressman to
intervene in the housing legislation and sets the renters group up
with the names of the congressional group appointing the committee
of reconciliation that is going to work out the details between
the senate and the house so that the renters committee can lobby
   them   it takes a couple of meetings dozens of phone calls and
maybe he helps them win this one   but in torrance all he can do
   is sit there and watch the black action group   and the
representatives of the administration and the board of education
and the teachers union people try to get through to each other and
   fail   then go back   to his office and write a report to his
   congressman
         if you include the number of times he has to go to
testimonial dinners or visit local city councils and to meet with
chambers of commerce or give talks to action groups its a job that
takes 60 hours a week and its a job that only the young can do
     and only for a while   till they decide what theyre going to
do with their lives

      so what is blaise going to do   he's thinking of going to
spain   his girlfriend has been thinking of going to spain
   she's bored with her job in los angeles and she speaks spanish
pretty well   though not as well as she speaks french   and she
thinks maybe she should go to spain and try to get a job there
   because its a pretty affluent country   and in a year she could
really get   completely fluent   it will probably help her in
her graduate studies when she decides to go   and blaise also has
pretty good spanish since he studied in guadalajara   and maybe
they can both get jobs there   and   live in europe for a year
   or two   blaise likes that idea   he's getting pretty tired of
trying to help people   and he likes the idea of living abroad
     so he thinks   well maybe i'll come to spain   but a

little bit later   because it seems that his congressman is going
   to make a run for the senate
                              if that happens blaise may want to work
   in his campaign   so he wouldnt quit his job   he'd simply take
time off at the end of march join cindy in spain and stay with her
   in barcelona   until the campaign starts   which would give
them five months in spain   but then she'd be coming back to go
   to graduate school in either new york or baltimore   while he'd
   be working in california   this is a real difficulty   but of
   course she doesnt know whether she'll be accepted into the
   graduate program in new york   and it's only a one year program
anyhow   and theyve been further apart before   when she was
   studying in lyon and he was studying in guadalajara   and they
dont really know what they want   she may want to work for
   the u.n. and he may want to be the next jewish senator from
   california   meanwhile he's in a state of suspense   he might
want to turn around and become a journalist
                                           does he want to write
   about the kind of life he's been living   probably not   does he
   want to become a political scientist?   a historian   a public
   servant?   when you're 23 it's hard to tell   you only know
   that you want to find a place somewhere in the world that you
havent entered yet   and so youre out there in space
            suspended   out of this world   waiting   maybe even
in a cheerful way   because you haven't yet stepped down into it

3. diversion

       there was a polish novelist living in exile   and one
wednesday he went out and bought himself a very fashionable pair
of lemon-colored shoes   he took them home put them on and
went out with his cape and cane and after a while realized that
they hurt his feet   the next day he went back to the shoe store
   insisted that they take the lemon-colored shoes back and bought
another pair of exactly the same color size and shape

4. digression

a woman got a job working for the state conservation district
in ramona   which is a little town in my part of california   it
was a small state-funded operation that offered assistance to
farmers   consultation   advice   pamphlets   she'd been
working as a secretary and she wanted a job doing something
socially useful and more intelligent than the kind of things she'd
been working on   and though the state of california didnt spend
a lot of money on this what they did with limited resources was to
make real environmental help available to farmers   but because
this was a low budget program the conservation district couldnt
afford space of its own   so they borrowed some space from the
county department of agriculture   and they shared this space in
a kind of garage-like cinder block building in ramona with the
county department   which did several other things in the same
building that they had their own people to take care of   but
there was one thing they wanted the conservation district to
handle in exchange for the use of the space   it was to take
charge of the sale of rodent poison to the farmers who needed it

it was not an onerous task the farmers didnt come in too often
the zinc phosphide came in small 5 lb bags   and she was
rarely so busy that the chance for some conversation with an
occasional farmer didnt provide a small but pleasant break from
her clerical work   and of course the farmers needed the poison
to protect their crops from gophers rats rabbits and the like   so
she felt she was doing her bit for the environment

she was the kind of person who derived satisfaction from the
fact that she was working at a job that contributed something
positive to society   and returned value to nature   she was one
of those people with a kind of green thumb   plants seemed to
flourish around her   she had filled her office space and   to
the delight of the other clerks working for the department of
agriculture   much of their common space with green plants
she had them on her desk on unused shelves and all around
the floor   and she would water them carefully in the mornings
as soon as she'd bicycled into work   bicycled because she knew
the problem the internal combustion engine was creating for the
atmosphere of southern california and she didn't want to be part

of the problem   and she was a pleasant and sociable person
who enjoyed sitting there surrounded by her plants that filtered the
gentle california light that came through the window over her
desk   and taking lunch with her co-workers from the
department of agriculture   though she never got her lunch from
the local mcdonalds but always brought herself a pita sandwich
with vegetables and sprouts and a little container of fat free yogurt
or a fresh fruit juice that she mixed in her blender in the morning
she was the kind of californian that you would expect to be
a runner or jogger or into yoga   though she wasnt at all   she
was simply into a kind of quiet wholesome living   a vegetarian
and a nonsmoker   and she was naturally fairly healthy
never got colds or physical problems of any kind   till
some time toward the end of winter she started getting terrible
headaches for the first time in her life   she wasnt used to any
kind of serious drawn out or repeated physical ailments of any
sort   and now she was suffering from headaches every day
she would come into work water her plants   work through
the morning   have lunch   and by early afternoon she would
have a splitting headache every day

at first she thought it might be too stuffy in the office and
she brought in a fan and propped open the door to let the outside
air circulate   but it didn't help   she went to a physical
therapist   a chiropractor   an acupuncturist   a dietitian
tried yoga   went to a psychotherapist   but   it was no help
her posture was all right her diet was fine her sex life o.k.
she started to meditate and it made her feel better while she
was meditating but the headaches came back   one of her
co-workers gave her some nuprin and it turned out this was the
only way she could control them   but after a while she was
living on nuprin   finishing off a bottle every couple of days
finally she went to a doctor who specialized in environmentally
caused disorders   and he went through everything in her life
with her   her foods her clothes her home and then he started on
the workplace   and she told him about the little bags of zinc
phosphide that she sold for the county

now the way zinc phosphide works is that its spread in the
form of a powder put on pellets of food that the gophers or squirrels
like to eat   and when they eat it   it comes in contact with

moisture   which causes it to release phosphine gas that will
   kill the animal   and in somewhat larger quantities would kill
a human being

        now the little five pound bags of zinc phosphide were kept on
the floor of a closet outside of which she used to keep plants that
   she watered every day   and cinder block buildings are
notoriously leaky   though southern california is a very dry place
   except in late fall winter and early spring   so that   while
the average rainfall in this area will hardly ever go much above 10
   inches for the whole year it hasnt reached that level in the last
four years   and in the times when it does rain it may rain very
   heavily   and the buildings   which are constructed on the
   assumption that the climate is very dry are not very leakproof
        so that the water from the rains and the overflow from the
plants she was watering would seep under the door of the closet and
   moisten the bottoms of the little paper bags   and the closet
would fill with phosphine gas
                                this is what her doctor finally told
her   but by then she had been sick for so long she had taken too
   many days off   she had taken several leaves and she had had to
quit her environmental job   and she was a little mad at the
   conservation district group that had not thought about this or
   informed her about it when they set her to selling the zinc
phosphide   and she was madder at the county department of
   agriculture for asking her to sell this poison that came in paper
   bags that were sometimes broken   and without informing her
that they required very precise and complicated methods for handling

        apparently the bags are never supposed to be stored on the
   ground   they have to be placed on skids or trays at least 4
inches above the ground and workers are supposed to wear masks and
   gloves when handling them   so it was understandable that she
   was disturbed and angry when she found out about this after she
had been to see a couple of doctors and a lawyer   and she naturally
   wanted some kind of remuneration   it was not a big case   she
   simply felt that she had lost so much time working   she had
to pay up her medical bills and finally had to give up her job   so
she felt she was entitled to something for all that   and she filed
   a claim for workmans compensation

but the county department of agriculture contested her claim
on the grounds that she had failed to follow the rules and
regulations for handling toxic substances which were fully described
in the appropriate publication of the department   had failed
to wear the appropriate garments mask and gloves that were
required for handling zinc phosphide   and moreover had allowed
it to be stored in a completely improper manner where contrary
to official regulations it had come directly in contact with the
ground   they also wrote several huffy letters to the state
conservation district upbraiding them for not informing their
employee of the appropriate measures for handling toxic substances
like zinc phosphide   to which the state conservation district
has not replied

she has also written several letters to the state conservation
district explaining her claim   reminding them of the sufferings
she had borne   the time and money she had lost   and of the
fact that no one had given her any indication of the danger of the
material she was being asked to handle or of the risks she was
being asked to run
so far the state has remained silent

5. destruction

now into this same ambience of california where i live
into this sunshine filled state   my wife and I have brought
our two mothers   my wifes and my own   because it was
the only way we could keep an eye on them as they were beginning
to fade   my mother is 86 years old   shes not someone i ever
had a close relationship with   i left home when i was 16 and i
felt great as soon as i left   i didnt hate her but i couldnt stand
being around her   so when i lived with her i couldnt stand her
but as soon as i got away i felt friendly enough to call her every
once in a while   and when it looked like i was going to get
married i came down with ellie to visit her   and when ellie
and i got married we would call her every so often and visit her
once in a great while   and i kept up this detached but friendly
relationship when we moved from new york to california

but at a certain point   around nineteen seventy-seven or

eight she became endangered   she felt she was losing it   one
day she called me up and started crying on the phone   she said
i had to help her   everything had gotten impossible everything
had changed   her neighborhood was dangerous   i had to do
something   get her out of there   take her to california   i
didnt look forward to the prospect of having my mother as a
neighbor but she sounded desperate   and as it happened in the
next few weeks i was scheduled to fly to toronto and i realized it
would be easy enough for me to drop into new york to check out
her situation and see if it was as desperate as it sounded

      so i did my talk in toronto and caught an early morning plane
for new york   sharing the empty terminal with a weary looking
older guy who turned out to be a nuclear engineer   whose job was
to go around nuclear plants inspecting them for safety   it was he
said a difficult job because wherever he went the managers and the
workers all seemed to feel that he was some kind of spy trying to
show them up   so they did all sorts of little things to show
they didnt like him   like letting him eat his lunch all alone
and he didnt care much about that   but then they were always
covering things up making his job that much harder   but there
was too much to cover up   a lot of the plants were old and just
deteriorating   pipes were repaired hastily with sloppy welds
and buried out in fields   like the winston salem plant   he
never could find out what was wrong there   but it was leaking
somewhere   because the tobacco fields around the reactor up to
three miles away were brown with blight   and they were fine
everywhere else   it didnt take much to figure out what was at
fault   but nobody was going to spend the money to dig up all
the fields and see where the leaks were   and if anybody knew they
werent telling him

      we flew together into new york and i took the brighton line
down to brooklyn because my mother lived on ocean parkway
      and getting out at the church avenue stop around albemarle
road would give me a chance to check out the neighborhood   it
had changed   it was poorer   there were fewer jews and more
black people and hispanics   but they werent destitute   just
struggling a little harder to maintain a decent working class
appearance   but i could see what the trouble was   my mother
was a racist   not the kind of racist who thinks black people are

inferior or wants to ship them back to africa   but the kind who
gets nervous whenever she's around them   as if they were some
    sort of unpredictable species that she's afraid of   and she
behaves around them the way she behaves around dogs   which
    she's also afraid of   near which she tries either to be not noticed
or is very carefully friendly   but mainly she tries to keep out of
their way   when i lived on court street i once had her over for
dinner and took her out for a walk to show her the neighborhood
        we were walking down the street toward a group of kids
        neighborhood friends i used to play catch with and i raised my
hand to wave to them when my mother clutched my other arm and
rushed me across the street   and they were only eight to twelve
    years old but they were black   so i understood one of her
problems   but when i got to her house i realized there were more

            as soon as i got there she told me youre going to have to help
me   i cant manage anymore   but she didnt mean money
        she simply couldnt handle things   she had gotten so afraid
of her changed neighborhood it was hard for her to go out to
waldbaums to shop   though it was only four blocks away   she
was afraid to go to her bank   which was about seven blocks
    away   and in fact the first thing she told me was that i would
have to help her with her money   and when i asked her what did
she mean she led me into the bathroom where she reached around
    behind the sink and took out a porcelain tile and set it on the toilet
seat   then she reached into the hollow space between the
porcelain and the water pipes and came out with a plastic bag that
looked like a large packet covered with plastic wrap and tied with
    rubber bands   she took these off and from inside removed
something resembling a large tobacco pouch that she opened to
    show me a great pack of single dollar bills and said you have to
help me take it to the bank   "so lets take it to the bank," i said
        but she said "we'll have to count it first"

                do you know what its like to count three
thousand dollars in single dollar bills?

        i said okay   i counted she counted   we differed by $10.00
        i said mom i'll give you the $10.00   let's call it quits she
said no we'll have to count it again   we got closer   it was
$4.00 off   i said mom lets take it to the bank $4.00 is

70

nothing its like a cab ride   we have to count it again   so we
counted it again   three times I counted $3000 worth or
thereabout   and each time it was a little bit more or a little
bit less but it was within shooting range   we were not enough
off to buy a decent meal   so forget it   but we counted it and
we counted it till we came to $3000   and then we counted it
again to see if we could stay there

      "now" she said "we can take it to the bank"   and i said okay
      "because there" she said "you can check my interest"   so   i
took her across ocean parkway up to church avenue and past the
little stores and markets that i dimly remembered as a little more
jewish and italian and a little more prosperous when i'd last
seen them and past the old beverly theater to the bank on the
corner of macdonald avenue   we get to the bank and we wait on
line to make our deposit   its not a long line and it moves
fairly fast because there is a very pleasant businesslike guy who's
the teller   who's very polite yet moving very crisply through
the people in front of us   but there's a problem   this very
efficient and good natured guy happens to be black   which
my mother doesnt notice till she hands him the money   then
i can tell she starts to get nervous   not so anybody would notice
but she gets a little flustered because he cant quite make out a
number on the deposit slip   and she starts to get belligerent
but he's used to dealing with cranky old ladies and he smiles
pleasantly and makes the correction for her and starts to count
the money   he puts on one of those rubber finger tips and counts
the bills   and he comes close too   he's within a dollar of
three thousand   i think he had three thousand and one   my
mother wasnt happy   i said "quit   while you're ahead
thats more than either of us got"   she says no count it
again   he counted it again and he got only 3000   this made
her very suspicious   she said please count it again   this poor
guy was so nice he didnt even roll his eyes   he counted it again
and got 3000 on the nose

      "mom" i said thats 3000 twice   its a winner   but she
said we counted 3004 and 3002 and i just want to be sure   i said
yeah but we also counted 2996   leave it alone   no   it had
to be counted again   the fourth time   the poor guy was going
out of his mind   he counted it again for her   he could see

71

that she was a crazy little lady in an orange hat   so he counted
  it again for her to $3000   and my mother was finally satisfied
      it was $3000   so i took her to california

              so she comes to california and i got her a nice little
place in an apartment complex in pacific beach that was managed by
  a big cheerful guy who used to work in the aircraft industry   it
    was a sunny little apartment easy to take care of and not far from
the bay or from the stores on garnet   to which the apartment
    manager who had a soft spot for little old ladies would drive her
for serious shopping on the weekends   but to which she could
  walk to pick up a few groceries when she needed them or visit
her local branch of the bank of america to get her interest recorded
          and she lived there alone for a while   almost a year before
it started getting bad   then she started worrying about the
apartment manager   because he was too nice   he must have
  wanted something from her   whenever she complained about
being a poor widow and all alone in a strange city he told her she
    must be sitting pretty retired with rich kids who could take care
  of her   nothing to do but collect social security checks and
pay the rent   so she was sure he was after her money   and
    then things started to disappear   little things but they really
annoyed her   her hairbrush   then a potato peeler was gone
          and finally her ice cube trays were missing   she decided
the apartment manager was stealing them and she told ellie and
me   and when we said that was crazy why would anyone steal
  ice cube trays   she said of course its crazy thats why he's doing
    it   to gaslight me

          that was when she started having trouble with san diego gas
and electric   they said she hadnt paid her bill   she was sure
  that she had paid the bill   they were sure that she hadnt
        they were threatening to turn off her gas and electric   she
had trouble with the phone company   there were people talking
  on her line   the people at the bank of america were very rude
to her   she used to go into the bank every day   sometimes
  twice a day to have them record the interest on her account
        then she wasnt satisfied theyd recorded it correctly and
insisted that they check it and make sure that they had recorded
  the right amount and then she often wasnt satisfied with that
        one time she was so insistent that the assistant bank manager

had to show her out of the building and she was very insulted
    so we moved her into a residential hotel "for active elderlies"
    it was a kind of hotel for people in various stages of decline
    some of them went out shopping on their own or to the
movies visited with friends   others hung out in chairs in the
lounge or sat on chairs on the porch or lobby waiting for meals
    but it had a social director who set up activities for them
    exercise classes lectures religious instruction educational
films   and a staff of underpaid ladies and mexican men who
prepared the meals that everybody ate in a common dining room
    cleaned up the rooms made the beds and maintained the grounds
    and i took over her finances

    this was a pretty good situation and lasted several years
    it was even better when ellie's mother jeanette started losing
her mind because we moved her in too and the two ladies kept each
other a kind of absent minded company   sitting together in
the large commons room sleepily through a bible lecture or a
national geographic film   and always being pleasantly surprised
to come together at their regular seats at the dining room table
    but then things suddenly got worse   or whats more likely
they were getting steadily but imperceptibly worse   the way all
things run quietly down and you never notice till something
suddenly crashes   and the people running the place told us we're
really not prepared to deal with this   they werent even prepared
    to talk to us about it   they said i had to come down and see for
    myself   and i did

    i went up to my mothers room and found out that my mother
had developed a kind of ritualistic relation to her own excrement and
had begun to make little louise bourgeois-like sculptures out of
    her own shit three or four inches high which she scattered
apparently haphazardly about her room   i would open a drawer or
i would look in one of her shoes   or in the medicine cabinet
    and there would be a little monument of nearly fossilized
shit three or four inches high   so i had to get her out of
there to some place where they were prepared to deal with this
    which was a nursing home

    i started to go round looking at nursing homes all over san
    diego   and the first thing i found out is that they all had

waiting lists   no matter how seedy or small or how hospital-
like large and new they were they all had waiting lists   and they
almost all seemed to be for people who were so physically disabled
that all the patients who werent lying around in hospital beds were
strapped into wheelchairs   apparently nobody who got into a
nursing home was able to walk   or else for some mysterious
reason they stopped being able to walk as soon as they got there
at first this seemed odd and nobody could explain it to me
finally i figured out that it was less inconvenient for the
nurses to deal with somebody tucked into a hospital bed or strapped
into a wheelchair sitting than wandering around the hallways of
bedlam in a loony daze   less inconvenient and in some sense safer

but i made up my mind to find my mother a nursing home
where they could deal with her excrement fetish and still let her
wander harmlessly around   and I found one   it was a pastel
colored postmodern nursing home called the carmel mountain
health care center and occupied a large one story building
between a small hospital and a high tech military contractor called
TRW on the way out to escondido in the middle of a nowhere razed
from chaparral country and called the avenue of industry one turn
off innovation drive

the nursing home was new and almost empty   the building
was a large quadrangle built around a desolate central garden that
was furnished with four or five little metal tables under umbrellas
where patients could sit in the shade with their visitors and its
mindless occupants ambled freely up and down the long corridor of
the ward reserved for them for the most part mumbling quietly to
themselves on their way from their rooms to the little common
room or the dining room where they usually took their meals
occasionally stopping and waving or demanding incomprehensible
things from the filipino nurses who usually smiled cheerfully and
ignored them   except for one athletic looking middle aged
guy   who always moved in a quick shuffle while emitting what
sounded to me like a continuous low scream that i finally
realized was supposed to be singing

so this seemed like a good place for my mother who   while
not a cheerful person as long as she still had most of her wits about
her   seemed cheerful enough now to join the procession

moving along the corridors exchanging some small joke with a
passing nurse   and the place itself seemed cheerful enough   it
was clean and new and the walls were all pastel colored   and it
seemed even more cheerful when ellie's mother came to join her
there   because we thought that the two ladies would keep each
other a kind of company wandering down the corridor together past
all the people lying in their bedrooms with tubes sticking out of
them on the way to the dining room   or out into the little
mohave of a garden behind the commons room   because jeanette
was a very charming cheerful little soul who chattered gaily and
melodiously in fragments of yiddish or english to the nurses or
patients or anyone in her general vicinity   and while my
mother was never really a charming person and wore a rather dour
expression much of the time   she was a physically healthy
woman with a mildly sardonic humor who was still capable of
coming out with a kind of cynical joke that even the nurses
would smile at when they had enough english to understand it
but the two ladies didnt recognize each other any more
or anybody else

they didnt recognize us either   although they seemed to
enjoy seeing us when we came by   jeannette was always
delighted to see eleanor whenever we came by   she might be
standing in the hallway talking seriously to herself but her face
would break into a sunny smile as soon as she caught sight of ellie
"youre so beautiful" she would say "you look just like my
daughter"   "but ma i am your daughter" ellie would say   and
jeanette would invariably say "how wonderful!"

but the two ladies were in separate wards now   they'd
finally gotten my mother into a wheelchair   my mother who
was a physically very healthy woman and   used to do push-ups in
the bathtub till she was eighty-four   but a couple of months ago
she fell and broke her hip and they operated they put a pin in the
hip and did a whole reconstruction of which they were justifiably
proud and they were giving her physical therapy   but there was
no way they were going to be able to teach her to walk again when
she couldnt remember who the therapist was or why she was
dragging her around by the arm   so they put her in another ward
on the other side of the nursing home with the physically disabled
crazies   and when we picked up jeanette ellie would take her by

the arm and the two of them would dance down the corridor past
the little old german lady with the sour face who kept muttering
"schwer schwer" and would never tell me "was ist schwer" but only
looked puzzled that i'd said anything to her at all   and ellie
would dance her past the soft shoe screamer who thought he was
singing and out the locked door that kept in the walking crazies
into the empty corridor that led past the deserted central garden
to my mothers ward   where we would usually find her lying in
bed or strapped into a wheelchair and we'd lead the two of them
ellie holding onto jeanette and laughing and joking with her
and me pushing my mother in her wheelchair while leaning
over her and petting her hair and trying to assure her it was really
me who was petting her
"you look like a very nice man" she would
say   "but who are you?" and when i would assure her it was me
her son   david   she would say   "then why dont i
recognize you?"   and we would negotiate them out to the empty
garden or the deserted reception room at the front of the building
where we would switch ladies   and i would talk with jeanette
because i understood her yiddish better than ellie and could make
a stab at speaking it   but it was always the same   in
melodious fragments   "the young people" she would say   "they
dont understand them   they have their own   i tell them
not to worry   but they have things on their mind   i
explain   its not the same   theyre different   but he doesnt
know   and what can you do   its not so good   and it
never gets better"

and i never know who they are who he is who are the young
but i try at appropriate moments   when it seems necessary   or
useful   to insert a comment that will help her go on   and if i
guess right it does and she goes on   and if i guess wrong she'll
look confused for a moment but go on anyway or start again
while ellie strokes my mothers hair and tries to say consoling
things to her in english and my mother looks at her as though to
say something and then claps her hands together angrily as though
she's punishing herself for something and tears come into her
watery blue eyes and then sometimes she'll smile   but the last
time we were there we had a hard time finding my mother   we
picked up jeanette   who was walking up and down the hall
chattering and waving to the nurses   and made our way to my

mothers ward but she wasnt there   and we checked in with the
head nurse who wasnt sure where she was but thought she might
be in the dining room eating   and we'd never been to this
dining room   but we finally found her there sitting at a
long table with about a dozen other people   who were also
sitting in front of plates of food at this long table   some gazing
down deliberately at their food   others looking absently toward
the dark screen of a television set on the other side of the room
     a few of them picking at their food   and a couple looking
in the general direction of a speaker who was gesticulating
intensely and delivering a kind of religious lecture to them   he's
a big man in a wilted white shirt and a pale gray business suit
who looks like a tv evangelist   a beefy handsome man with a
noble profile and his pale yellow hair brushed into a pompadour
     and he's working hard at it   stabbing into the air with his
arm to emphasize some of his points
                                                            but my mother is eating
deliberately bringing the mashed turnips to her face   because my
mother likes to eat   and takes her eating seriously   when she
eats turnips nothing can take her mind off the turnips   she
     wouldnt even look at me   till she was finished   and the
preachers talk is finding hard going in the overheated common room
     his face is getting red and he's taken off his jacket and rolled
it up under his arm   and he's saying to the little cluster of
people seated around him   "you say you forget and youre worried
about forgetting   but god also forgets   he forgets lots of
     things   there are too many important things to keep on his
     mind   thats why we have prayer   to remind him"
                                                            and the
people who were picking at their food continued to pick and the ones
     watching the darkened tv screen continued to watch it   and
the people sitting around the minister stared right into the air over
     his head while my mother continued to eat and jeanette started
humming in her beautiful birdlike voice while the minister
     continued to justify the ways of god to man   "and you say i
have pain   why do i have pain   if there is a god why do i have
     pain?" and he leaned across the table and stared right into the
     face of an elderly gentleman who slowly lowered his head into
his plate so that his face was buried in the mashed potatoes
     "god wants you to have pain because he has pain   he has
lots of pain and he wants you to be like him"

77

David Antin

* * *

     my mother has finished eating and she looks up at me blankly
       so i start talking to her   i tell her about blaise   how
blaise is working for a congressman in los angeles   how he has a
   pretty girlfriend and i think he's going to spain   my mother
sits there   he's going to spain to get a job or he's not going to
  spain   i can make it up any way i like   i say he's going to
spain   my mother sits there   he's not going to spain   she
  also sits there   i say barcelona but maybe he'll go to madrid or
maybe he'll go to brooklyn   i can say all of these things and i'm
  waiting to see if i get a response   i dont get any response so
i ask her if she recognizes jeanette   jeanette is talking to ellie
  about the young   "of course" she says   "of course i like
the young people to come to my house   i prepare things   i
  think theyll feel better   i talk to them"   and ellie is just
nodding her head and smiling and listening and the preacher is
  finished has put on his coat and gone away   and through all
this my mother is just sitting there silently   and jeanette
starts to feel cold and is suddenly shivering   and i put my jean
  jacket over her shoulders and ellie says "she looks so thin" and
wraps the arms of the jacket tighter around her   and jeanette
is very depressed and says "its so cold in here i feel so cold"
  and i think she's feeling cold because my mother is in a daze
and she cant get any human response out of my mother who has
turned into a vegetable and she's beginning to get frightened by
  it   so eleanor takes jeanette by the arm and jeanette dances
off with her   jeanette dances off with one arm in the air looking
gay and crazy in a sort of happy bedlam   and i'm sitting there
  with my mother   sitting there and i'm trying to think of what
to say   and i'm just about to say something when she says to me
    "i cant help it"
    and she doesnt say another word

Money

Aleksei Parshchikov

— Translated from the Russian by
Darlene Reddaway with Michael Palmer

Walking on Stone Bridge
playing at star wars visions
I suddenly felt the air
tissue into whispered layers.
Albania will triumph in global battles,
descending toward depths of another world,
the wobblings of fleeting ether
amplified, piercing me through.
Within frenzied swarms of multiplication
devoid of primordial zero
a point opened on Stone Bridge
from which I strode through a "three-ruble" bill.

We have an intuition — the more-than
of our very selves. A family of astral figures,
flaring up, snailing helices behind.
Money lacks a more-than. Tempestuous hens
take the Dutch guilder on a stroll
along with the royal family busts —
as many hens as people need
strut about, pecking at eternity's eyes.
The bills are the trace of touch,
they could take the place of eyes, of ears.
Monies, to the State you're the same
as lateral line to a fish.

And I stepped off the bridge on the count of "three."
O golden freebie!
I fell from the inside of money
to the inside-out of money now.
There I strolled the gallery

Aleksei Parshchikov

and saw Presidents from behind
sitting, straighter than hafts,
peering out the windows of their bills.
I saw how easily they change
the world's scales from point zero.
And with a precision that ignites us
they tense like a bullet in a cage.

I understood that money was a statue
jammed together by finger-people,
a passion-hot vacuum,
for Russians and foreigners alike.
Galloping on the final steed and growing brighter,
it stings people's faces,
yet not we, but our figures
of intuition combat it.
Like wind-up messiahs, they race across seas,
tacking nimbly between watermarks,
which darken bicarbonate ships
in sickening chasms.

These figures are not programmed;
they resemble: a stick striking
a light bulb; their traits:
in bondage they don't
create; they hide behind
the belted eight, ahead of
the speeding shell. Like a hole in the chest
they can't be exchanged.
Recorded in the "Diamond Sutra,"
they're the mere shadow of soul, barely etched.
While we bathe in the nacreous suds
of passivity, they pave our way.

The bills flew, skirting riches,
their shelf-ridges branched,
they looked like mushrooms layered on a tree
robbing the universe of its safe
transported by the horseman of the void, king of finances,
all the world's money on his back.
The Kremlin chimes struck twelve

and the horseman turned to me.
Rippling like a biker's leathers,
a Scout caught out behind the barn,
I heard his sybiline voice ascending:
Well, why the stallin' over a three-ruble note?

Figures of intuition! They live
in the desert, their pupils pierced
by spines. Their holy
communes sit high toward the source
of time's river. We have vistas and e-mail,
embraces and earth, and lightning in a bottle.
Death can't afford
what they have to sell.
They are three-year-old Mozarts.
It's night, the heights exacting, the yearning brute.
Now the figure of intuition grows more visible.
It walks alone from both ends of the bridge.

Lettuce-green three-spot, beet-red twenty
and jaundiced-ten!
And I wanted to wander free of charge
in those clouds where nothing
resembles them, and where "Cinzano" still flows
in the Bar of the Beards,
and where our threesome, beneath lightning at Black Station,
is bound tighter than an atom of water.
But again the mimeo machine of People's Freedom
bated the dreams of teens, and the Pale Horse flew in,
his rash gallop so torn from the earth
that each leap was like a trigger squeeze.

The goal draws us on, traps the cold
larva of a second goal within us.
The future's spirit enthralls the eye:
comparing goals gives rise to prices.
One bill admires itself in another, but not eye to eye,
and from the viewpoint of progress, it seems
to whisk my penniless fate
into a periscope curl. Nevertheless
the bills smell of leather and gasoline,

and if you sleep with an open mouth, they crawl in.
I walked around their property, like Osiris,
backside forward, to deceive them.

History is a sack, an abyss of money inside it.
But the sack has its own story.
Who will draw it into a knot? Who will carry
these powerful centuries on a stick?
Where does the bearer go?
And does he know what a mirror is?
And a wheel? And where does he dwell?
And how much did he pay for a jar of milk?
Could he have gotten lost or stopped
while I walked along Stone Bridge
and spent violet ink?
And who was a figure of intuition to whom?

From 707 SCOTT STREET
A Journal
for Billie Holiday

John Wieners

March 8, 1958

Saturday 1:30 PM

The sun shines. Miss Kids is across asleep on the couch. She wakes and says "I dreamt I just put on — " I can't hear the rest. She goes back to sleep. Dana is asleep in the bedroom beside this one where the sun fills three windows. Miss Kids' dark glasses sound/ crack on the floor.

I must forget how to write. I must unlearn what has been taught me.

Last night I dreamed Alan appeared in a hallway where I leaned against a lintel; there were open doors on all sides and he presented me with a doll, his doll, the country one whose dress he ironed 3000 miles away. He was smiling, a great smile and I still see his white teeth and the black beard on his face. She was dressed in black, the doll, and her long thick hair was tied back the way I had left it. He had put it on top of one of those innumerable chests he had around his house. And I take it as a sign that all is well, I am and he is, today with the doll handed between us, he wanted me to have what he named was his. It is only Miss Kids and Dana who have hangovers. I must not let them hang me up.

She awakes again and asks "Is it cloudy outside yet"? I say "No" and an automobile horn busts our ears and the Chinese kids overhead beat and stomp on the floor.

These days shall be my poems, these words what I leave behind as mine, my record up against time. It is all very sad that we have to fight it. Possibly I may come to love time and its taking of my days.

"It wee may be, I don not think I would"

John Wieners

Right now, it is very fine. The cable car track shuttles in right inside the street and they empty the mail-box. A motor-scooter or motorcycle guns its motor and what bright flesh runs on Leaven- worth Street. The 80 bus stops. Miss Kids has the Mohawk blanket that we (Dana and I) bought in the Morgan Memorial up to her eyes and her hair, her yellow hair is all over the pillow and her shut eye-lids. The cable car conductor rings the bell twice. It also stops. Only man and time move. And the space we are given to inhabit, so fast it is thru our fingers.

I must learn how not to write. I must watch with my 5 senses.

"the 5 perfections that are the 5 hindrances" and I must nail down those who would, all that would hang me up.

The 80 bus going the other way, to Market Street sounds its squashed beep, peculiar to San Francisco, where they are afraid any loud noise would start another earthquake. And yet we all go around screaming.

There is not enough sound in the air. Miss Kids and Dana have headaches from last night.

I must stop being wise. Miss Kids wakes and says "Is it late?"

"Almost two."

"Another day ruined." She stretches her long wax arms (parafin) on the mohair couch. "I feel fine now, Kids." The sun puts gold on her nose. "Kids, they're after me." I tell her "Kids, you look like a fucked Alice-in-Wonderland. And your hands are swollen."

She looks at them. "Dana did it."

Sunday March 9
    8: AM

I make this very very short otherwise it would last forever. I have walked all dawn, all night. Without control. I am forced to stop what I am doing if I want to survive.

I came home and there is a strange man-boy in the bed. Dana must have brought him home although he has never before — and where is Dana. Whatever, I am tired and my arm aches too much to write. Detectives again tonight but why and later I shall tell what they look like.

He does not snore.

July 22

She has brought her treasures out into the sun and I spring
                    to write them down.
4 stills of Charlie Chaplin, "2 by 2" walking on the road
                    then THE END,
                                        spread out in a circle on
            top of the table, ½ an orange rind, the top
of a crystal water jar, a sugar tin, driftwood, green stones
thrushes, my head is still heavy with sleep, the brain cells
not open from the dream.
                            Of night and the junkies
stealing my bicycle and books. I love them because they are the
            boys of my childhood who would chase me home
from school and leave this same terror.
                                So that even here by the sea,
the objects of my life return, from another life that never dies.
                            Fish bones, a pin
She brings me in
another tin
                    charcoal burnt newspaper.
                            I tell her
                            my dream, how they stole
the bike and I think some clothes because they gave us cigarette
papers to redeem them. Red Sharpe's car and when I got my
clothes back they had someone else's name sewn on the label. An
old name I will not reveal,
                    as I do
the contents of table. The black circle drawn around the hole
in the center, the clinking of pewter as she moves the objects
around. The wash of the waves under us.

7/22/59

It has to do with jazz. This dark symphony brought to birth by
brothers, to Hell, to junk. There is a reason for the vocabulary we
use. The demon means we use to extend our life on whatever terms
we can make. An infinite extension. Hold on, fond wanderer, when
you come to this to whatever you are involved in, with every atom
of your body, for this is eternity. And cannot be turned away from,

John Wieners

at peril of your death. The voice comes out
               from the microphone
                  megaphone

20th century r.

          I'll remember April and the way
          it turns in the night the town
                        to snow,
          See the streets banked high and the men
             midgets between them.
          How we walked, under the trees and lights
          laid down in the ice and made love.
          No more. This is a city of the sun.
          Nocturnal dreams are out of place,
          the acts we no longer live return to
             haunt us in our dreams.

            ———————————

I would rather live my dreams at night than
dream them out to fill the morning with pain.

Over I think but the melody
      lingers. I am too
        taken away
by sense/impulses flying me off
        anywhere.
But so it is and here
           I go again
             taking a chance
On love.
   Its gentle barges drift me up
             a hundred new
   channels. Clanging out a
          jungle dance
          man makes under the moon
in whatever clearing he can. Sun
             burnt on my back. Bearing
      her crescent on his breast.
Walking over the land
        like hands beating out a rhythm I do not

understand.
Listen. It is
Morse code from the goddess,
And jingle bells in the
jungle.
Mambah.

July 22

And so now I sit alone in the house with the lights on and
Lex Baxter beating his drums
on the phonograph.
The woman and the 2 children asleep on the porch
covered in blankets.
Night I think with wild cries
and a cymbal clashes somewhere in the jungle.
An uptown beat.
Tempo. Try to maintain control
of the tempo, don't fly off
like the evening star
Venus
from the sea.
How red she is
tonight
Love descends on the land. The record
ends. With
no other words but hers
in the night. Two tin cans
take over this poem. A skin
stretched over bamboo
blows out Cuban blues in the night like
Chicago. East in
the city I dont wanna go no more.
I wanta be
free as the breeze
that blows the waves
onto the shore.
Picks up speed
the tide does
with the rising of the waning/   moon.

July 23

He thought: What next to do? He wanted to stay in
the house beside her, her spirit moving thru
the rooms; the door was open to the porch and the waves were
there. The boy was crying, rather whining in the next room. He
would stop. He was bored. He was not stirred by the rising of the
waves. They would roar for aeons on this beach after him. Who
would be here to hear them. The boy had been sent outside. He
came back in sobbing to the bathroom, and the girl was sucking a
honey dew melon. Motor boat roared in the bay. It was July and the
dog days. He thought what's a poet doing writing prose? Where are
the phantoms he had called down with night. Gone with the night.
Writing he knew was an agony. From what source it sprang he did
not know. That the gods were not with him now he knew. But he
felt that the recording of that fact was important. The crying on
the doorstep had begun again. And the girl came in calling: *Mommy,
do you want to see a sailboat?* I am a silent man, he thought. How
can I ever amuse a woman? Fill her life with a structure that would
support her and prop her for the life they had left together. The
wind is a woman, he thought, but he knew that was not true. And
that this compulsive writing not a productive act for the house.
But the house is a woman, he thought and so he went outside.
    He sat in the big green chair overlooking the sea. He had changed
pens from a ball point one to a fountain. He had taken off his shirt
and there were grapes in his left hand.
        A machine whirred on the porch
            next to theirs
and the waves lapped at the pilings behind him. He ate a grape and
spit the seed into the sea, crushing it first by accident between his
teeth. It is terrible, he thought, to be a reporter of the instant. One
has to be there all the time. He ate another.
    There was a hill behind the house, like a gargantuan guardian of
the house. Its summit reaching a peak exactly in front of their
front door, which opened onto a boardwalk which led to a piece of
land not wider than 5 feet which ran between the hill and sea, along
that little bay of houses which she called *Cat Fish Row.* Across the
bay was another hill which she pointed out to him last night looked
like an Egyptian mummy. He said Gulliver. She said what. He said
Rip Van Winkle. And later, reminds me of a drawing by Blake, you
know the old man with the long white beard. She went inside to

fix the rest of supper and he had smoked. Later she came and got him in the doorway. Sending waves of her being thru him as he stood in the doorway there, holding onto his wrist and causing his belly to bounce in that queer way, like he too was at high tide.

Now it was a new day and he sat in the green chair above the sea with only dungarees on and they too had a hole in the seat. He finished the grapes and threw the vine down. Then the last seed between his teeth, his fingers, he shot it out and it bounced back off the wooden slats which fenced in the porch. Except where he sat which opened directly to the liquid quicksand of what was called Pacific Ocean. The motor picked up speed next door. "Mommy" came drifting out from the house, soft and liquid as the sea. Women really are that, he thought. Even the young, and he would hate, he thought, to anger any one of them. That was why he was such a sibilant around them. Not really bothering them, but always on the lookout for what pleased them. Rather than himself which he reduced to a kind of helpmate around them. Help me God, he thought, to be a man and keep this woman and her brood. Of course it was her house and she brought the food. And he just sat in the sun and let the sweat roll down his thighs. But they were good together at night, she let him know that. And she was his first woman. And despite other lovers, she gladly came back to him, courted him and made him feel at home. Her and her friend Margo up the row. That was good for him, he thought, rubbing orange stains off his belly and spitting his sinus mucous into the sea, pulling part of his skin off his back as he moved too quickly, stuck as he was somehow to the green chair! The sun made his eyes squint and the nasal cavities behind them to discharge their flow down the back of his throat. He liked the taste. That was one thing he got being by the sea, sinus.

And a gull bounced on the waves before him. Another thing. Brown with black tail and black beak, turning to face him as he wrote that down. How a poet controls the universe, he thought. Had not his master taught him: He who controls rhythm, controls. There was a rumble behind him and he half turned but saw nothing so came back again to his book. And the wind cooled him, as the jazz boys would say. And the land loved each new arrival that the wave dumped upon it. And the speedboat across his ears further out than the cruiser, was a caress. Why not? Be a sensualist. Take the pleasures, richness another master had said.

Damn the references to my lords, I must set myself up as absolute,

and as he bent to write it, a black shadow of some winged thing
passed over the white paper and the memory of it made him sit
there for a long time rubbing his running nose.

                                                    July 23

                    A poem for the storyteller

There are many here where I am
                    right now, the ranks of
                        fabled dead, shadows
fall across this paper. Names. Cleopatra
            lists her beloveds gone underground:
                        Anthony, who is to me
                        or I to him
            that I should name him courtier to that heavenly
                        crown.
                                    Oh lush

                life
come to me out of your graves,
            it is the day
    the dead shall rise and populate
                            the skies.
                        They are tears
                        in my eyes,
Mists that lie along the land
                to the west, gray blue spectres
                that have no names,
                    but play
an enchanted game with our minds. Childhood stories,
                we never heard
                till now.

                                                    July 25

                O God of the dawn
                    birds protect me
                            from the dangers of this world.
                As I sit in the dark with the crab

                            90

as my ashtray.
   Dreams reveal
      how much in danger we are,
but across the room in the new blue light
    a little girl sits up, her eyes
        wide open staring at me, and
I know it is your sign.
     No matter what disease gets caught
        in my throat.

The waves wash in on the shore and
I find my solace there.
     Comfort against the coming
       of the storm,
     The trial
   arranged by our betrayers.

   On H

running the most beautiful blue water
      in the sink
vomiting strawberry and green.

               July 27

There is the flute
      that sings
in the dead of the night.
The word that writes itself
   only in the dark.

There is the woman that sleeps
   now and rises in the dawn
      the note
that dances in the air
      on ten toes.
  Then silence.

And shadows on the wall
  that look like snakes.

91

No scheme. Only acts
fragments of the act
that is my life and
that of the fellows around me.

My book is before me
why dont my fingers move over it

July 28

A cricket sings in the morning

What to do with the definite article. And
prepositions. How to
connect
without them. I want language to be taut
as the rope
that holds a teapot over
the fire
for hot water.
We pour it. Into the strainer
thru sweet leaves

"The living spirit grows and even outgrows its earlier forms of
expression; it freely chooses the men in whom it lives and who
proclaim it. This living spirit is eternally renewed and pursues its
goal in manifold and inconceivable ways throughout the history of
mankind. Measured against it, the names and forms which men
have given it mean little enough; they are only the changing leaves
and blossoms on the stem of the eternal tree."   p244   Jung
Modern Man
in Search of
a Soul

This is a stone house built on a ridge in the Big Sur mountains of
Southern California. If it were not for the mist which has surrounded us since we arrived, blocking out the sun but not its glare,

we could see miles out on the Pacific Ocean. There is a garden built on ridges behind the house. The animals have eaten all the plants. I found two sunflowers at the edge of an abyss, one of which I propped up with pink scarf and stick. They face southwest, giant servants to the sun. We stay in doors all day, the mist being a bright gray glare that is like a wall around and below us.

The house was built in 1919 by a man named Lapler. It is in good condition except for the roof which has been used over the years for firewood. We live primitive on a stone floor, mattresses over wood slabs which give an excellent night's sleep. It is an hour's climb from the road, so all supplies have to be brought in on one's back. There is a large stone fireplace to the right of the doorway which opens West. To the East the kitchen and backdoor. All doors are wood. All else is stone. Finely built and of careful craftsman-ship. Except of course cabinets and table and stools, which are handmade from the woods which slope off from this ridge on three sides.

I have trouble with Mass Media

July 28

The sea rolls in the sky. Why
at twilight do I
have to write
all the world dropping off the West

July 29

Even my piss runs golden
in this time of plenty
all spring long one lovely
flowering of my life, and
now in summer I come to
this mountain, this morning
while below the mist rages. I range
here clear in the secrets of
my own being.

John Wieners

Let the peaks be blocked from view
the woman walks thru the room and
brother and sister sit together on the step
    of this stone house.

Lizard under the stone,
bees buzz around us
    in the morning
the two trees full of *canaries* and
    in the burnt grass
        yellow poppies.

The air is alive with sound

                    Aug 24   Sunday

Across the eye come images from another world. They slide on
and off the screen. Bits of tree, four fingers, a silver scissors. They
twist and coil with a shape, a life of their own. Seaweed.
    I am a spy from another scene, sent here to steal your secrets.
Do not speak them before me.
                  I see two leaves
                  Soon they are three.
                  Who is the woodsman
                  that cuts down my tree?

The show's over now. The drug has entered our heads and there
will be peace. Or the black magician rules over my head. There
are other things to do I think than write this. Images flash again.
Language gives way or is funnelled to the tongue there to dart out
as a viper when the right fly lands before its eye.
        Colored paper rose, blue spots, ink spots Boston in 1949,
the sound of cellophane. The sky is brought down. A black boat
scudding in a purple fog. My life with all sails a-furl, the small
town
        left behind, a new soul on the horizon.
        Mark it, make it
            your own.
    Catch up with the colors, be extravagant.
        Spend all that you find
            Shimmy the horizon.

September 5
Saturday
Labor Day Weekend

And what do I care
what they say about me
when it's you I hunger
and pant for over the
whole face of the world.

You and the night and the music
is the song they send to me on the Divasadero.

And of course I turn to my words when the rest of the world runs
out.
They flee from me
that some time did me seek.
Care is what I work for. That no matter what I do
I do it
with some measure of love and time. Take it easy
Tempo Duncan said over the heads of the
audience.
The black tree on the wall spreads its ominous form
thru my brain. I am in no rush, not looking for the universe
through binoculars, see
the blonde girl bend
over two Japanese dolls.
Their black hair as straight and short as hers.
Their eyes roll and their arms and legs bend.
Le style est l'homme.

· · ·

the offal of ancestors
in the hands of a scribe.
Pressure yr. tribe.

The night of December 26   1959
Received 25 dollars
on loan from Trumbull Higgins Family
2500 N. Street
Washington
DC

95

John Wieners

And what is the message? The message is
a discrete or continuous sequence of measurable events distributed in time
is the birth of air, is
the birth of water, is
a state between
the origin and
the end, between
birth and the beginning of

another fetid nest

is change, presents
no more than itself

And the too strong grasping of it,
when it is pressed together and condensed,
loses it

This very thing you are

    • • •

How awe, night-rest and neighborhood can rot

    • • •

I pose you your question:
shall you uncover honey / where maggots are?
    I hunt among stones

The mechanics of the consecutive order of events
in any repeatable sequence

For 711

I may be anybody to you
but you're still Miss King to me.
On the top, planes fly
dogs, bark at men.
Cry in the night, the girl
    downstairs
sends her mother up to get me.
Cuz somethin's on the fire. And

it may be me. So
blow
out the blue smoke. Where
all sound dies in the night. And boys
hitch their trousers
at the moon. Move
through the under brushes.
bird heard out loud.

In the green shadow of the lamplight absolute reality is all I am
interested in, the light shining on the silver edge of these keys, the
magic formation of the letters in rows upon the green field of the
paper, looking like the shadowed corner of a garden, elaborating on
none of this, entering into communion with it, picking up speed
as I go further in, looking out that nothing disturbs me from it,
this place, which cd. be called,
magic, but which
is not, is only
here, 707
Scott Street, San Francisco

AFTERWORD

"707 Scott Street," the journal of John Wieners, dates from 1958–59, the years
when Wieners was composing *The Hotel Wentley Poems*, as well as many of the
great lyrical poems included in his *Selected Poems* (Black Sparrow, 1986). The
journal contains versions of some of these poems as well as others that have
never been published anywhere. "I must forget how to write," he states on the
opening page. "I must unlearn what has been taught me." And then later, a bit
less portentously: "I must learn how not to write. I must watch with my 5
senses." Wieners was twenty-four, still grasping for the ineffable "other" that
would somehow connect his various selves and give his life meaning, yet he
was already fully formed (in many ways) as a poet. The question was how to
define the "other," how to get there through invocation, sex, poetry, drugs and
magic. He knows he has his "whole life" ahead of him, but what does that
matter? Conversations transcribed on the spot (easy to picture poet in corner
of crowded room with journal open), dream narratives, a list of potential contributors to a new issue of his magazine *Measure*, quotes from reading (Witt-
genstein, Jung): everything's permitted, nothing's excluded, poetry and prose
passages alternate, while the emotional pitch centers around loss of love,
frustration, love's inaccessibility, the transience of every encounter. There's a lot
of overly self-conscious romanticism, always redeemed by Wieners' innate

97

John Wieners

ability to step back from and enter into experience simultaneously, as if it were possible to be totally hot and cold at the same time. The journal conveys the sweep of a whole life lived in this way.

In 1972, William Corbett and I visited John in his apartment at 44 Joy Street in Boston with the hope of getting poems from him for our new magazine (edited with Lee Harwood), *The Boston Eagle*. I remember John opening a trunk filled with ledger-sized journals with old-fashioned marble covers. "I'd love to read them someday," I said, thinking out loud, but Wieners caught the genuine interest in my tone and presented one to me. I was initially shocked that he would simply hand over one of his intimate journals to someone he didn't know well (casually, as if he were offering me a taste from a box of bonbons), and without even looking through it, but I accepted the gesture as an act of trust, a gift, an offering. Sometimes giving and taking and accepting is frightening but this moment seemed perfectly clear and unthreatening. My next memory is sitting at a desk on the top floor of Bill's house in downtown Boston; it's the Watergate summer, Bill and his family are in Vermont, and I'm listening to the hearings on the radio and transcribing John's words on my portable Smith-Corona electric. When I was finished I had 77 manuscript pages, a book. On the inside cover of the ledger there was the title: 707 Scott Street, for Billie Holliday. I published a few pages of the journal in an issue of *The World*, the literary magazine of the Poetry Project (an issue devoted to autobiographical writing which I was guest-editing); then, for almost twenty years, the transcript of the journal disappeared. It was the interest of the poet Peter Gizzi, who had heard that such a journal existed, that made me go searching for it. I never presented John with a finished copy of the transcript, though I do remember visiting him again and returning the original, not that it would have mattered (or so he led me to believe) whether I'd kept it or not.

— Lewis Warsh
April 1992

Friends: 1689

Adam Thorpe

IT WAS NOT SNOWING when we set out. The barest places can look heavenly under a bright moon and it was so then. If it had been in any way otherwise I can assure you we would not have set out.

The funeral of good Reverend Josiah Flaw had been fitting but full of sorrow. His assiduousness did cause his death: one stormy evening had him out to administer his flock, whereupon a chill came upon him and he forthwith sunk into the lap of our Lord.

Though his living was as mine and bore barely a roof yet he too was at every beck of those 'twas his ill fortune to mediate for betwixt the ire of the Lord and their gaming and fornication and drinking and covetousness and all the customary excesses, my children. O horrible oaths likewise do our ploughmen bellow, our sowers bark, our reapers bawl at every interposing stone. But when I have flung up my hands at their wantonness, Josiah Flaw was ever zealous for their betterment, that every peasant in this parish might praise the Lord as they delved and not scandalise the very corn.

His being the parish of Bursop.

It too does have its gaggle of ranters. It too does have its precious life-blood sucked, a cheating zeal that sups up as the east wind among the rabble, and leaves our churches hollow.

You shalt see how deep to the heart hath this poison entered, my children, when this true history is wound up.

'Twas not snowing nor in any ways foul when we set out. We thought to foot it back in no more than two hours, the said parish not being unknown to most of you as lying on the northerly edge of our chalkland yet, alas, without a convenient road between us on account of I know not what but those customary reasons that come betwixt convenience and human kind.

The snow already fallen the yesternight was soft no more than a thumb deep. Thereafter was iron.

Then we three left without foreboding. Our curate, our clerk, and thy minister.

Without foreboding did we set out illumined by a round moon which made the snow all abouts gleam and our hearts exult so virgin did the world seem and blameless.

And upon that vast blamelessness of snow the Lord espied us and craved to mantle us in His safekeeping for some have maintained. He did abandon us or that He was full of ire for none other reason than mine own inadequacies.

I have heard the whisperings.

What presumption.

As if those small faults, those thinnest fissures from which we are none of us caulked lest stopped up by death, were worthy of God's ire whilst all about be poxed and gaping.

My children.

The draught be about your legs. My voice cries out of the stone. List, list, we are empty and void. Our walls are smitten with breaches, and little clefts, and our roof is as the furrows of the field, and the stink of neglect doth come up unto our nostrils. Doth the Lord sift us in these days of famine, that is not a famine of bread, nor a thirst for water, but of hearing the words of the Lord, that good grain only doth fall upon the earth?

And the seed is rotten under our clods.

And the drunkard is with drink. And the ploughman is with his oxen. And the inhabitant of Ulverton doth loll fleshly abed. And thus saith the Lord, I will send a fire on the wall of Gaza, and of Ashdod, and of Tyrus, and of Edom, and of Rabbah. I shall smite you with blastings and mildew. For ye have turned judgement into gall, and the fruit of righteousness into hemlock.

Rejoicing in a thing of nought.

Woe.

That our piety is no longer snug with companions.

That we are spaced so, like scattered candles in the dark.

That we are cold.

Woe.

Woe.

For a zealous wind doth blow amongst us, withering the vine.

And the armies of the flashing mind devour the poor secretly.

Then beware, my children.

And that no conjecture further rot amongst you into malice, I shall relate the true history. Not a false whisper upon a filthy wind.

Beginning upon that track that runs higgledy-piggledly worn by shepherds and their more manageable flocks between Bursop and this habitation but rarely by folk making betwixt the two, for it runs along the crests and is not the crow's way, and trusting in the fine light, and William Scablehorne having the way well, being once a shepherd's boy, we soon took to the maiden downs, and were not troubled in any wise by having at our feet but immaculate snow.

For one happy hour we proceeded, my children, across that waste, fortified by our faith, by reflections on the good character of the late lamented and instances of this, and by my fine brandy which, though it was partook of eagerly by William Scablehorne, did barely wet the lips of Simon Kistle our late curate. And even merrily did we proceed, like true pilgrims, towards our holy harbour, for we could mount any drifted incline without sunken shins, and our swift pace hindered the cold from entering our bones. Even merrily, despite our mourning robes, did we proceed across that white waste.

So it was that Adam awoke in the garden that fateful morning teeming with light, unaware of the leadenness which was to befall that very noon.

There is a shame which bringeth sin, and there is a shame which bringeth glory and grace.

Cast a stone into snow and you shall hark no sound. Whip petty Vice and he shall howl but pettily.

Purge, purge, my children.

Purge those false whispers from the foul wind that have set your ears to tingle and your eyes to crowd with base lying images that rise like dust betwixt us. Rather feel inly that rawness of the very first morning of the very first day of creation before the zephyrous balm had blown through the avenues of the universe and scatter the dust that lies upon your judgement like a filthy cloud and freeze the canker-worm that eats thee up unto the last hair and make white, my children. Make white and bruise not. Do not cast a stone to bruise the snow, do not welt the innocent back nor slaughter the lamb.

Do not presume to judge from a dung-hill of ignorance a ragged stinking deformed beggar, let alone thy minister!

Or is the hour come with toleration that the basest scum can judge the appointed, can lift on the heap of great waters of this modish freedom, and engulf all?

If so, woe.

O how virgin lay the snow, how darkly across those bald flanks that no ploughblade has yet delved but the lips of sheep crop we three light hearts and easy minds of the sure in faith, forgetful of the inward rottenness, the hidden of the land, the blistering poison that thrives unseen, progressed. How uncomplainingly did we our bread that I had in my pocket from the funeral feast chew upon the empty scarp at Goosey Hill. With what heartiness did we slap William Scablehorne off of snow after he did tumble, and set his wide crown back upon his head, and slow descend from the high crest onto Furzecombe Down.

O how pure are the eyes of the unknowing, when iniquity lies all about them!

One fact let me make plain.

Our Adversary has many subtle devices at his disposal.

But that which was not expected but which so suddenly approached and overwhelmed us in that vale was in no wise owing to his actions.

God, but God, controls the seasons and the winds, my children.

The seemingly unreasonable changes therein.

He maketh his sun rise on the evil and on the good and sendeth rain on the just and on the unjust.

Nay.

Stealthily, stealthily, doth our Adversary work.

Inly he thrives, breeding in our corruption the filthy spots that shall consume us, threshing from our sins the rotten stinking putrefying heap of our damnation, fattening upon the smallest waywardness that he might belch forth its sourness at our last breath and plunge us without stop unto the ovens of Hell.

Trust, then, in divine grace.

For may we remember the agonies of Mary Brinn late of our parish whose ague did cleanse her unclean stomach and did pour forth upon the pillow the sweat of her redemption that she did embrace with a fearful and devout mind unclouded of drink's affections. And may we remember the sufferings of Thomas Walters late of our parish whose scall was endured as Job's and whom I visited in his humble abode not a stone's throw from this our holy house at his moment of release and whose ancient visage, ravaged though it was, bore upon it a smile sweeter than any I have ever beheld because he had had broken upon him the light of our Lord. O wicked are the ways of the flesh and the disease therein yet blessed is the state of the soul in bliss as I did witness only last week in this our habitation God rest their souls amen.

Yea, out of the whirlwind comes the still small voice.
   Out of the howling wind.
   Thou didst cleave the earth. Thou didst walk with burning coals before Thee, and the clouds were the dust of Thy feet. Thou didst break asunder and scatter the mountains and Thy wrath was terrible, O Lord.
   O my children.

On Furzecombe Down I tasted of despair.
   Yea, on Furzecombe Down the whirlwind came and filled my mouth and the snow stopped up mine ears and I chewed on ashes and was blind.
   O my children.

In mine own parish. In mine own parish far from succour I did grow weak in faith. In that sudden tempest so small and feeble I did feel bowed down before the wrath of the Lord I called as Our Saviour Himself did upon the Cross, I lapsed into the greatest most horrible sin of all yea as if I had never once known Him or ever entered into the house of our Lord or as if my attire was but so much stage costume or rags as it did feel like in that ferocious cold and as my companions did appear to resemble whipped by the wind that made their cloaks blow before them and their hats to come off.

And Hell is but a single tiny thought away, my children.

You may well shift.
   But you are looking agog at one who has felt the hot rasp and icy nip at once in his bowels and on his cheeks.
   The fires and frosts of Hell's perpetual kingdom.

Whatsoever be the talk of holy frauds. Whatsoever be the modish jabber of those inly lit up, as by some angelic taper. As by some luminous blossom.

Now this, my children, hear closely.

At the very moment of my despair and numbness in which the sudden inclement weather and its great gloominess all but obliterated my senses my Reason like our single shielded lanthorn swung by my hand endured and I reckoned that one amongst us was not feeling his suffering as he ought.

Nay, hear me out.

For it is in this point that the nub even the fruit of my sermon lies. For in these moments of extremity our greatest challenge comes and I do not speak of bodily challenge though that be severe. I speak of those challenges to our intellect and to our faith more subtle than the momentary clouding of that faith in despair which has doubtless chilled each one of you at some time in grief or in melancholy or in sickness and which is overcome when the light of Reason is restored or not at all. Indeed, I might add that those momentary nights of the soul are as limberings up that exercise and stiffen faith and our resolve. They imitate the night of Our Lord. But our Adversary has subtler ways still.

Nay, let me proceed.

One amongst us namely Simon Kistle our late curate, God rest his soul, who came to us on very tender pinions out of his ordination and was barely fledged and had as you recall but a downy beard, was beckoning out of the foul wind that blew our cloaks about our heads for Mr Scablehorne and myself to shelter in the lee of a small hummock.

This hummock being but the sole swelling on a waste of snowy furze.

And Mr Scablehorne and myself did make for the hummock with our hoods held tight to our faces that we might not be blinded by the snow and did crouch there, it affording in the lee some shelter from the blasts.

Then think, my children, what degree of horror came upon your minister when poor Mr Scablehorne did lean across to me and did part my hood from mine ear and did whisper that our comforting protuberance was none other than that place where certain of the spiritually distracted in our grandparents' time fell into unspeakable depravity and cavorted lustfully in nakedness upon its flanks and that is called thereby the Devil's Knob.

Yea, and how often have I cried out for these heathen spots, like that great mound high upon our own southerly flank, called by some filthy name, that I shall not blister my lips with repeating, but that flaunts itself at this our humble house of God — how often have I cried out for these to be removed as a black wen from a face, that no canker might work unseen within, to pollute and foul the rabble? Yea, who was it but he whom ye now see stood before you that rooted up and broke upon a great fire the seven stones of Noon's Hill?

Think what degree of horror coursed through my frozen joints. And I bid immediately Mr Scablehorne and Mr Kistle to pray aloud, that though our words might be obscured by the loudness of the blasts, we might scatter this wickedness. And I bid to cease from his sniggering poor William Scablehorne, whose wits were already turning in that exceeding discomfort.

My children.

William Scablehorne our clerk for forty years, whose rod was ever vigilant amongst thee for the smallest yawn, whose pitchpipe did clothe the poverty of our singing with its asseveratory flourishes, whose hand remains in our register as a meticulous record of his attention I perceived was already slipping, my children.

Yet when I did turn to Mr Kistle who was clad in his customary hat and coat that you might recall as being as threadbare as the times, and out at one elbow, and wholly inadequate for the present great cold, I did perceive that in spite of his shuddering exceedingly every limb, he bore upon his face an expression I had never previously viewed upon his attenuated countenance, but which I swiftly ascertained was one of a comfortable elation.

List, my children.

I had indeed been amiss in not keeping a more eager watch on my curate. The dull chafe of our duties oft wears us to forgetfulness. Yea, my despair at the scandalous practices of this parish was all but consuming my will and my attention. Even on that very day not more than one month past when my curate returned from London with an excitable air I discovered, upon entering our vestry, a certain lackey of this village pissing upon the floor. And having with my heaviest candle-bearer cudgelled him out he did swear at me and declaim that it was the action of no Christian to strike a poor man who has Christ seeded inside him. That no fellow, however ragged and mean, might be condemned by those set up above him by riches. And that I was a dunce.

Nay.
    Snigger not, my children.
    Weep, rather.
    Weep that you have sunk this far.

This thine holy house become a piss-pot.

List, list.
    Mr Scablehorne being of a sudden flung into a fit of coughing that did spray me with its bloody phlegm, my attention was drawn from my curate. But holding Mr Scablehorne close to me, cradled in mine arm, with a handkercher to his mouth, and the lanthorn up in mine other hand that I might view the sick man and his eructations more proficiently, I was able to turn my head once more towards my curate.
    And I did dimly see him staring outwards, with a smile upon his face as of one latterly taken, and I thought he had indeed been taken but that his limbs were still shuddering, and I bid him turn up his collar, and come close, that we might endure together until this wrathfulness had blown itself out.
    But he was as the dumb stone, laid over with the gold of my lanthorn. As if there was no breath at all in the midst of him.
    I clamoured to him, and putting the lanthorn beside me I shook his arm. And he then did turn to me, moving his lips as if in supplication, that were very blue.
    But at that moment Mr Scablehorne being vexed exceedingly with coughing, erubescing the virgin mantle before us with his fluids, and quite sopping my handkercher, I was otherwise preoccupied.
    Though putting the bottle of fiery brandy to my poor clerk's lips, and leaving it there in his ebbing grasp, that he might relieve his agony, I could turn again to my curate. And lo, he was moving his lips.
    And leaning closer towards him, I did feel his cold mouth chafing upon mine ear, and the rasp of his collar upon my cheek, and did have the following words deposited in a whisper, but clear as a bell, from my curate:

'I have Perfection.'

And somewhat startled by this curious yet in these teemingly blasphemous days familiar eruption, I did bid him repeat it.

And again he deposited in mine ear-hole this drop of venom that blistereth as it touches:

'I have Perfection.'

And putting my mouth to his ear likewise I returned the following:

'Mr Kistle. Pray tell me what Perfection it is that you are having.'

And he did smile broader, and did say, from Matthew 5, Verse 48, that I did recognise straightaway:

'Be perfect, as your Heavenly Father is perfect.'

And put his chill hand upon my shoulder. Like a father might do to a son.

Too well in our own humble parish of Ulverton, my children, know we this chill hand upon the shoulder. This eructation of Perfection.

Of the Light within. Of the Seed of Infinite Wisdom.

Being once the rantings of fools and madmen who are now the quiet of the land, blighting.

Too well. Ah, too well.

Too well know we the enemies of the cloth and of the steeple, of our Church and of our God, my children, that draw the ploughmen from their ploughs and the clerks from their offices. Too well know we the filth glossed over with a semblance of our raiments, breathed forth sourly in every meeting house, that is open to every Revelation of any lying Enthusiast e'en as ridiculous as that of Mahomet, as a broken roof is ope to every drop of rain.

The fig tree shall not blossom, and the labour of the olive shall fail.

Yet I will rejoice in the Lord.

Yea, in that day sing ye unto her a vineyard of red wine. I the Lord do keep it. I will water it every moment. Lest any hurt it, I will keep it night and day.

Think, my children, of what horror there was within me when I heard Simon Kistle speak into mine ear of Perfection as to a dunce. Think how near to the quick has come this blight that mine own curate was breathing it over me and turning it in my bowels who had trodden in my house and prayed with me, and performed numerous services in my name upon mine own horse when I lay afflicted with the headache, and whom I had trusted as one might a son. Think of my horror.

But ever regardful of the vexed state of our situation, that the blasts or the evil nature of that afflicted place might have deceived mine hearing, after administering to myself some heat from the bottle poor Mr Scablehorne would barely relinquish to me I did turn to Mr Kistle and say to him, in a loud voice, though his nose was but inches from mine own:

'What is it you mean, that which you uttered but a few minutes past?'

And through the scouring of the wind that was having at us still in the lee of that wicked place he did set his glimmering face up to mine and his whole body shaking or should I say quaking he of a sudden grinned and stroked my arm and answered:

'My fruit is being brought forth to Perfection. I am ripe in Christ. For Truth requires Plainness and Simplicity and my seed is sown. For the sorrowful nights of affliction are over, and the sun is burst upon us.'

Imagine my children what astonishment I received this with, I that was almost stuck fast with cold and could barely see my hand before me in the extremest danger of death and no allaying of the storm in sight with the words of the late service ashen as it were in my mouth and the wind whipping my hood almost threadbare and poor Mr Scablehorne's span almost up beside me. Imagine my astonishment — nay, even fear — at those fateful words that appeared to me familiar and awful, except that I could not bring myself to imagine that the quaking habit had fallen upon mine own curate and rather imagined that this extremity of exposure had bred in him a kind of despair, or foolishness, and that he was not in his right mind.

And so, not wishing to break the truth of our situation too quick upon him, I put my hand upon his that was without glove upon mine arm and said:

'It is meet that your thoughts should be filled with sunshine, Mr Kistle, for the inward man is the vital, and is fed by the Scriptures, which are the very Light of life.'

And I reached into mine pocket which was already sodden and bringing out mine holy Book laid his hand upon it and sought the lanthorn and did hold it above the holy Book, that the feeble rays might illumine sufficient to bring my curate out of his distraction.

And I did call out, through the great noise, 'Herein are all things necessary to the eternal life. Though we cannot read we can lay our hands upon this Truth and think on our sins, and on the Day of Judgement. This shall be as the bread for the hungry, and the wine for the thirsty, and our mantle for the cold, Mr Kistle.'

But he then straightway seized hold of the Book that is the Light of our Lord and the Word of God and the path to our salvation if rightfully understood and inwardly digested, and did pull it violently out of my hands, and did hurl it from me, into the blackness and misery of the night, so that for a moment I was stonied into silence and could utter no word but a sort of gargling.

Bereft as it were of the Word itself, viciously cast into darkness.

And so astonied was I that my fingers let hold of the lanthorn, that straightway rolled across the snow throwing out its light as a wheel till snuffed by that motion.

And all was as blind as in the beginning before the Spirit of our God moved upon the face of the waters.

And despite my poor clerk being seized at that moment with a most severe coughing that did send his bloody gob forcefully against my cheek I could not turn to him in mine own extremity, but instantly did hurl myself forward into the night's blasts, searching upon my knees for our holy Book. But so forcefully buffeted was I by that horrid tempest, that I was cast to the ground and did thereupon weep in the snow for my staff and our salvation. And when I rose again I was as the seed thrown upon the wind hurled hither and thither till my hand alighted upon a cloak of wool, being manna in that desert fastness, which did thereupon crumble to ashes in my mouth when I did handle it further and understand that it was but the frozen carcass of a sheep, withered almost to fleece and bone. Yet so distracted was I that I dragged it towards our poor shelter, and laid the sheep upon Mr Scablehorne's legs, that had but the thinnest of leggings about them otherwise.

And still in that severe cold the beast did have a smell about it. O let us pray the Day of Judgement doth swiftly come, that our corrupt bodies may put on the mantle of innocence and our black and unwholesome bile be scoured and the blown flies fall away that our flesh and bones may walk cleanly into the house of our Lord.

Then instantly turning and fumbling in that blackness for Mr Kistle's collar, that I soon found, I tugged him, as it were, out of his exultations.

For wrath is oft just.

'Mr Kistle,' cried I, 'what mean you in throwing from us our holy Book, that is our Staff of Life, we being in such extremity and so near to death as it may be we are?'

And he did shout out, in a high voice:

'Welcome the Resurrection! The Scriptures are but the way not the means!'

And I replied, in a trembling voice:

'They are the Word of God, Mr Kistle!'

And he cried out again:

'Worms might have God's Word for supper, I say! Welcome the Resurrection!'

'What are they then, Mr Kistle, if not the Word of God?'

'Christ is within us! Open thyself and be free! Cast off! Cast off! Welcome the Resurrection!'

And other such roarings.

Then hanging though he was from my grip upon his collar, he did bring his mouth to mine ear, so that I could smell the sourness of his feeble breath, and uttered, quite certain of his wits, the following:

'The Scriptures are but the declaration of the stipulations of the Saints, Mr Brazier. Let the worm now have them. Open thyself and be free.'

And at that moment the clouds tore asunder before the moon and a brilliant light was cast through the rent and indeed Mr Kistle's collar choosing to tear at that same moment he fell from me onto the snow, so that I was delivered of the frightful vision of his glimmering face that the moon had illumined.

But still disbelieving of the filthy stinking blasphemies that had pierced the blasts, and fearful lest the wicked nature of the hummock had infected us with its fumes, I lifted up Mr Kistle from where he lay upon the snow upon his face, and asked him what need the Scriptures, and my ministry, and his curate's post, and the Communion of the Church of England, if he had the Word of Christ within him and naught else needed. And raising his arms on high and shaking in his error so that I well nigh lost my grip upon his hair he did shout out that naught else was needed, that he had Perfection inwardly and God was in his conscience and that if I were to understand this I would cast aside my vestments and blossom. And the moon shone upon a sheet of snow that had adhered to his face within which his eyes and his mouth shifted constantly and so filled with horror was I by this vision that I stepped back and tripped upon William Scablehorne or rather the sheep about which his arms were held for he had evidently derived comfort therefrom. And sprawled beside him I saw that the bottle was drained at his lips, and that a mess of his fluids lay upon his cheek, and that he was no more in the living realm than the withered beast bound by his arms, against whose poor flayed skull his own face did nestle with a like grin.

I see in your own faces, my children, a mingling of horror and sorrow. We know not when the sickle of God will sweep deeply into us. His harvest obeys not summer. Mr Scablehorne now rests, my children, in the quietest of sleeps, sure of having performed his small round. And having filled his narrow way with an abundance of song and inward rejoicing and general diligence most especially witnessed in the white cleanliness of this surplice of which only having one, such is the thinness of my living, it must needs be cared for mightily, in all this lies the reward of a greater life, a peck to weigh in the scales and naught to scoff at.

And having ascertained his state I speedily administered the appropriate rites and fervently prayed for him even in mine own extremity of cold that was beginning to seize me like a vice. And I would indeed have covered his face with his own coat, but his limbs were exceeding stiff and I could not prise them from about the aforesaid sheep.

And so left him, alas, uncovered.

As ye have no doubt known of.

As ye have no doubt known of, and lamented thereof, from out of a whisper on the filthy wind, though not the worst that hath carried its poison amongst thee! A whisper carried calumniously against thy minister who did through his own trembling lay that soul to sleep nevertheless, my children, with the words that are ever fit.

That I must utter when your time comes. Without a slip in the utterance. Such are my responsibilities.

The business with the deceased complete, I turned towards Mr Kistle who had gone.

And just then the moon again was lost and a great gloominess once more compassed me about as if I had been cast into the deep as Jonah in the midst of seas, for all thy billows and thy waves passed over me, O Lord.

111

And though I did shout none heard me in that infinite desolation, save the Lord.

For on climbing the declivity with slow and labouring steps, so feeble did I feel, that I might view round about to better vantage should the clouds once more rend themselves and light be let out, my hand did seize by chance the heel of a boot, as Jacob took his brother by the heel in the womb.

And when I looked up, lo, I did see my curate by moonlight again with arms outspread above me, vexed by the buffets and blasts of the storm upon that chalky top but stuck fast, as it were, to their exceeding cold as if upon a cross.

And after I had reached beside him and urged him in his ear to descend, he only cried out, through a numbed mouth, that which was at first hard to comprehend, but on the third repeat had blasted mine own ear more than the snow upon the whirlwind, and was the following:

'I am set free from the burden of sin!'

And seeing that his cloak was more out behind him wildly than about him, and that beneath his cloak his shirt was loose, I made the latter fast with the utmost difficulty, my fingers being chilled to the bone, and wrapped my arms about him and might have brought him down but that we slipped and fell and in this tumble I placed my hand upon a small furze bush concealed beneath the snow and did give myself great hurt from the thorns thereon.

And Mr Kistle did remain upon his back in the snow, and did shout to me many things through the blasts. He did shout that the spirit of Christ was rising within me. That I must put off all worldly things and taste the sweetness of a humbled life and this mortification of the flesh that was sent by God to prove our inclinations and set the seed within us to leaf and blossom, and that the perfume of His ointment was all about us for we both dwelt under His canopy and were bathing in a river of unspeakable joy.

O my children.

Never was our miserable state of sinfulness and wretchedness more clear to me than on that chalky summit, bowed down beside my ranting giddy blasphemous curate whose stinking spewings forth I had not the strength of body to smother or e'en answer, my lips being quite helpless with the cold, that a burning firebrand might not have melted them.

Simon Kistle is no more, my children. But what you will be asking in your hearts is more to the matter than his end. It is the after-
life that is the pith. Whether his gross and obnoxious Enthusiasm
was intact at the moment of his passing, he being taken with all
his infirmities and downright blasphemies ripe in the husk as it
were but incorrigibly poisoned and rotten. What didst thou our
minister do to save his soul to cling to he who was your pillar nay
your companion in extremity?

List, my children.

The scuttling of mice in our poor thatch or the wind under the
door or the squeaking of thy boots shall in that other life of happiness be transported into harmonious music the like of which we
cannot imagine, save were we to come of a sudden out of a city's
huff and clamour and stink by chance into a vast nave filled with
the loveliness of a choir dropping from the sweetness of their
mouths such songs as might move our bowels and make us walk
upon the high places. For the other life be perpetual music, my
children.

And in these vain and jesting times we must tune ourselves to
that which is harmonious and lovely for in Hell all is grating, and
freakish, and loud with misery, like a knife upon a whetstone perpetually pressed betwixt the grindings of teeth in torment.

And now imagine how similarly vexatious to my ears was that
blasphemy of my curate mingled with the fearful clamour of the
storm. And fiercely in my soul did I desire to stop up the sluice
from which his hope of salvation was already flooding, that he
might though he be taken be raised into life everlasting, when the
Last Day comes and the trumpet be blown.

So I rose and went to him still upon the summit of that desolate
slope blasted by the storm and bent to him and with my left hand
under his head I did plead with him to leave off his ramblings and
this Enthusiasm that had come upon him so suddenly no doubt
owing to the touch of this infamous place and to come down into
the shelter of our Lord, into the lee of the Scriptures, to throw
himself upon the mercy of the Lord and His Word. And I shouted
to him those words of David in the Psalm:

'Thou art he that tookest me out of the womb, thou madest me
to hope when I was upon my mother's breasts. I was cast upon
thee from the womb, thou art my God from my mother's belly.

Be not far from me for trouble is near.'

And I also recalled to him the words that did begin my peroration this morning, my children:

'When our heart fails God is the strength of our hearts and our portion for ever.'

He was shivering and his teeth chattering and his face and hands were exceeding cold, but he raised himself upon one elbow and shouted loud unto me,

'You are mistaken. This blessed state has not come upon me suddenly, but has been growing within me for several months, since God led me to a certain book I saw in a window and took home, that was the Christian Epistle to Friends writ by George Whitehead. And Barclay and Fox I also read, and others, that persuaded me of my own state of ignorance and blindness and it was as if the sun had burst upon me and the scales fallen from my sight, and all that I had thought mad and foolish I saw might not be, but I was fearful of telling anyone though I found no satisfaction in my employment and in the shapes and shadows of religion, flaunting words that are so much dust to the lascivious people, who nevertheless doff their hats to the steeple and enter in to the ceremonies, but have never tasted the banquet that lies within themselves, but only stuff their mouths with the serpent's food.'

I was much astonied to hear this Enthusiasm had been on him so long, and called tremblingly into his ear:

'What am I, then, that feeds them this dust that is the serpent's food, and has command of the steeple, or rather tower, under which they do doff their hats, Mr Kistle?

And he made reply, with an obnoxious sigh, so that my ear grew exceeding hot, the following:

'Thou art the fat and wanton smotherer of their souls, Mr Brazier.'

My children.

Snigger not.

For this Mr Brazier is the very same Reverend Crispin Brazier of His Majesty's Church of England that doth stand before ye now, and hath command of this parish, and maintenance of all its souls, and is our Lord's minister on this base earth. O wherefore lookest thou upon them that deal treacherously, and holdest thy tongue when the wicked devoureth the man that is more righteous than he? O what thick and palpable clouds have descended upon this our land, that our anointed guardians of the Faith must rail against the revelations of blockheads and the wisdom of creeping things, yet be mocked!

O thou didst walk through the sea with thine horses.

O thou didst slay the nations.

Give them, O Lord. What wilt thou give? Give them a miscarrying womb. Give them dry breasts.

Woe.

List, list.

To touch the very marrow of the matter now.

I ask thee: is not that man that runs toward Death willingly more culpable than those poor Gaderene swine, for he does it in full knowledge of his trespass? We are weighed in the balance and are found wanting and if the grapes be not fine the wine-press cannot be trodden into sweetness. The Lord it is who decides when the tender grape shall be gathered, when the reaper shall bow with his hook and the ears of the barley fall. To cut ourselves untimely off is to wither on the vine, to foul the streams of Lebanon, to worm the apple and bring frost to the garden of our souls and the chafe of despair upon our necks, O my children.

For Mr Kistle did then rise stiffly and took off his coat and gave it to me, saying, 'Take this. I wish to embrace the Power of my Lord. To come into his presence as naked as the babe and as helpless and as innocent, washed of all my sins. For my soul is one with God and my seed blossoms.'

My children, he did take off his garments one by one and I was helpless to interject.

He it was, he alone it was who rended his garments from himself.

Not as the foulest whisper on the filthy wind hath dropped it amongst you, infecting with its calumnious poison.

Against thy healing minister.

Who was so near death or so I felt and not able to stand and my heart hard against him for I saw he was foolish and drunken, but not with wine, that I could not interpose myself betwixt his foolishness and his action.

Adam Thorpe

Meaning our late curate.

And he did toss his garments to me, calling them after Isaiah but filthy rags of righteousness, and did thereupon halfway out of his worsted stockings fall heavily and nakedly upon the snow. And did not tremble.

My children, whither his soul went I cannot say, but his breath did not melt the snow at his mouth.

And on perceiving he was no more, I besought myself to seek succour, but on stumbling out for but a few moments I was so cruelly whipped by the storm that I returned, and laid myself at the mercy of our Lord, huddled in the lee of His compassion whose comfort is ever nigh e'en in the most fearful of times, and that did, thanks be to God, did come with dawn in the bodily guise of a shepherd and his dog, as ye well know.

And if I had indeed swaddled myself in the garments so venially cast to me, so foolishly cast off, who says I did evil?

Seeking life.
As the reasoning soul must.

Yet the ear of jealousy heareth all things, my children.

Though he that toucheth pitch shall be defiled therewith.

Two Poems
Elaine Equi

THIS IS NOT A POEM

the poem exists
always and only
in the mind
of the reader

and these words
can never be more than
arrows, breadcrumbs

a map of abbreviations
however crude or elaborate

the poem comes into being
as the writer reads
and the reader anticipates

one can fill every inch
with writing and still
be no closer to the poem

as it lies there
a liar with a beautiful voice
that is often mistaken for silence

Elaine Equi

POEM

Like a window
open in winter

I look to the edge of
hair, teeth, nails.

Too busy to be internal
libido calmly rushes

in one orchard
and out another.

Its knotted weather
spreads brightly.

Its peach thread melody
is squandered away.

Three Poems
Carl Rakosi

NARRATIVE OF THE IMAGE

It appeared to me
in broad daylight,
imprimatur unknown,

a mouse scrounging
in the dirt for a moral
(sic). The image was in

transcendental air,
yet in my mind, complete
as Buddha's smile.

If there is meaning
in a look, it spoke.
I waited, man as spectator

sans rhetoric, not knowing
whether I was witnessing
a parable or pineal chemistry

(no, that's matter)
or a masque staged by
the poet's local imp

in which the mouse
was a capriccio
(or vice versa), a guise

with more disjunctions
and abortions than are
conceivable in reason

and on earth. According
to signor mouse I was not
quite the man I thought.

But in what way had I
failed to measure up?
Had I been presumptuous?

Or trespassed, God forbid,
on someone's avant garde?
Repondez s'il vous plait.

I waited for my imp,
who likes to jive oracles,
to answer but he had

disappeared into the
literary and nobody could
figure out his point.

THE NEW WORLD

I am Uchida
5 foot four

I speak
German

English
Japanese

German is
very strong

On the other
hand I can be

very vague
in Japanese

English is
the clearest

I try to
be clear

Carl Rakosi

MEDITATION

The widower
        lies under
a stone
        anon

sans eyes
        sans code
sans I
        the observer

with a
        damned subject.

Alas,
        metaphysician.

James' Games
Dennis Silk

Persons

Jane, a girl in her twenties
Jim, her admirer
Charles, her admirer
Jane's confidante
Accordionist
Jane's dressmaker
Maid
Priest

ACT ONE

Scene One

Jane's room. Jane and her confidante, seated. Scattered stools, a table beyond the stools.

Confidante: Jim's your oddest admirer. Where did you find him, Jane?
Jane: Between times, I imagine. Loitering in the gap between two admirers. Lounging, really. Yes, Jim knows how to lounge.
Confidante: He's playing dominoes downstairs with Charles. It's odd to watch him humped over the table. All the expression was in his shoulders.
Jane: The two rivals. He and Charles. Kids playing dominoes.
Confidante: You're odd as Jim. He's so inexpressive. How do you sort out what's going on up there?
Jane: There's a kind of attractiveness in his lack of expression. It allows one to attribute the kindest motives to him.
Confidante: And Charles, poor, put-away Charles?
Jane: A girl really needs a Mohammedan number of partners and to be the man. Charles? Yes, I suppose a straight line could be

steered through life with Charles.

Confidante: He seems built around some idea which may not be inimical to you, Jane.

Jane: Yes, a ruling idea. It juts out in his forehead, his eyebrows.

Confidante: Such relentless eyebrows.

Jane: Surrey's full of people leaving their visiting-cards and what's one to do with them? The cards pile up on the plate, the names cry out: *Help, help!* And I'm a green girl.

Scene Two

A dark stage except for Charles and Jim, at a table stage center playing dominoes. Charles faces the audience. Jim, his back turned to it, is hunched over the table.

Charles: Are you with me, Jim?

Jim: To the last pip.

Charles: You're so negligent yet you'll win again. I could be angry almost with your negligence.

Jim: Don't be, Charles.

Jane strolls in, looks over Jim's shoulder.

Jane: James' games.

Charles: Don't laugh at us, Jane.

Jane: Counting the pips, Jim?

Jim: If you say so.

Charles: I'd like to talk to you, Jane.

Jane: Is that all right, Jim?

Jim: The game's over for the evening.

Jane beckons, Charles and she exit together, Jim turns round and reveals he has no head. He begins to replace the dominoes in the box.

Scene Three

Jane's room. Jane and Charles, seated.

Charles (leans forward): I want to talk to you about Jim.

Jane: Charles, on that table over there you'll find an aspirin.

He knocks over several stools on the way. He grimaces.

Jane: Ow!

Dennis Silk

It's odd, Charles. You can't work your way through my stools yet you talk like a traffic-controller.

He bangs against a table-leg.

Ow again!

He seats himself, offers the aspirin bottle. She takes a pill with a glass of water. He again leans forward.

Charles: Don't you think Jim's a little inconsequent, a little airy, up there?
Jane: I'm tired of consequent suitors. I've the right to a year's dawdling with Jim.
Charles: Something in Jim's working against me.
Jane (seriously): What could it be?
Charles: Could it be the charm of headlessness?
Jane: Don't be impertinent.
Charles: Perhaps he's an esprit of the hosiers. The spine foundered at the neck. It could go no further.
Jane: You're trespassing.

Scene Four

Jane's room. Jane. Jim walks in, picks up stools Charles knocked over. He sits down.

Jim: Charles is our problem.
Jane: I like Charles.
Jim: Charles is very serious.
Jane: Charles is sincere. He thinks a lot.
Jim: I wish Charles would not come here.
Jane: I like Charles. I find him diverting . . . diverting and gray.
Jim: Charles has a head too many.
Jane: Don't be hard on him. We make Charles suffer.
Jim: Charles makes us suffer. Always talking about definite things. Nasty.
Jane: There is something a little specific about Charles.

She rises.

Will we go for a drive today?
Jim: Anyway, we have each other.
Jane (thoughtfully): Yes.
Jim: You're glad about that?

124

Jane: Where shall we go?
Jim: Where our wheels take us.

Scene Five

Jane and Jim drive across the stage. Their car is a chassis. Their working legs, visible underneath, provide the horsepower. The car stops, they look out through binoculars at the landscape.

Jane: That must be . . . yes . . . that must be . . . Shall we take a look at it, Jim?
Jim: Um . . . what about that game of SNAP?
Jane: Nothing too taxing, Jim? Hand me that *Guide to Surrey*.

He hands it to her.

There's nothing like a guidebook to make you sad. Even your binoculars look sad. Yet we shouldn't be always in disarray. Sometimes it's immoral not to know what one's looking at.

She consults the guidebook.

"Guy de Strange held out here for fourteen months. He would not budge."
Jim: He was acting against his own interests.
Jane: Why?
Jim: It's not nice to stay in one place too long.
Jane: Scatterbrain!
Jim: What about that game of SNAP?

They climb out of the car, pull out a rug, sit on it and play SNAP.

Jim (happily): SNAP!
Jane: It's funny how you manage always to win. How do you get there first? *(She caresses his no-head.)* I love that humming place where your head should be.
Jim: Maybe *you'd* do better without a head. It's giving you trouble, Jane. It would rid us of the problem of Charles, also. He'd disown you. We could have a lifetime of unplanned excursions.

Jane looks troubled.

Scene Six

Jane and Jim sun themselves on deck chairs facing the audience.

Jim: Sitting's tiresome.

Jane: You have to be very determined to sit long.
Jim: All those waves tiring themselves out. I think I'll build you a sand-castle. Would you like that?
Jane: I would like that very much, Jim.

Jim begins building a sand-castle.

Jim: How many floors, Jane?
Jane: Anything you say, Jim.
Jim: Lots.
Jane: Looks as though it will be quite a stronghold.
Jim: Can you imagine, Jane and Jim rushing up the staircase, looking out through all the windows at once?
Jane: That would be very nice, Jim.
Jim: Wouldn't it, Jane?

Scene Seven

Jane and Jim

Jane: I do dote on you, Jim. Why?

She nestles up to him.

Jim: I don't take a serious view of things, that's why. If I did, I'd sprout a head in no time.
Jane: Jane has aims. *(She sighs.)*
Something's coming up through the shoulder blades that quite attracts me, Jim. You've a kind of funnel of nonsense that I rather like. Do you think I could take a look?

She tries to take a peep; he gently restrains her.

Jim: Let's leave it at that, Jane.
Jane: It's . . . mysterious.
Jim: I think you're being a bit bookish. I find it ordinary.
Jane: You're not very ordinary, Jim.
Jim: Ah Jane! let's nestle up a bit.

They do. She props her head on his shoulder.

Jane: Your head.
Jim: My no-head.
Jane: It's kind of springy and comfortable.

End of Act One

Dennis Silk

Entr'acte

Jim sings and dances a solitary polka. An accordionist accompanies him.

Jim: You should see me dance the polka,
    sang Jim the headless groom.
    I steer through fog like a blind man's dog,
    or in my dear bird's room

    Where the mantelpiece is period,
    and the suitors perch on stools,
    I'm the wisest of the very odd
    among straightforward fools.

    I've no love-locks like Lord Byron,
    my looks are rather plain,
    yet my silky song is the siren
    that lures my dear bird Jane.

The accordionist places stools in Jim's way. Jim dances through them, wags his finger at the accordionist.

Jim: Naughty-naughty.

The accordionist throws him coins, Jim catches them. The accordionist throws cards in the air, Jim draws a revolver and shoots. The accordionist picks up a card, examines it, displays it to the audience.

Accordionist: Right through the queen's heart.

Jim stands on a stool, shoots at the audience.

ACT TWO

Scene One

Jim and Jane. Jane wears trousers throughout Act Two. They move and act as one up to "the parents will like them."

Jim and Jane: Two matching right black shoes.
    Two matching left black shoes.

They draw up their trouser-legs.

127

Two matching right green socks.
Two matching left green socks.

As for our trouser-legs
it goes without saying
the parents will like them.

Jane: Oh Jim, the parents will think you such fun.
Jim: Your bandanna goes very nicely with your complexion.
Jane: And your tie goes very nicely with your *(looking a little desolately at his space)* . . . thingamajig. Dearest Jim, are you ready for tea with the parents?

They march off arm in arm, determined.

Scene Two

The parents' drawing room. Jane's parents, Jane, Jim.

Jane: Jim, meet my parents.
Mother: Lady-killer!
Father: Jane's talked about you a lot.
Mother: She finds you restful. After all those hectic colors. Not that Charles is so hectic. For Jane you're a . . .

She looks fascinatedly at Jim.

Jane: You were about to say something, mother, when you interrupted yourself.
Mother: . . . middle distance she can project onto.

Jim begins a series of gurgling noises.
The mother picks up an ear trumpet, shows it questioningly to Jane.

Will we need the ear trumpet, dear?
Jane: Certainly not.

More gurgling noises from Jim.

Father: Jim has something to say.
Jane: It's just that he's a little shy on formal occasions.
Father: All the same . . .

He takes the ear trumpet from Jane's mother, applies the small end to Jim's shoulders, addresses him through the wide end. (When he tries to coax Jim into a reply, he applies the wide end to Jim's

128

shoulders, the small end to his own ear.)

Father: What's that, Jim?
Jane: Don't be brutal, Father.
Father: Brutal! It's a practical expression of my sympathy.

Jim undulates his arms.

Jane: Jim's saying he'd like to be one of the family.
Mother: How do you know?
Jane: There's a kind of pathos in the shoulder blades.
Mother: That's enough of the trumpet, Arthur. Teatime!

She bangs a gong, a maid wheels in a trolley, they all seat themselves. The mother begins to pour tea for a now completely withdrawn Jim.

Father (through trumpet): How do you manage for nutrition, Jim?

He reverses trumpet, sits in listening attitude.

Jane: Jim doesn't like analytical minds. He likes to loll a bit.
Mother: It's father's objective curiosity, dear.

To her husband.

General conversation, dear. Nothing too archaeological.

Father (again reverses trumpet): Speak up, sir!

Jim pulls the wide mouth of the trumpet toward him, bends his shoulders to speak through it.

Mother: What's he saying?
Father (grimly): Untea-like things.

Scene Three

Father and mother in their drawing room.

Mother: What a waste of tea on a headless man.
Father: Some say Jane has been tricked.
Mother: It cannot be hypnosis.
Father: Probably he courted the pedagogue in her. Jane likes to reclaim people. We must insist. A groom with a head or no wedding.
Mother: Yes, it will be a kind of trousseau.

Jane returns, radiant.

Jane: Isn't he fine?
Father: Even the ear trumpet blushed.
Jane: Oh!
Mother: We respect your reclamation schemes but . . .
Father: Can't you ask him whether he has a head? Perhaps he mislaid it?
Mother: It will be hard to acquire an entirely new one.
Jane: To ask would be to disturb our friendship.
Mother: An answer would confirm it.
Jane: I allow him a certain leeway in information.
Mother: Think of the consequences for the neighborhood. All the tailor's dummies in Surrey will get ideas above their station. Young girls will develop odd notions of companionship. And it's all because you're high-minded.
Jane: Charles says the opposite. He says my mind loiters.
Father: Charles is no use in an emergency. When the sideboards see him coming, they cower in the corner. How can he cope with a mislaid head?
Jane: Very well. To appease you, and because I am a tiny bit curious, I will ask Jim. You should know what I risk. Jim may take flight when he detects a framing question.

Scene Four

Jim and Jane. Jane's seated. Jim stands behind her, moving her head gently from extreme left to extreme right, then back again.

Jim: What about it, Jane?

She places her hands over his, their hands continue the same movement, there and back.
He bends to say

It will unscrew so softly.
Jane: Tempter.
Jim: You wouldn't have to see yourself in the looking glass. Sensing would do.
Jane: Not today, Jim.
Jim: Tomorrow, maybe?
Jane: Who'd represent you?
Jim: We'd sleep all day.
Jane: Jim, did you ever have a head?
Jim: I got rid of it early.

Jane: What did you do with it?
Jim: Wrapped it up in a school report. Buried it in the attic.
Jane (removing her hands, turns around): I'd like to take a look at it.
Jim: Peeper.

Jane rises, takes his hand in hers, leads him off.

Scene Five

They tiptoe through the attic together. Pedestals with dolls' heads on them, a couple of old trunks.

Jane points to head.

Jane: Who's that?
Jim: Mum.
Jane: And that?
Jim: Dad of course.

Jane points to trunk.

Jane: What's in there, Jim?
Jim: Crummy things.

She begins to open trunk, looks back at him.

Jane: Let's peep together. Baby shoes. Quite touching. Cigarette cards of the English cricketers, circa 1938. An incomplete set. And this?
Jim: A bottle of cricket-bat oil.
Jane: Reading matter, too. "Bulldog Drummond Strikes Again," heavily annotated. You did once do some reading, Jim. What's that wrapped up there?

She pulls out an adult and smiling papier-mâché head, claps her hands.

It's you, Jim. Quite good-looking. I suppose it was warm down there, you just kept growing.
Jim: Responsibilities!

Scene Six

At the dressmaker's. A tailor's dummy. A large looking glass. The dressmaker sits before her sewing machine. Enter Jane, leading

Jim by one hand, holding a sack over her shoulder with the other.

Jane: Forget about that wedding dress. I'm betrothed to a headless groom.

She points at Jim. The dressmaker throws up her hands in horror.

Have you the sewing machine that will put him together again?
Dressmaker: What's that in the sack?

Jane produces Jim's head.

The dressmaker inspects it, picks up a tape measure, measures the head, measures Jim's shoulders and back.

Dressmaker: Chancy work.
Jane: You will not lose by it.
Dressmaker: It will be sew and hem all night.

The dressmaker brings up a pair of steps, stands on it, begins to sew Jim's head onto his shoulders. Clearly, it is hard work.

Jane wheels looking glass up to Jim so he can watch the work.

Jim: Charles would laugh if he could see me now.
Jane: Forget about Charles. Jim, this has got to be a good fit. Try to think straight.
Jim (dubiously): I'm beginning to rethink our relationship.

Jane clambers onto the table, holds the lolling head as the dressmaker works away.

Dressmaker (to herself): Baste and baste away.
Jane (shouts): Gather yourself together down there. Think along the spine.
Jim: Stop bellowing down. I'll imagine I have a headache.
Jane: A world of headaches awaits you.
Jim: Ours was a fine relation.

Tries to back away. The women pull him back.

Jane: Now's not the time for flightiness.
Dressmaker (to no one in particular): These ambitious brides!

Jim extricates himself, puts on a woman's modish hat he finds on the table, tries to exit. They pull him back, Jane removes the hat.

Jane: What an impatient Jim you are. We haven't made our adjustments and already you want to show off your headgear.
Jim: How much longer must I stand here?
Jane: Do you know how long the bride sews away at her trousseau? Can you have less than bridal patience?
Dressmaker: I've managed to sew the head on. Perhaps, in the course of time . . .
Jane: . . . the connection will be organic. Jim, how do you feel?
Jim: I've lost a gap and found a grin.

Jane picks up another hat.

Jane: Try on this homburg.

He does.

Jane: Charles will be jealous.
Jim: You think so?
Jane: There can be no doubt.

Jim adjusts hat and tie, looks pleased. Jane writes out check for the dressmaker, who accepts it with one hand, combs Jim's hair with the other.

End of Act Two

ACT THREE

Scene One

Jane and Charles.

Charles: Jim looks quite *nouveau riche* with that head.
Jane: Don't mock us.
Charles: It's hard to get used to that *us*.
Jane: It was his deficiencies that won me.
Charles: I couldn't fight *them*.
Jane: We need you, Charles. The family's lined up against us. Won't you be best man at our wedding?
Charles: For old times' sake, Jane.
Jane: Thank you, Charles.

Dennis Silk

Scene Two

The dressmaker arranges Jane's bridal veil.

Jane: It's difficult for a girl to know what to do with herself.
I did want to loiter.
White seems so definite.
It's nice just chatting.
Hovering.
Helicopters.

She falls asleep. The dressmaker has to prop her head up. She continues her work on the veil.

Scene Three

Accordionist at side, priest at stage center.

Accordionist: It's that heady wedding march again.

He sings.
Here comes the bride
all dressed in fright.

As the wedding party enters, he continues the tune on his accordion. Enter Jane, furiously yawning, in wedding dress, and Jim, Charles, parents, dressmaker. The dressmaker runs from Jane to Jim, shaking Jane into consciousness, and patting down Jim's head. The party makes a circuit of the stage, stands before the priest. The accordionist provides the chorus, breaks it off to maintain his tune, returns to his role as chorus.

Here's the nodding bride.

And groom wanting not to nod.

Lucky the dressmaker found that strong thread. I reckon it should see bride and groom through an important twenty minutes of their lives.

Here's the laughing groom. He must have a terrible headache. He's got both hands up to his neck. In fact, he seems to find it difficult to slip the ring on—that eternal ring, you know—he's clutching his head so hard. Jane's mother persuades him to let go. He bends over Jane, laughing. OOPS.

134

Charles takes a long pair of scissors from under his jacket, and quickly snips off Jim's head, which falls at the feet of the parents and Jane. All raise hands in horror.

Jane: Charles, you cad!

Charles exits laughing.

Scene Four

Jane and Jim. He holds his head under his arm.

Jane: I thought of you as a young Brighton boy trying out machines on South Pier. Now you look as though you need help. That means me, probably.
Jim: There's that trade union of head-owners who surround you. They know where they're going even on their deathbeds. They've reserved the best rooms in the next world.
Jane: Don't feel ragged, Jim. I'm with you. At least for a little while, Jim.

Exit Jane, holding Jim's hand. Charles follows behind.

End of James' Games

Three Poems
Melissa Townsend

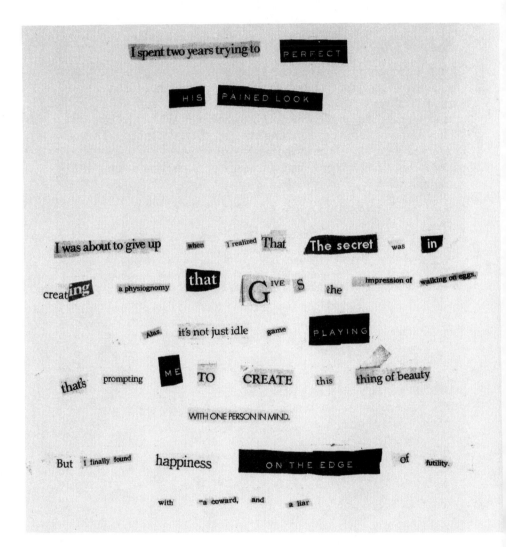

I spent two years trying to PERFECT

HIS PAINED LOOK

I was about to give up when I realized That The secret was in creating a physiognomy that G IVE S the impression of walking on eggs. Alas, it's not just idle game PLAYING that's prompting ME TO CREATE this thing of beauty WITH ONE PERSON IN MIND.

But I finally found happiness ON THE EDGE of futility. with "a coward, and a liar

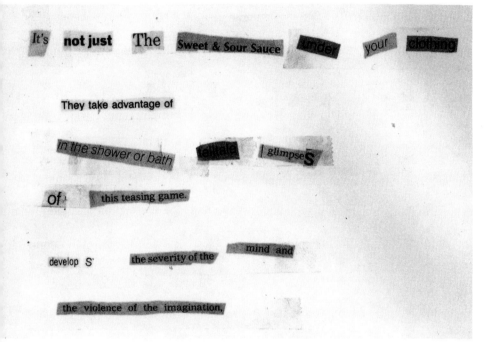

It's not just The Sweet & Sour Sauce under your clothing

They take advantage of

in the shower or bath telltale I glimpses

Of this teasing game.

develop S the severity of the mind and

the violence of the imagination,

Melissa Townsend

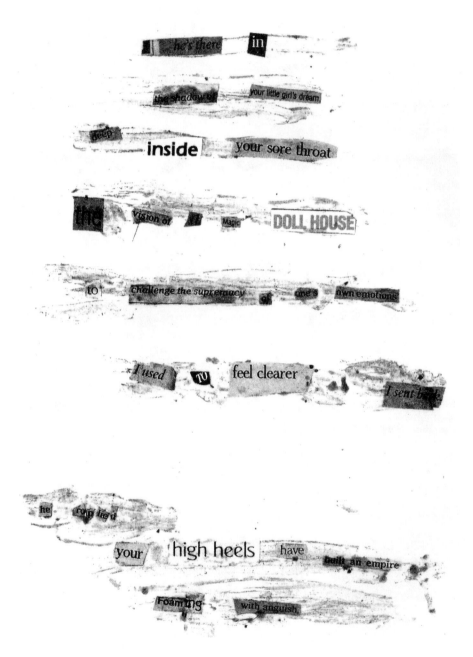

he's there in
the shadow of your little girl's dream
deep inside your sore throat
the vision of Magic DOLL HOUSE
to challenge the supremacy of one's own emotions

I used TO feel clearer I sent back

he replied
your high heels have built an empire
Foaming with anguish

Herculaneum
Thom Gunn

1

I dropped into the Theater's tiers of seats,
Then from the central well I crawled along
        Tight galleries that flung
All ways as if to parody the streets
They bored through, rich seams far beneath the crust.

And still I lose my way. Is this the Slum,
The villas, Forum, Baths, or Pastry Shop?
        Creeping from prop to prop,
I broach the past of Herculaneum.
Choked on itself, seeking some clue to trust.

I scrabble for it, sifting a town's dirt,
Named for a muscle-man. Some dedication!
        I think its implication
Worked out too well, for at his end a shirt
Burned off his human traits, doubt, self-disgust,

Greed, whatnot, when it freed him from his breath
Into a god,
        prefiguring in its way
        Vesuvian lava's stay,
Which cooled, as an arrested grace, in death,
The aiming arm that never got to thrust.

Thom Gunn

2

Perhaps if I could reconstruct the hour
Before the flow, I'd find myself among
   The attitudes of the young,
Where beauty for a moment looks like power
(As if such poise could make an order just).

Reckless, then, on the track of the unmarred,
I smash away, mosaic or stable-stall,
   And burst through villa-wall
For perfect bodies, for the ageless hard
Cold curve of pectoral or pale glare of bust.

3

So, Marcus,
   you! whole on your marble horse,
Athletic youth upraising your white hand
   In gesture of command,
To which obedience is a matter of course.
Yet I make out a slight frown of mistrust.

For all the correct controlled ease of your seat,
Feet dangling loose in their soft riding-shoes,
   Your mouth seems to refuse:
The lips incredulously will not meet,
The lower lip reluctant to adjust.

And thus the spoiled rich boy, I like to think
— With combed Augustan hair each tousle in place —
   Asks questions in his face:
His very selfishness brings him to the brink
Of some revolt — any would be robust.

4

At last I move on to the skeletons
Of slaves with bones deformed by overwork:
       These are the finds I shirk,
Without hope after Spartacus, the ones
Who nanny, groom, or drudge because they must.

The clues I saw were clues I hoped to see,
Beauty subverting military order
       While still part of its border,
With bulging calves and armed revealingly.
— And Hercules! that bully died of lust.

The dig is maze-like now, what clue is left?
The House of Carbonated Furniture,
       Now only that is sure . . .
Marcus, your nose-hole is a jagged cleft.
Here are your ribs like road-kill in the dust.

(specifics derived from
HERCULANEUM, by
Joseph Jay Deiss)

Fix Me Up
Pat Califia

LENA PLASTERED HER BODY, thin as a zither and as tightly strung, full-length against the big window. It gave her a silly little rush to know that nothing but a thick pane of glass held her up, fifty stories off the ground. It was late Sarday afternoon. Rain had been pissing down all the dismal day. The moment the sun fell, a wind was going to come up, a mean wind that would pour itself through the canyons between the ziggurats and gleefully slice through the poor, wet drones and plugs trying to slog their way home. She was up too high to see the bright colors of the advertholos, chasing pedestrians, or hear the illegal ads blaring bad music and squawking about their wares. The neon and pastel shades of the commercials and the shop windows would be reflected back by the puddles on the street, making rainbows like so much spilled snake oil. Lena never went down to the street if she could help it.

The lines of rain thickened, darkened, blew in diagonal lines like a shower of poisoned abo spears. Lena smiled, and felt her teeth click against the glass. No matter how devil-may-care David's streetboy act was, he would get his cute little ass inside before that wind bit him in the butt.

She had spent the last hour just tidying up. Nothing major like floors or laundry. She had gone down to the twenty-fifth floor breezeway and gotten a few groceries and some tequila. Then she had come home and wandered through her apartment, sucking on a lemon and a shot glass, touching this and that, arranging things, making sure she knew where everything was. During the week it was so easy for the smaller props — the vibrators and dildos, wigs, her stethoscope, the rubber hood, the pacifier, the nurse's cowl, the bug-gloves and bug-face, the military cap, the riding crop, the poppers — to get misplaced. She wasn't waiting for David. He wasn't that important.

She had covered the computer terminal and unplugged the video camera and the earphones. Today had been surprisingly busy for a weekend. She did most of her business between working hours, when office plugs could make surreptitious use of company lines or stop in a private booth during lunchtime. There was another flurry of biz for an hour before and after corporate roll calls, when sweats could use the databooths on the way to and from home for a quick fantasy fix. Today, she had done two baby calls, a cross-dresser, one pioneer-and-aborigines scenario, a full set of military calisthenics, a castration, a bug collector, and six straight fucks in various imaginary positions and costumes — seven men, five women, and a herm. The Virgin alone knew how many of them were transies.

She was pretty quick at the keyboard, but she still needed to do some costume changes to augment the visuals, or customers complained. One of them had called from home with deluxe, full sensory plug-in, which meant she had to create three hundred and sixty degrees of erotic experience incorporating all five senses. She hadn't had much practice with the software for taste sensations; luckily, most people didn't know what real sex tasted like any more, and were happy with a sugary substitute.

Lena felt like a worn-out drive that's been erased, reformatted and written on so often that its ability to hold on to the data was deteriorating. So she did not want to look at the terminal tonight — or tomorrow, if she could help it. She moved involuntarily toward the keyboard to check her credit balance, but restrained herself from lifting the dustcover; made herself just sit in the comfortable work-chair that gave perfect back support no matter which way she tilted. She stared into the mirror behind the computer. Tonight's events might have nothing at all to do with sex, but they were something she surely desired. After so many hours of catering to other people's desires, her own (no matter how arbitrary, no matter how destructive) seemed very precious.

No, she had not been waiting for David. That was the difference between them. He was the one who waited on his missionary, who waited until it was late enough in the day that he could drop by her place pretending he was on his way to someplace else — a show, a party, a jump-off. And she knew just what he would say when he came in the door. Every time he saw her, he said it earlier and earlier, with less and less preliminary conversation.

He would say, "Fix me up, Lena."

And she would. After he paid the price. That was one factor that carried over from her job — the expectation that everyone who wanted her had to give something up in return, at a rate she calculated and demanded without negotiation.

She ran a finger over her eyebrows, made sure the peak was still there, that crooked place in the curve that made her look so dark and disapproving when she raised one brow. Even when she smiled, her face had a sharp, satirical look.

She got up and stretched for the mirror, bent over and looked at her own ass. She was wearing her favorite pair of shimmerlegs. The inside seams, the ones along the upper thigh that always wore out first, had been mended with wide leather patches, a dull black that absorbed the colored lights which twinkled in the fabric. Mirror studs ran down the outer seams, emphasizing the length of her legs. Tonight she wore a mirror for a belt buckle, also. Her knee-high boots were silver, and the spike heels were studded with rhinestones. She was wearing a very old, neon-pink T that had been worn down to the thickness of a sheet of paper. In the right light (or if it was wet), you could see her tattoos through it, the black spiderwebs that spanned her shoulder blades and breasts and collarbones, and the red jumping spiders that waited there for a thrumming touch on the web to bring them to life.

These were primitive engravings, made by actually implanting pigment beneath her skin with an electric needle. The process was illegal, but you could always find some ex-con, derelict or artist with a passion for quick cash and live canvas. She had no patience for the holos that other people wore like a bracelet or a mask. This was no jewelry, this was an alteration of the map of her body, its boundaries, and it was a way of saying: This comes with the territory.

David had never commented on the way she looked. Still, why would a top-bunk boy approach you in a bar full of his peers when you looked like an old witch, especially when you wore your pistol in a very visible shoulder holster and a large buck-knife in one of your boots, if he did not find you attractive? He had brought her a drink back from the bar on a fucking tray. Hadn't spilled it, either. Then he disappeared into the crowd to return with something a lot more interesting. He had had the good sense to precede her out of the bar—not get behind her and make her nervous about her back. And he had touched her only once, on the back of the hand, an instinctively submissive gesture that had charmed and irritated her.

She had not been back to the kite bar since. And it had been much longer than she liked to think since she had actually strapped

herself to the cross-pieces of one of those dangerous, fragile con-
traptions and accepted an aerial duel. It took a serious stretch of
sobriety or celibacy to make the walls of her home seem more dangerous than the outside world. She had to be forced onto the street
by furniture that resented taking her weight, mirrors that were
adding years to her face, kitchen drawers and bathroom cabinets
full of ways to take her own life.

She had picked that place because she knew there would not be
any other women there. There weren't any covens any more; a
room full of women would have made too tempting a target. Still,
dykes managed to claim corners of other people's clubs. But she
would rather be among resentful male strangers than run the risk
of taking a woman home. Lena had another bad habit she preferred
to romance. She knew she could not give it up for the sake of love.
And when you combined lust with religion — well, it was just too
dangerous. She had been just a kid when she learned that, dumb
enough to believe somebody was going to save her.

It was tricky, finding a good old pioneer place that didn't want
you but wouldn't throw you out. Women were rare but not unheard
of in the kite scene; Lena was careful to be neither obnoxious nor
servile. Her presence titillated some of the men, and made most
of them skeptical. It seemed to her that the hetmen who got hostile with her were painfully attracted to machas, but assumed
they were not available. No wonder they were nervous. Since the
plague had killed half of the planet's women of child-bearing age,
most females had been locked up by their families or husbands. If
you saw a woman on the street, she probably carried a sidearm.
Rumors that woman-lovers were somehow, perhaps by magical
means, invulnerable to the disease had made any woman who was
perceived as a witch the target of gang rape. This was still a frontier planet. The law responded by authorizing members of protected classes to carry firearms at all times. It was cheaper than
paying the cops or the courts or a commission to take care of the
problem, and satisfied the vague requirement that members of the
Planetary Trade Co-Operative "recognize human rights issues."

The whole society was just inches away from martial law anyway since the bugs had come out of nowhere and taken the first
batch of humans off their ship. Rumor had it that the bugs were
responsible for the plague. It was germ warfare from outer space.
Another rumor attributed it to the government. Something it had
cooked up to kill the aliens had gotten loose by mistake. Lena

145

found trips to the firing range and a heavy investment in rubber goods more productive than such speculation. What did it matter where it came from? The fact was that fucking around could give you a slow and ugly death. Just believing that, the simple truth, was more than most people could manage.

Lena had always been the kind of woman who went places men would rather keep for themselves. She felt immune to their threats — the verbal ones, anyway — because she didn't consider herself unavailable as much as undesirable. She hadn't found that many women who were interested in what she had to offer, either. So she was amused by the occasional startled look on the face of a breeder boy who had just felt a pang of desire that would make his buddies guffaw. Let him feel freakish and undesirable, also. Do him good, it would.

But then again, Lena thought, I am not just a dyke, and David is not just a cunt-lover. She unrolled her bed-of-nails across her tatami, a leather hide liberally studded with metal prongs. She touched one to reassure herself of its sharpness. David and I have something in common that brings us together. It's rather touching, in a way, his fear of needles and my fascination with puncturing the skin.

Maybe Joey the Bag is right, she mused, and David is just a re-pressed little faggot who needs a daddy with a big dick to put him on the proper path to submissive, cock-sucking clamhood. But somehow I doubt it's that simple. Might work if he could find a daddy who came Angel Piss. The Bag is just jealous 'cause I got me a better-looking boy than he does presently. Not that I want to be anybody's daddy, you understand. And where is the kid? she asked herself. My mind is wandering. Time for more tequila. It helps me focus. Where's the damn bottle?

The doorbell rang, and she jumped. She hated the sound of bells. Telephones, doorbells, sirens, curfew, ambulances, fire alarms, anything like that made her grit her teeth, hold her ears and will it to stop. She was standing by the speaker plate at her front door, so it would have been the work of a few seconds to press the buzzer and let him in. She placed her finger on the button, but didn't push it down. Let the little fuck-hole sweat it. The pisser. How much longer, she wondered, was he going to be able to keep these visits down to a weekly thing? She had told him in the beginning that she would only see him once every ten days, and if she ever caught him letting anybody else stick a plunger-and-point into his arm, she would blot him out of her retina file.

The doorbell went off again, and this time she didn't wince. She counted to ten, fifteen, under her breath, then hit the buzzer. The door in the lobby crashed shut. The stairs rattled as he came up. When she had met David, he was wearing lace-up shoes, cheap sidewalk shock absorbers. But the first time he came back to her apartment, he was wearing steel-toed boots. She wondered if he had done that on purpose. But people like David tended not to make conscious choices about how they appeared to others. They just let things happen.

Which is how she got away with little mind-fucks like making him wait again at the front door of the apartment, making him wonder if maybe he'd hit the wrong button by mistake and got buzzed in by somebody else. What if the bitch has gone out? she imagined him wondering, and when she popped open the peephole, there did seem to be a little extra shine around his hairline. Sweat, maybe? Sweat was almost as good as blood, just more difficult to obtain in quantity.

The peephole signaled recognition of the pattern behind his eyeball. She smiled sweetly and threw the door open. "Get your sorry ass in here," she snarled, and kicked it shut. "You smell like a wet dog."

"Aw, Lena, didja have a bad day?" He was already pleading with her. His blond hair needed cutting. His hands were filthy. And had he lost some weight?

"You look like shit," she said, ignoring his question. "When did you eat last?"

"I hadda samwich," he mumbled. One of his worst nights with her had started when she caught him eating some cold leftover soup out of the refrigerator, without her permission, with his fingers, yet. "I'm not going to feed you," she had shouted. "You damn well better eat before you get over here, pinhead, pincushion! This is not a date, boy. I'm not running a baby wagon here!"

"You hadda samwich," she mocked him. "When? Twoday?"

"Aw, Lena, don't be mean."

"Aw, David, don't be stupid. If I wasn't mean you wouldn't be here."

"I brought —" His hands were shaking when he pulled the zipperbag full of glassine envelopes from the front of his red leather jacket. Was it new? She liked the way it looked on him — its color, the quilted shoulders, the fur collar and the tight, corseted waist. Under the jacket he wore his usual gold and black leopard-spot T and tiger-striped tights.

Her eyes narrowed. There were many more glassine envelopes in the bag than usual. How had he gotten this much religion? Probably sold some major piece of his comfort — a cycle, a music console, one of those appurtenances that seem so expendable when you are turning yourself into a convert, a true believer, a steady user. It always seems to you that you are on the brink of getting something so much better and bigger, but you never do, you just learn to live on less and less. And more and more.

She took it away from him. Really, there has to be something wrong with me, she thought, that I get such a rush in my crotch over these little struggles. He does not want to let go of his dope, but he has to, if it's going to do him any good.

"Party favors, sport?"

"No, no. Um, they were going to be a present."

She did not understand. "What?"

"If you want it."

Well, no matter how well you think you know your chattel, he can still surprise you. She looked hard at him, not exactly pleased.

He sighed, hunched his shoulders, and pleaded with her again. "You always say I have to bring enough for both of us, so, well, I thought maybe if I brought extra, um, well, that you would, well, like it. You could get high without me underfoot, if you wanted to. Maybe. Lena?"

She slapped him. He started to cry. It was one of the most touching things about him, the fact that he actually shed tears in her presence. They just jumped out of his eyes while he looked surprised and humiliated and wiped at his cheeks.

"Haven't you got it figured out by now, asshole, that the best way to get yourself in big trouble is to think for yourself? You little freak. Just because I keep you company with your lousy habit, don't you try to make a believer out of me. Did you figure you could get some more control over me this way, by giving me more religion than I can handle? What other favors did you think I might start to do for you to keep you preaching? Got visions of yourself as some bigtime switchboard cowboy with a stable of operators? Shit! Think again. You are talking nothing but shit. Bug shit."

She slapped him again, and he staggered a little. Her arms were hard and long. His own body was more muscle than fat, but she had never seen him raise his hands above his waist while she was hitting him. He didn't even make a fist. He just hugged the outside of his own thighs and kept on crying.

It was enough to make you want to come.

"Go clean up," she said roughly. "There's some potato salad and cold-cuts in the fridge. Eat some if you can quit bawling long enough. Boil some water while you're at it. Then get your butt in here and let's get this over with. I got things I have to do."

In the shower, David soaped his body for the second time that evening. He would never dream of showing up on her doorstep dirty. She had some kind of thing about hygiene. The whole apartment looked like she cleaned it with a toothbrush. But then, if you hardly ever go outside, he guessed you had a lot of time to keep everything spotless. Sighing, he picked up the fingernail brush and scrubbed his hands again. Cabinet-making left a perpetual black stain on his fingertips, cuticles and knuckles. Sometimes he had burns or patches of epoxy stuck to his skin. He didn't blame her for shying away if he made the mistake of trying to touch her. His hands looked awful. He scrubbed them until they were bleeding a little, then rinsed them under scalding water. Come to think of it, she probably didn't even know what he did for a living. She never asked him any questions. He must have walnut-stained three hundred keyboard benches this week. It was a bug-headed fad, people wanting good, clean, durable plastic to look like something that gave you splinters and rotted away. But overtime pay was double-time-and-a-half, and all that had gone into the zipperbag that had just gotten his face slapped.

So why am I happy? he asked himself, stepping out of the tub and toweling off. His cock stood out in a shallow curve, no more than the beginning of a proper erection, but when he thought about her hand connecting hotly with his cheek, it jerked upright so fast it took his breath away. But he didn't touch it. If I was going to do something that simple, he thought, laughing quietly at himself, I could have stayed home.

He put his stripes and spots back on, padded into the kitchen, and filled a glass with water. While it cooked in the hotbox, he stuck his head into the refrigerator. There, as promised, was a tub of potato salad and a plate of cold-cuts. He ate some of each, although he wasn't hungry. He wished Lena would let him take her out to dinner sometime. But she always pretended she had someplace else to go and was gonna kick him out as soon as they got the angels to come down. Every Sarday night for the last three months, the same damn routine.

She had lost weight, he thought, rolling up a piece of ham and sliding it into his mouth. The circles under her eyes kept getting larger. Animal protein, for War Mother's sake, and being able to afford it was no excuse. Didn't she know what it did to your heart? There wasn't a slab of soy or a sheet of seaweed in the house. She didn't get enough sun or exercise. He checked the vegetable bin. It was full of single servings of carob and cola pudding. She didn't have any vitamins, either. He had checked every shelf in the kitchen. But try and tell her she ought to take better care of herself, just try. Worth your life. Damn woman would rip your arm off and beat you over the head with it just to prove she was in better shape than the Big Bug Queen.

"Hey, you looking for an escape hatch in there?" she jeered from the living room. He put the lid back on the potato salad and licked his fingers. His stomach tightened. She was in fine form tonight. Maybe the dope would slow her down. About as much chance of that as getting off on derms. Which are legal, yes, all you have to do to get them is sign up at your local health center and get three extra digits punched into your id. Being on the government's narco list makes you exempt from the draft, so you don't have nightmares about being trapped in a ship with a hull about as thick as a balloon while aliens uglier than centipedes take careful aim, disable your vessel, come inside, and take you all away. Carefully. Tenderly. Alive. While they tasted you with their mouth-parts, full of pulpy pieces that looked like rotten fruit, and tickled you with their antennae and stuck their jointed, chitonous limbs that were covered with fine hairs down your throat and up your —

Those three extra id numbers entitled you to pick up so many derms a day at the pharmacy of your choice. If you wanted more, you had to go back to the health center and sit around most of the day until you saw a doctor who would tell you to consider cleaning up before he doubled your 'script. But you had the time to sit around once you got registered, because there were so many jobs they wouldn't let you do if you were on the list. Like the job he had now, for instance. Let an addict handle power tools? Joke.

The skin patches were always reliable because they were made under carefully controlled laboratory conditions. Nothing like the unpredictable, kick-ass stuff that loco alchemists cooked up from flowerbeds of illegally cultivated seraphim that could give you a heart attack or bring on the rapture. Bless the double-sexed aborigines for showing us that trick before they all died of the common cold and venereal warts. By comparison, the synthetic heroin-fourteen in derms is about as much fun as an artifical vagina. Even one that can talk dirty to you. Give me Lena any day.

Whatever you want, he said silently to himself. Whatever you want. Just so I can look at you and be here for a little while, I don't care. Do whatever you want.

"Coming, Lena," he said patiently, and walked into the living room, carrying the glass of boiled water.

Lena had her T off and was wearing a leather vest that was open in front. It made his perineum ache when she did something like that, take her shirt off like a man and just walk around completely unconscious of her tits and what they did to him. He liked the whole shape of her, lean and somehow coiled up, springy, inside her tight, glittering clothes. And he could see the spiders. The first time he ever crashed at the foot of her futon, sleeping on a pile of cold, greasy chains, he dreamed of being held captive by big and extremely intelligent spiders who intended to sting him repeatedly and then eat him a little bit at a time. It had been unpleasant but fascinating, the kind of thing that made you shiver half the day and wonder how shit like that got into your brain.

The witches seemed to like bugs. They all wore jewelry and laserpix with crawly things on 'em. Well, why not? The deep-space bugs never took women. Just crawled right over 'em to drag out the dudes. He'd heard a rumor that Major Aerospace Corp. was going to start hiring women-only on their security teams. The union would have fits over that. Any day now the army would probably start drafting women. Wouldn't that shake things up, now? Oooooh-eee.

Lena looked a little like a soldier, the first time he saw her, or a b-vid space pirate. He had actually gone up to her at the bar instead of just looking because some prick-pisser had made a very bad-taste crack about a bunk wearing a chain-mail vest and dueling spurs. Though he must have been just a novice kiteboy himself, because he still had all his fingers and none of the nasty facial scars you got from glass-impregnated string sawing across your face. Not to mention the damage the spurs could do, although those scars tended to be invisible in most social situations and created odd rumors about the sexual kinks duelers had to develop to compensate for the loss of vital parts.

Instead of uniting them in joint distaste, the insult had suddenly made David's own tastes very clear. That, something inside him had said, is one fine woman. Put on your welfare-office manners, junior, and go find out what this is gonna cost you.

"Shall I light the candles?" he asked.

"Yes."

He liked asking her what to do and waiting for her response. When she said yes, it was as if he had anticipated a need and provided for it without challenging her supremacy, and that made him feel a little proud. It was a good trick. When she said no, it was as if something had reached out and held him in check, and it was annoying, but it was also reassuring. It told him she paid attention to what he said, evaluated it. It gave him a place in her regard.

So he lit candles, trying to move quietly and not bump into anything. He knew better than to light the lamp on the table where her paraphernalia was laid out neatly as a surgeon's tray. She always lit that, striking the match with one hand while she held the spoon full of water and powder in the other — a piece of arrogance that had pissed him off in the beginning, her taking a chance of wasting that much of his salvation. But she had never spilled any yet, and by now he didn't care. It was her ritual, and it meant so much to her, it made the whole thing mean something to him, too. That sense of doing something important, following a plan, got him off as much (well, almost as much) as the needle.

He noticed the spiked hide on the tatami and got a lump in his throat. He had not seen that before. New games kept things interesting, but you never knew how you were going to perform. The probability of fucking up increased. And fucking up increased the probability of more new games. Sometimes David thought she didn't like him very much. But to be honest, most of the time he didn't care. Did he?

The anxiety became a little much. "I don't want to hold you up," he lied, placing the spent matches in her single ashtray. "Lemme have my shot now?"

"Follow the form," she reminded him irritably.

"Lena," he breathed, "please, would you fix me up?" It was so embarrassing.

"No. Not yet. Tell me how bad you want it."

Now he discovered that the cold fire of a spike sliding into his arm, and the subsequent diffusion of warmth up to his heart, his head, down to his loins and his toes, was something he wanted more than he could stand. "Please," he whispered. Then he whined. "Lena, I really need to get out of my head. I've been working so hard this week. And you know I can't do it for myself. I always mess it up, please."

"Not yet. There are a few things I want you to do for me first."

This was the form. He was on familiar ground, but he was miserable. "Do I have to?" he cried.

"No. You can leave."

"I can't."

"Then get down on your knees."

Nations have surrendered with less grief.

She had told him to get down on his knees. He fell like a bird in mid-flight. Now she told him to strip, something that was hard to do in that position. But he contrived to make it look pretty. Enticing. He took his boots off first, giving up the whole idea of protection along with their steel toes. His fingers lingered over the riptabs at the shoulders of his leopard-spotted T, and it fell seductively, revealing his well-defined, smooth-shaven chest and the small, inverted nipples. Without being told, he rolled the T up and tucked it neatly into one boot. He had never needed to be told to fold his things and stow them out of her way, take up as little room as possible. Sometimes it seemed to her he even breathed considerately in her presence, careful not to use up too much of the good air. She thought about his deftness, the strength of those hands, and her knees went a little weak. It made her want to slap his face bloody. When he pushed down the tiger-striped expandex tights, he had to straighten his thighs, then lift each leg and peel the stretchy, clinging material off his calf, and maneuver it over the awkward angle of his ankle and foot. Then the tights were folded once, rolled and stuffed into his other boot.

His liberated dick was a fat sausage. It could hardly swing from side to side, it was so heavy and swollen. But he was careful to keep his hands away from his genitals — another habit (along with keeping himself shaved) that she had taken pains to reinforce. He came here to have her do things to his body that he could not do for himself. Very well, then, let him relinquish all attempts to give himself pleasure. It was just part of the price. And she loved to see him in need.

Looking at him felt like getting rich. No vid could ever approach the glory of doing it in person, or making somebody else do it. It was such a pleasure to look her fill instead of dressing, posing, acting, editing an image to be seen. People had gotten crazy about sex since the epidemic. Erotophobic. Everybody knew you couldn't catch it by just being in the same room with somebody else, but that "knowledge" didn't quiet the visceral fear that the virus would crawl into your bloodstream via the mere presence of lust. One of her clients had even demanded that she put on rubber gloves before she touched the keyboard to upload his fantasy.

Was David crazy? Because he didn't seem to care, he was shameless. Even now, he was crawling toward her with his tongue out, as if there was nothing to be afraid of. She let him lick the leather patches on the inside of her thighs. In a minute or two, he would try to wheedle her out of her 'legs, start talking about how much he loved to eat oysters. Why did hetboys always think that was what machas were looking for?

I am shameless, too, but I'm not careless, Lena told herself. I want to live forever. Sure, he says he doesn't do this with anybody but me, but people lie to get sex. They lie to get anything that makes them feel good. So he can do what I say and we'll both stay healthy, or he can go to the local piece-a parlor and fuck in a body bag, or he can ask death to go dancing.

Even through the shimmerlegs, she could feel the heat and wetness inside his mouth. It must hurt to lick the fabric — the metallic threads were sharp. But he lapped at her repeatedly, until the pressure became uncomfortable, and she slapped him away. Tears ran down his cheeks. "I could make you feel real good," he said, and the next slap bloodied his mouth and tossed him onto his side. She kicked him then, and took her time about it, walking around him to pick her spot, sure he would not try to get away. He didn't even curl himself into a decent ball or cover his head, just laid his hands on his thighs and bit his lip and moaned. Mostly she used the side of her boot, or the sole. But a couple of times she planted the pointed toe deep into the muscle of his naked buttocks, then she kicked him over so he lay on his belly, and literally walked all over him. He bore her weight patiently, even though the spike heels were making bloody holes in his back. He did not scream until she stepped off — onto his upturned palms.

From there, she went to her favorite chair, and sat, legs crossed so she could squeeze her thighs together at the sight of him crawling, dragging himself forward with his injured hands, to cradle and kiss the boots that had hurt him. He could take the entire heel into his mouth. She liked this spurious fellatio, his Eve's apple bobbing as he struggled to cope with the intrusive object in his throat. Maybe it would help him develop self-control. The Virgin knows he needed some.

When she took her boot away from him, he rolled over onto his back, and she rose to her feet, balanced on one foot, and placed the other foot on his face. She did not have to put much weight on it to make him hyperventilate and squirm. The toe was pressing on his mouth and chin, and the sharp heel rested in the hollow of his throat. "Do you want it?" she teased him, and he could not say yes or no. "Would it get you off, or is it just too big, David?" She saw from the look in his eyes that he understood the reference perfectly. When she lifted her foot and walked away, his sign of relief was loud.

You won't be glad for long, sucker, she vowed to herself. It's going to take you a long time to get off the hook tonight.

It was his job to crawl after her. Tonight this was coming easily. That was a relief. Sometimes he froze. Hands and knees refused to carry him, and she had to drive him forward with pain or with threats. That was baffling as well as mortifying. David suspected it was the little, nagging discomforts — the pain in his ankles, the irritation of the carpet against his palms, the soreness in his lower back — as much as the humiliation that sometimes stuck in his craw. Why did Lena have to make him crawl? He would have been glad to run to the bathroom, if the mood was on her to make him suffer there. He would even have sprinted to the leather bed-of-nails on her tatami, which is where she led him now.

He chuckled at himself, silently, deep in his throat, afraid she would see it on his face or hear it and think he was deriding her. If I wanted to crawl, she would make me run, he told himself. All we both want right now is to pump as much religion, chapter and verse, as we can before we got too fucked up to find a vein. And it's dangerous. It's a desire that cannot be consummated. If you try, you engender nothing but more desire. So Lena won't let me do anything just the way I want, for a long time. To prove we have enough control to finally do it, do the thing we want, and handle it, stay in control. She is taking care of me, a perverse nurturance, training me in denial to prepare me for indulgence.

The calves of her long legs, swaying ahead of him, were plump in the tall silver boots. He wanted to sink his teeth into them, taste the flesh encased in the metal. The rhinestone heels that had worn his tongue to shreds winked sardonically at him. Would Lena taste of flesh, or of mylar and zircons? His mouth was dry, making it hard to swallow the little bits of dirt left there by her soles. Does she notice me? he wondered. Does she care that I am crawling well tonight, that I do not hesitate or stumble? Or does she only notice me when I fail?

Behind her, Lena heard the slight, rhythmic scraping of his palms and shins on the rug. She made him stop at the low table by her tatami and hand her the bowl full of rubbing alcohol and used needles she had placed there earlier. She had been saving the points she used on him ever since he started seeing her. But the way she would use them now was something new. She wondered how he would respond. "Keep your hands down, David. Don't move."

She pinched up some flesh at the side of his upper arm, pulled it away from the bone, and ran a needle through his skin. He winced, but did not cry out. She repeated this on the other side. He looked at her mutely, begging, like a dog who has done something wrong. She smiled and put a third needle in below the first one, then inserted a fourth one in the loose skin of his other arm. When she had six of them in each arm, she put eight of them in the front of each thigh. The skin was not so loose there. The skewered flesh bled. He was shaking and making noises that were not quite words. When she started to rub and pinch his nipples, his bloated cock swung up like a tusker's trunk, and he blubbered for mercy.

"Later for you. This is for me." She could smell the blood. It made her mouth water, and she clamped her lips together. Too bad she was old enough to have developed a taste for it, before the plague. Look all you want, touch, smell, but don't swallow, she told herself. You can always make him bleed a little more to make up for it.

She thought it was best to restrain herself to a pair of needles per nipple. She ran them parallel to each other, at the top and bottom of the brown nubs. Here, too, there was bleeding as soon as she put the points in. Now, wasn't it a good thing she made him shave? Hair would distort the thin red paths, soak them up, make them less vivid. "You're making such a mess," she said. "Straighten your back." It would make the blood flow in straighter lines.

He was coming along nicely so far, but she didn't want to lose him. So she turned around and made him bend over and unzip her boots with his teeth. Then she stepped out of them, took her belt off, threw it on the tatami, and rolled her 'legs down over her hips. Unlike David, she didn't fold them up neatly and stow them away discreetly. She wadded them up in her hand and tossed them into the corner. He spread his thighs in anticipation, and she stepped between them, pressing his nose into the latex bikini she wore under her clothes.

"I'm tired of hearing you brag about how many oysters you've swallowed," she said. "So put up or shut up. Now."

She was wet enough to feel his tongue gliding over her, despite the thin sheet of rubber between them. When he sucked at her clit, it was wonderful. But there was no reason to spoil him. She turned around again, and bent over.

"Spread my cheeks," she said, then thought, Have you gone crazy? Letting him paw you with his sweaty little mitts? But his hands on either side of her furrow were surprisingly gentle and dry. He opened her only enough to allow his tongue complete access, and he didn't try to cheat and get a taste under the strap. Getting rimmed this way was much better than having him go after her clit. She let him do it until she was dizzy from hanging upside-down, and by the time she turned around, the blood was dry on his chest and thighs.

But his cock was still up, and she crouched between his legs to grasp it. Her erect nipples grazed his cheek, and he pulled his face away from her vest, afraid of seeming forward. But his mouth was still open, and a thin string of saliva fell from his lower lip. "What a good hungry dog," she said. "What a good boy. Oh, David, do you really want to be a good, good boy?"

He nodded, and she ran the first needle through the underside of his dick. He jerked, and she laughed, low and sexy, and said again, "What a good hungry dog." Then she pierced the loose skin of his shaft again. She put one in every inch, and his erection just got firmer, his balls tighter. With praise and with pain, she kept him pumped up until he would have let her put a needle through his tongue if she had promised to kiss him first.

Then she produced a ball of black and silver twine. First she wound it in figure-eights around each set of upper-arm piercings. Then she cinched each nipple to its mate. The long threads that were left over from binding his tits were woven back into the piercings on his arms. She drew the twine so tight, his shoulders were cupped forward. The holes in his arms began to bleed, and his wounded nipples opened and released more thin threads of scarlet.

She laced up each of his thighs. He guessed what came next, and shuddered, but could not form a coherent protest. It was awful and wonderful at the same time. Thigh was bound to thigh. Then his cock was bound — twine going completely around it, up and down — and his nipples utilized once more as anchors, to keep his pisser pointing toward the ceiling.

Lena stepped back and regarded her handiwork. He was holding absolutely still. To move at all would cause him excruciating pain. The idea of having his skin penetrated and violated so often had put him in a near-catatonic state. The piercings themselves were not that painful, but the stress the twine put on them jerked the pain up to a level that she found it erotic to witness. I actually want to play with myself, she thought, I want to make myself come just watching him kneeling there, trying to save himself some hurt by not breathing deeply. And resisting is absolutely out of the question. That would just pull everything out, split the skin in a dozen places.

She put her fingers under the latex strap of the bikini and manipulated her own thick sexual lubrication, the thin and rubbery lips, the spongy mouth of her opening. She let him watch her. Let him know, let him know, let him know — what this did to her. It was a reward. It was a threat.

David shook, and willed himself not to shake. Every needle blazed. Every needle froze. The skin around the piercings heated and swelled. The rest of his skin was clammy and cold. And she was perfect, in front of him, her face a bestial mask of sadistic lust, masturbating at the spectacle of his willing vulnerability, the suffering he offered up to her, the bleeding wounds he had held still for her to make, and allowed her to bind. He wanted . . . everything. Consumption. To be used, to be used up completely. To be absorbed into her eyes, her mouth, her sex, to become part of her substance.

When he tried to tell her this, stumbling over the inadequate words he could barely string together, she pushed him over onto his back, onto the bed of nails. He choked and cried her name. She laughed again, and picked up her crop. She struck him on the piercings. She was careful, aiming the crop in such a way that the needles would not be caught and ripped out, but she hurt him a lot.

She even found his nipples, within the hollows of his shoulders, and beat them. She made him lick his own blood off the crop. And she used the large flap of leather at the tip of it to flog his cock and balls. The stock was used to beat him across the thighs. He saw white light every time she hit him. The force of the blows sent him back into the sharp points embedded in the leather. Slivers of pain went deep into his back and buns and upper thighs. He had never done anything so difficult.

Then Lena said, "Roll over, David."

Oh, the bitch, the bitch, the unfeeling loveless heartless dried-up cunt of a bitch. She wasn't even going to help him by kicking him over. He was going to have to do this all by himself. He did not deserve this, he did not know how he was going to obey, it was hard, too hard.

He must have spoken at least part of this aloud, because she was reaching inside the black latex bikini and smearing something on his face. "Oh, far from dried-up, David dear," she said. "Of course it's hard. But it gets you off, too. I know you. So do it, David, do it now. Do it because I want to watch you. I promise I'll make it worth your while, David. Lay on your pain, boy."

With a groan, he went over, and screamed. There was no way to help himself land. He simply fell on the piercings, and there was nothing but more needles to fall upon. He was held up in the air on spear-points. Broken. A victim.

Then she beat him. Hymen! As he howled, he thought, When she cropped me before, she was toying with me. Trying to scare me. Now she's just trying to cut me in half. I hate this, I hate her, and there's nothing I can do, because I want what comes later, I want — I want — I want this, even this. Even this. Because she cannot cut me in half, she cannot diminish me, even this I can survive, thrive on, so go ahead, you bitch, I can take it, and more than that, I can love it — almost come from it — but I can't stop screaming. And I can't scream any louder. When will it end?

He could not get up by himself. He could only roll from side to side. And that meant rolling on the needles, rolling on the spikes in the leather. He hated that riding crop. Hated its thin, leather-covered, flexible stock. Hated the noisy, floppy piece of leather on the end of it. Resolved to buy her something thicker and less stingy, a razor strop, maybe. Then she threw down the crop and started to use her belt, and he changed his mind. Let's not buy Lena anything. Let's not give Lena any ideas. Let's just hope we live through this.

When she was done, she rolled him over with a hand on his shoulder and a hand in his hair. She showed him his own face in her belt buckle. He was a mess — tears and snot, hair every which way. But his eyes looked serene, his face was relaxed somehow. Virgin, Birth Mother and War Mother damn it, she always does it, she makes me feel . . . safe. If she's crazy, we're a pair.

Lena let him rest while she untied the twine. She removed the needles carefully, wrapping alcohol preps around each point before pulling them out so the stinging antiseptic would be drawn through the wound. Then she dabbed antibiotic salve on the punctures. Had she really let him put his mouth on her panties, earlier? Or had he dreamed that?

She was bending over him with another needle in her hand, a different kind, just a slender, hollow tube of chrome with no plastic end to connect it to a syringe. And a gold ring. "I want you to wear this, David," she said. "Just for tonight."

On his finger? What? "OK," he mumbled.

She grabbed his right nipple, shoved the needle through it, fit the end of the ring into the hollow butt of the needle, and pushed it through. A tit-ring? Indignation almost made him bolt off the mat. "Just for me, David, just for tonight," she reminded him. "Nobody else needs to see. Nobody else needs to know."

A ring, going through an actual hole in his body. Might as well say in public, I'm a hype. Nobody else wore them. They were too fucking primitive, permanent. An advertisement that you liked to put needles in your body. Unsanitary. Spreads disease. Spreads the plague. Unnecessary. Illegal. Sick.

She was bending over him, closing the ring. Her vest fell open enough for him to see that her nipples were still hard. And why not? He was still hard too, and she was squeezing him, making him gasp as the salty sweat on her hand made contact with the fresh needle-marks.

Then she left him, and he was so lonely, he cried out for her. "Lena!"

"Don't worry, I'll be right there. Time you met the heavenly host, boy. Lay still."

She returned carrying the alcohol lamp, the water, and her wooden box. This was another break with tradition. Before, she always fixed him at the table. If they got really inspired, they would slide to the floor, but they started out facing each other, sitting primly on chairs. He was confused, and decided the best policy was to be absolutely passive. As usual. Lena knew what she was doing. He didn't know. So he should just hold his tongue and watch.

She handed him a foil packet. "Put this on."

It was a condom. She had made him wear one before. She liked to make him jerk off in them, then save the contents to punish him with later. Cum tasted terrible when it was cold. He rolled it on.

Lena sat down at the little bedside table. She took a mirror from the wooden box, tipped half of the contents of one of the glassine envelopes onto its silver face, and began chopping the yellow flakes into powder with a single-edged razor blade. When it was fine enough to suit her, she slid the razor blade beneath the tiny heap of gold dust, and dumped a portion of it into the ornate silver spoon. The bottom of its bowl was permanently blackened, and the handle had been bent to make sure the precious liquid in it stayed level. She lit the alcohol lamp, drew some of the clean water into one of the syringes, rinsed the blade off into the spoon with careful, tiny squirts, ejected the rest of the water into the glass, and held the spoon over the flame.

"Keep it up," she warned him. The air over the spoon sizzled. She put it down and pinched a bit of cotton off one of the large white balls of fluff, rolled it tight, then dropped it into the spoon. David handled himself, watching her chase the cotton and finally pin it down with the needle, and draw the plunger on the syringe back, filling the glass barrel with piss-colored fluid. The slow masturbation wasn't necessary. He wouldn't lose his erection or shoot until —

She was shimmying out of the black latex bikini. He gaped at her shaved sex. She put one foot on each side of him, and spread herself with her free hand. It looked like a woman wearing a hooded cape . . . or a woman with wings.

"Hold it up for me," she said, and sank onto him. There was no time to be grateful or surprised, and barely enough time to be helpful. David tried to position his sex so it would go in smoothly, at the proper angle. "Help me," she said, waving the rubber tourniquet at him. He put out his arm, and she somehow managed to pull it tight and tuck one loose end under, so it would put just a little pressure on his bicep. She shook the syringe, flicked it with her forefinger to get rid of the air bubbles. Between two fingers, she felt for his vein and held it still, and rested the point of the needle where it should go.

But she did not put it in. Instead, she moved on him. He stopped caring about the spiked hide under his back, if that was the price he had to pay for being ridden this way. Lena had put down the needle and had both hands on his shoulders. Her eyes were closed. He lifted his hands, knowing this was an unpardonable crime, and slid them beneath her vest. Her breasts were small and firm, and he touched them as lightly as he could, hoping she would ignore the touch or maybe not even feel it.

But Lena did feel it. Her eyes popped open, and she showed him her teeth. "Better get a decent feel while you can," she hissed. "Grab them, stupid, pinch them, hang onto them, you might never get another chance." Yeah, so a real mistress always insisted that her submissives treat her with absolute respect and gentle tenderness. Shit on that. She hated being touched that way, the way you pick up something disgusting — tentatively, afraid to make contact. He was almost mauling her, but it felt good, good, and that was what he was there for, to make her feel good.

She was fiercely happy to have David inside her. Show him what that big thing was good for. Something besides getting it slapped around, punctured, and jacked off. She was breaking too many of her own rules, but she did not care, not yet. She could worry about it later. She never had to see him again. After tonight, she could send him away. If she hadn't finally scared him off for good. She rested one hand on his pectoral, heard him groan, and looked down to see the ring. She would make him give that back first, of course. It was 24-karat gold, and he'd never dare keep it in long enough for the piercing to heal. She tugged on it anyway, just to remind him that he was a marked man, then leaned on his other pec, the intact one.

He wouldn't be able to resist coming for much longer, and neither would she. The only difference was, if she came now, the party could still go on. If he came, the party was over. Might as well perform the rest of the experiment. She picked up the hypodermic and got his arm in the right position again. This time, there was no tease. She slapped at his vein, and it bulged the way his cock did when she hit it. All she had to do was lean on the needle a little, and it broke the skin. She had barely retracted the plunger when a miniature geyser of blood appeared. He was so easy to do. She gave him nearly three-quarters of a cc, more than his usual dose. He wouldn't be able to come now until his drugs wore off a little. He could lay there and get a head start on salvation while she sat on top of him and cooked up a fix for herself. It would be awkward, but interesting.

Then she began to hear music — or almost hear music. Or was it her own voice, singing? Somewhere something sounded delicious, heavenly, and there was a golden light around everything. David looked as if he were miles below her, as if he had fallen from a great height and landed on his back, his wings spread out behind him. Maybe they weren't wings, exactly, but a nimbus, a radiant cloud of . . . benevolence and goodness and warmth, a blessing, a . . . melting. As if everything bad or painful or confusing was melting, dissolving, running out of her, out of the whole world, disappearing, and what was left behind was so simple, so good, it was no wonder she could hear everything singing, music everywhere.

The power of so much beauty made her want to cry. When she touched David's hair, light came off of it in rainbow glints, it hurt her eyes. And when she closed them, the visuals turned instantly into a rush of heat in her gut, between her legs, and she used him hard, again and again, knowing he could not prevent her, did not want to, would have given his life to see this look on her face, her helplessness, pleasure, his tormentor losing control while she still controlled him absolutely. When she finally tired and slowed down, he put his hands under her hips and helped her keep moving, and the drug had filled her with so much sweetness that she did not mind. She knew that even now, David would not come until she allowed it, released him from her service. And so she pounded it out of him, demanded it, and he obeyed this order like all the others, not knowing why both of them were flying together, seeing, being angels together.

It wasn't until the music faded out of earshot that she got mad. For her to catch his rush, there had to be skin-to-skin contact between them. The drug could pass through one mucous membrane into another, especially if there was enough friction to wear away the outer layers of protective cells. She wasn't sorry, and that was what made her so angry — that she had needed him, needed him to pleasure her, but also needed him to go on and reach his own climax. How could this have happened? He was a toy, he was recreation, he was like your favorite vid program or a hobby. This was not a relationship. She did not have relationships. Especially not with boys half her age who were stupid enough to be hypes

163

and bent enough to love getting spanked.

This could not be her fault. Somebody would have to pay.

David was out of breath, panting, watching her through half-closed eyes as she came up and off of him with a wad of rubber in her hand. "Broken! Shithead! Can't you even put on a scumbag right? What is *wrong* with you?" She threw it at him, and David winced as it hit his chest and smeared slime across his nipple.

His chest contracted. He felt as if he had just murdered someone. "Lena! No! I was careful."

"Are you arguing with me?"

"Yes!"

It was the first time he had ever crossed her. They stared at each other, furious. He started talking again, fast, afraid she would find a way to shut him up. This was too important. "Lena, I am sorry. But I have been using those things since I was eight, and I've never had one break yet. Maybe it was old. Maybe we just got carried away. But it shouldn't matter. I had a blood test just a month ago. I am *clean*. And I have not been fucking or shooting up with anybody but you. I swear."

He remembered the bad teeth and bald head of the bartender at the High Flyer, whispering in his ear when he came up to get Lena's drink, "Better take her something a little more potent unless you want just a handshake. Talk to Shaky over there, that drowned-rat character with the shoulder pads, he knows what her usual is. Hope you know what you're doing, son, she's fifty miles of bad road." It seemed like such a long time ago. Giving Lena her drink, trying to look like he really did know what he was doing, figuring if you want to be cool you talk as little as possible, so all he said was, "If you really want a party I'll go talk to Shaky." She had just glanced up at him and barely nodded. And him afraid to ask the missionary what was in the envelope that had cost too much money, afraid to ask Lena, too, just letting her take the lead. Until now.

"You swear?" she shouted. "You swear? You pisshole. If I hadn't had the brains to shove some foam up there before you got here, you would be dead, sucker. I would call the cops and report you."

"Report me? That's hysterical. Have you lost your fuckin' mind? You better grab the rest of this religion and flush it down somebody else's toilet before the sheriff kicks down your door. You better wipe your hard-drive and cook an extra set of books to hand the tax-man, unless you're the first sex-jockey since the first moron microchip got stuck on a board to give Caesar his due. You better pray real hard that nobody in this building hates you enough to claim that you been seeing johns on premises. The very nicest thing they'll do is revoke your license, Lena, and you can work off your fine down at the corner of Fifth and Grand, and hope Joey the Bag will buy you a drink once in a while so you can get off your achin' feet."

David realized he had gotten closer and closer to her, until he was yelling at her just inches from her face. He grabbed her hands, backed up a step, and lowered the volume. "Don't make a bug raid out of a bat bite. This is going to be okay. You want me to get tested again? I will. Come with me. I'll sign for you to get the results, and you can tell me if I'm clean or not. Lena, please, it was so fine, don't make it ugly, it was an accident. I would never do anything to hurt you. Please."

She twisted out of his grip. "Oh, yes, you'll get tested," she said. "Tomorrow. And a month after that. So will I. And you will stay here with me until you do. So I know where you go and what you do. And if I get sick — "

"If you get sick, you can shoot me up with a needle full of your own blood. You can do it now. I'm that sure I'm clean. Are you? Are you that sure?"

She didn't answer him, just grabbed her knees, put her head down, and rocked. He left her alone, went into the kitchen, and found half a bottle of tequila sitting by a sticky shot glass. He rinsed the glass, looked in the refrigerator for a lemon, couldn't find anything but cans of lemon-flavored iced tea, and settled for taking the tequila and a clean glass out to the tatami. He poured her a shot, made her drink it, and persuaded her to give him one of her feet to massage. Finally she started to cry. He wondered if that would make it better or worse. Would it ease her terror, or would it make her ashamed?

Lena was panicking. He was being too good. But he had done something awful. Hadn't he? Had she? He was picking her up, moving her off of the tatami, putting her down, and unrolling the futon. Her bed. She never let him up on her bed. And there was something extremely scary about how easy it had been for him to lift her off the floor and put her someplace else. She didn't like being reminded that he was that strong, that he really had a choice about obeying her. Then he picked her up again, put her on the bed, and stretched out beside her. His naked hip was warm. She

wanted to stroke it, she wanted to touch his cock. She made a fist
instead and went to get off the futon.

David touched her shoulder, gave her a tissue and some more
tequila. He was kissing her, making her lie down while he cooked
up some more religion. "Second-hand can't be as good as the real
thing," he said, reaching for her arm. He looped her belt around it,
cinched it tight, gave her the end to hold. Lena was too heavy with
grief to stop him. She realized then that she had never actually
seen him fuck up his own hit. He didn't seem to be having any
trouble doing it for her.

His hand was in her. After everything that had happened, the
idiot had put on a rubber glove. And he was touching all those
places that a cock never reaches. All those places only women had
touched. The dangerous women, women who could make you do
anything, say anything, buy them anything, follow them anywhere
for their attention, their smiles, the sex, this sex —

Just one woman, really, Lena thought, a woman who knew how
to make you happy even if you wanted to die, knew where to get
it, the doses, showed you how, laughed at you for being such a
goon the first time you got religion and you knew this was something that could take you over. The woman who claimed she never
would have sent you to heaven if she'd known how young you
really were. But then said it was better if you did it with her, at
home, so she could take care of you. That woman carried a gun
before it was legal and swore she would shoot the man who made
you leave home if she ever ran across him on the streets. He wasn't
your daddy, but he made you call him that all the time, even when
your mouth was full of his wrinkled prick. That was a memory
with poisonous spines. It was easier to think about the woman
who had a beat to walk every night, in shoes that should have been
worn only in bed. While you waited all night at a dirty table, feeling squeezed by the vending machines that lined the walls and the
fluorescent light that beat down from the ceiling so hard there
were no shadows, not even under your chair. Waiting for her to
come back and give you some more cash and take a few more
rubbers. She would tell you to wash your face and ask you what
you were reading, promise to take you back to the library tomorrow. The woman who serviced vice cops in the dark and didn't tell
them she was bleeding because "I know I'm dead, and some of
them are coming with me." The woman with an illegal child that
would never go to school or be a taxpayer because of its imperfect

DNA, the child who lived with its father who was almost female, who always wanted more cash for the kid and for hormones and surgery. The woman who one night decided not to turn anybody with the numbers 3 and 7 in their license plate because she could swear the bastard who'd tried to choke her yesterday had a license plate with those numbers. Or was it 8 and 9? The woman who had broken some of the bones in her right hand beating a trick who tried to take his money back. That hand hurt her on rainy nights.

The woman and her sore feet, the woman and her kabuki make-up and clown wig and chipped purple nails, the woman with a dagger tattooed between her breasts, the woman who laughed at her own horrible stories, the woman and her habit could shatter your whole life, if you ever got a chance to have a life apart from her, apart from the messed-up adults who could not help themselves, could not help but be predatory, unpredictable, draining. Feeling this good couldn't be good for you. Oh no, oh no, not me, not me, I am an atheist, I am an agnostic, I can take this or leave it. Leave her. Leave her. Find another way to get a bed for the night. Join that gang of kids that boosts stuff from the market. Find a rent-a-daddy and hold his cache. Get some fake id, chase some other rooster out of a bar, and keep the patrons supplied with whatever it's illegal for the bartender to sell. Break into cars, co-ops, street vendors' booths. Sell expired film, bootleg vids full of static and broken designer watches to tourists. But never walk into the headlights and stop your own drivers, keep your own paranoid list of license plate numbers. Never pour your whole life into the spoon and the needle. And never be able to do without it, either. Because the pain of living does not go away. You need to treat that pain. Or you need to die. Lena did not want to die.

Or was it really just that she left me? Forgot to come back for me? Until I got sick of chugging vending machine coffee and couldn't face the place in daylight, and went off on my own. Did she find somebody older and smarter who could take care of her, or was it somebody as young and scared as I was when she first met me? How could she abandon me? We had absolutely nothing, but it was still more than anybody ever wanted us to have.

Every other woman in Lena's life had her own story, but it was the same story. She is jealous because religion means more to you than she does. Or you get jealous because of the things she does to get to heaven. You have been trying to clean up only she asks you to hit her because she has the shakes and then she tells you how

167

good you are to her and she has extra, let's get off together, let's party. Please. She is scared, and you are so strong. Strong enough to do without it. Then you do, you fix, and she says now she knows you will never leave her. Only later she leaves you to clean up. Or she leaves you for somebody who can get her high three times a day. And the only reason you are surprised, the only reason it matters, the only reason you stick around for the end of the story is because you care. Loving her makes you stupid. So when she hurts you you have no one but yourself to blame, you should have known it was coming, you shouldn't even feel sorry for yourself. You're sick and you need medicine, even if taking the medication *is* your sickness, and it all makes about as much sense as falling in love because you don't want to be lonely.

David's other hand fell on Lena's nipple, and it was full of strength and love. The touch was angelic, too sensitive, too completely pleasurable to be human. "Hush, Lena," he said. His honeyed voice was resonant, set off vibrations that hummed in her belly, tickled her throat and made her thighs roll apart. Her body was hollow, it was tuned to his voice, he was like a clapper in a bell. "Listen. Hear the music? Good, I'm glad. I'm so glad."

Lena realized that the spaces in between the words were even more delicious than the sounds that David was making. She wished he would just shut up and let the sweet silence hum around her. But he kept on talking. "You're so beautiful when you smile like that. All I ever wanted to do is make you happy. Would it be so terrible, having me around? The shop owes me two months of vacation. I wouldn't get in your way. I know you have to work. But I could feed you, Lena. I could cook you really wonderful things to eat. At night, you could sit down and relax and have a hot, nutritious meal for a change instead of all that takeout crap. And I'll clean up after myself. I could keep the whole house together. You'd save so much money."

Lena put her hands up to cover her ears, but David intercepted one of them and carried it to his breast. "I'm not going to take it out, Lena, I'm going to leave it in. The ring. Feel it? I'll leave it in. And I'll take care of you. It'll be okay, sweetheart. I'm a big, strong boy, and there's nothing that I can't fix for you, if you'll just let me."

She opened her eyes, and everything in her apartment was a weapon.

From Posthumous Fragments of 1798
Novalis

— Translated from the German by Alexander Gelley

[6] In every utterance there speaks an incantation. Whoever summons spirit — such a one appears.

[12] In its most authentic sense philosophizing is — a caress — testimony of the deepest love of reflection, of an absolute passion for wisdom.

[17] The supreme form of the sciences [*Wissenschaften*] must be poetic. Every proposition [*Satz*] must have its singular character — must be a self-evident individual, the vestment of a witty idea.

[18] The first synthetic proposition is, as it were, the first seed. One proposition after another detaches itself from each of the extremities according to the rule of attraction of the seed and, by virtue of having passed through the first proposition, becomes assimilated to it — and so philosophy expands to infinity, both outwardly and inwardly — It seeks, in a sense, to fill out the infinite space between the extremities.

[19] The highest tasks preoccupy mankind at the earliest stage. In his first thoughts man most urgently experiences the need to unite the highest goals. As culture evolves his efforts diminish in respect to genius but improve in practicality — and this leads him into the error of turning his energies only to the more immediate and restricted elements while abstracting altogether from ultimate things. But he cannot fail very soon to notice the deficiency of this method and to consider the possibility of combining the advantages of the first with those of the second, and thus to augment both. Now it finally occurs to him to seek in himself, as absolute midpoint of these separated worlds, the absolute means of fusion — He suddenly realizes that the problem has *realiter* already been solved through his own existence — and that the consciousness of the laws of his existence is *kat exoxen* [par excellence] the science [*Wissenschaft*] that he has so long sought. Through the disclosure of this consciousness the great puzzle is, in essence, solved. Just as his life is

real philosophy, so is his philosophy ideal life — the living theory of life. Scattered circumstances turn into systematic experiments. His path is now mapped out to eternity — His occupation is the expansion of his existence into infinity — the dream of his youth has become a lovely reality — his earlier hopes and intimations have turned into symbolic prophecies. The apparent contradiction of the original task — the tasks — resolution and non-resolution in one — has altogether disappeared.

[21] There are certain poetic conceptions [*Dichtungen*] in us that seem to have an altogether different character than the others, since they are accompanied by a feeling of necessity which can in no sense be justified on external grounds. It's as if mankind were engaged in a dialogue [*Gespräch*] where some unknown spiritual being prompts it in a wondrous manner to develop the most palpable, manifest ideas. This being must be of a higher sort since it relates to man in a way that would not be possible with any being that is bound to appearances — it must be homogeneous since it treats man as a spiritual being and only very rarely incites him to autonomous activity. This Self of a higher kind is related to man as man is to nature or as a wise man to a child. Man yearns to become like it just as he seeks to identify the N[ot]-I with himself.

This is not a fact to be explicated. Everyone must experience it for himself. It is a fact of a higher type that only the higher individual will encounter. Yet all men should strive to induce it in themselves. . . .

[31] Poetry elevates every single element by means of a singular attachment to the rest of the whole — and if philosophy, in setting forth laws, prepares the world to submit to the efficacy of ideas, poetry is, as it were, the key to philosophy, its purpose and its meaning; for poetry fashions the beautiful society — the world-family — the beautiful household of the universe.

Just as philosophy, by means of system and statehood, *strengthens* the capacities and power of the individual through those of mankind and of the world-all, making the individual an organ of the whole — to does poetry in respect to *life*. The individual lives in the whole and the whole in the individual. The highest form of sympathy and collaboration, the most intimate *communality* of the temporal and the eternal comes about through poetry.

[32] The poet, just as he has begun the procession, brings it to a close. If the philosopher puts all in order, sets it up, the poet dissolves all ties. His words are not general signs — they are tones —

magical words which set comely groups into motion all around. Just as the clothes of saints still contain wondrous powers, so is many a word blessed on account of a marvelous remembrance, having become almost a poem in itself. For the poet language is never too poor but always too general. He often requires familiar words, worn out through constant use. His world is simple, as is his instrument — but just as inexhaustible in melodies.

[41] The mime vivifies in himself the principles of a given individuality *arbitrarily*.

There is a symptomatic and a genetic form of imitation. The latter alone is vital. It presupposes the most intimate fusion of the imagination and the understanding.

This capacity of truly arousing an alien individuality in oneself — not merely of simulating by way of superficial imitation — is still wholly unknown — and hinges on a most wondrous *penetration* and spiritual mimicry. The artist turns himself into everything that he perceives and wants to be.

[42] Poetry is the great art of constructing transcendental well-being. The poet, then, is the transcendental physician. Poetry works its ends by means of pain and longing [*Schmerz und Kitzel*] — pleasure and displeasure — error and truth — health and sickness — It mixes all for its great goal of goals — the *elevation of mankind above itself.*

[46] Poetry dissolves alien existence into one's own.

[47] Transcendental poetry is a mixture of philosophy and poetry. Fundamentally, it includes all transcendental functions, and in fact contains the transcendental in itself. The transcendental poet is the transcendental man in general.

[48] The elaboration of transcendental poetry should lead to a tropology which would encompass the rules of the *symbolic construction* of the transcendental world.

[74] We seek a *project* [*Entwurf*] for the world — and we ourselves are this project — What are we? personified *almighty points*. But the execution, as the image of the project, must be like it both with respect to spontaneity and autonomy — and vice versa. Thus the life or the essence of the spirit consists in the creation, the nativity, and the education of its like. Man, then, is fit for marriage and family only insofar as he is capable of maintaining a happy marriage with himself — of constituting a good family in himself. Act of self-embracing.

The love of self must never be acknowledged to oneself — the secrecy of this avowal is the life-principle of the only true and eternal love. The first kiss within this compact is the principle of philosophy — the origin of a new world — the beginning of absolute temporal reckoning — the fulfillment of an infinitely enlarging self-covenant.

Who would not be attracted to a philosophy whose germ is a first kiss?

Love popularizes the personality — It makes individualities *communicable* and *comprehensible*. (Understanding through love.)

[81] I wish that my readers would read the remark that the origin of philosophy is a first kiss while they were listening to a deeply felt rendition of Mozart's composition "Wenn die Liebe in Deinen blauen Augen" ["An Chloe," KV 524] — unless it were in a moment when they themselves stood in expectant proximity of a first kiss.

[105] The world must be romanticized. In this way we may recover its original meaning. Romanticizing is nothing but a qualitative potentiation. Through this operation the lower self becomes identified with the better self. Thus we ourselves are such a qualitatively potentiating series. This operation is still wholly unknown. Insofar as I give the ordinary an elevated meaning, the commonplace a mysterious aspect, the familiar the dignity of the unfamiliar, the finite an illusion of infinity, I romanticize it — The process is inverted for what is higher, unknown, mystical, infinite — it becomes logarithmized through this linkage — and assumes a familiar designation. Romantic philosophy. *Lingua romana.* Elevation and abasement in alternation.

[125] The world has a fundamental capacity to be activated by me — It is actually activated by me a priori — One with me. I have a fundamental tendency and capacity to activate the world — At present I am incapable of entering into relation with anything that is not oriented according to my will, or is not congruent to it — Thus the world must have a fundamental disposition to be directed by me — to be congruent to my will.

My *spiritual* activity — my realization of ideas — is thus not a *decomposition* and transformation of the world — at least not insofar as I am — could be — a *member* of this particular world — rather it could only be an *operation of variation* — I will, irrespective of the world and its laws — by means of these — be able to arrange, order, and fashion it for me. This higher formation is not in conflict with the lesser — It follows its path irrespective of the latter — and utilizes the world, which is world precisely because it is not

172

completely and *totally* determined — and thus is susceptible to determination from multiple sources, for whatsoever purpose — which would not be the case for a totally rational individuo. . . .

[134] The act of overleaping oneself is everywhere the highest, the primordial point — the *genesis of life*. Thus the flame is nothing but such an act — Thus all philosophy originates where the philosophizing element philosophizes itself — that is, at once consumes (determines, necessitates) and again renews (does not determine, leaves free) — The history of this process is philosophy. Thus the beginning of all living morality consists in acting virtuously against virtue — therein begins the life of virtue, whereby perhaps the capacity augments to infinity, without any limit whatsoever — this is the condition of the possibility of losing its *life*.

TRANSLATOR'S NOTE

This selection is drawn from a group of some 442 notations that Novalis (Friedrich von Hardenberg) prepared as a source for future fragment collections, which, however, could not be realized in his lifetime (he died in 1801). He had already prepared an integral collection of 125 fragments, published in 1798 in the periodical *Anthenäum* under the title "Pollen." His characterization of these new notations as "logological fragments, poeticisms" reflects his sense of the inextricable fusion of the speculative and poetic.

This translation utilizes the German text in Novalis, *Schriften*, ed. Richard Samuel in collaboration with Hans-Joachim Mähl and Gerhard Schulz (Stuttgart: W Kohlhammer, 1960), II: 522–57. The numbering of that edition has been retained.

for Peter Pastreich

EL DORADO

Part I. A Dream of Gold

JOHN ADAMS

John Adams
An Interview with Aaron Jay Kernis

IN 1977, at the age of seventeen, I traveled what seemed as far away as possible from my home in the mall-lined suburbs of Philadelphia to study musical composition at the San Francisco Conservatory of Music. I was assigned to work with composer John Adams for the second semester, and got to know his newly written Minimalist pieces, *Phrygian Gates* and *Shaker Loops*, through hearing first performances of them that year. I had already developed a keen interest in the Minimalism of Steve Reich and Philip Glass, whose music I'd discovered on an underground Philadelphia college radio station.

It was with great excitement that I came to know those early works of Adams's, for it was clear from the start that he was doing something special, pushing past Minimalism's inherent boundaries, molding its steady state, no-beginning-no-end quality into music with sensual surfaces and dramatic shapes that reflected romantic emotionalism instead of the purer, classical formalism of Reich or Glass.

Those early works, along with his first major success — the choral and orchestral *Harmonium* — have provided the cornerstone for one of the most rapidly ascendant careers in the world of new music. For the past fifteen years, Adams has produced a stream of distinctive and provocative compositions, including the high-profile operas *Nixon in China* and *The Death of Klinghoffer* (both in collaboration with director Peter Sellars and librettist Alice Goodman), and the instrumental works *Harmonielehre, The Chairman Dances, The Wound Dresser, Fearful Symmetries, Grand Pianola Music, Short Ride in a Fast Machine, Common Tones in Simple Time* and, most recently, *El Dorado*. Adams is the most performed of living American concert composers, and his works are as frequently enjoyed by enthusiastic, diverse listeners as they are reviled by modernist composers and critics. *Nixon in China* is already acclaimed as a classic of its time, while *Klinghoffer* — which deals with the death of a crippled Jewish American cruise-ship passenger at the hands of Palestinian terrorists — has been met with a more divided response that was somehow appropriate to its subject.

This interview took place last February in the newish, uncluttered house that Adams shares with his wife, Deborah O'Grady, and their two young children in Berkeley, California. Before our talk, we drove around the ruins of the 1991 Berkeley/Oakland Hills fire — his house barely escaped devastation — and passed scores of empty foundations just beginning to pulse with shockingly green, lush overgrowth.

AARON JAY KERNIS: I've always been struck by how *American* your music is — in its overall sound and its frame of reference. I wonder how you see your work now that multiculturalism is the current measure of artistic relevance.

JOHN ADAMS: Well, I've always said that what really interests me about a work of art is its ethnicity. The Frenchness of Debussy or Ravel, the Russianness of Dostoyevsky or the Italianness of Monteverdi or Verdi. I acknowledge the old saw that says art is a universal language. But it *is* and it *isn't*. Yes, you can appreciate a work of art strictly as a found object, without any cultural awareness, but what really interests me, what gives me great pleasure in a work of art, is its reference to the time and place and its social milieu. So it's given me a great deal of pleasure while composing to acknowledge through my composition that I am an American, living in the latter part of twentieth-century music, being inundated with American culture. And for better or worse this is reflected in my music.

KERNIS: What about political and social concerns, which have shaped your operatic and instrumental works increasingly, most recently in *El Dorado*?

ADAMS: I think that there's an eternal pendulum in the arts between art which is very introspective and very hermetic, and art which is socially engaged and reflects its historical milieu.

KERNIS: So you feel we're coming into a time now where the pendulum's swinging back toward engagement?

ADAMS: I definitely do. I see evidence of it in a lot of artists and composers who are younger than I am. I think that we're emerging from a period, particularly in music, where formalism has been

176

the persuasive aesthetic. Call it modernism or whatever, but we all recognize the period from 1950 to 1970 to be one governed by a fixation on materials, form and method. Now, this doesn't mean that other kinds of art didn't flourish within this period, but within western Europe, the very small limited world of western Europe, America and possibly Japan, that kind of art gained an immense amount of prestige — composers starting with Webern and the Darmstadt composers (Boulez, Stockhausen, Berio, Donatoni, etc.), and in this country people like Babbit and Carter and so forth. And we must also include John Cage in this. There's an enormous formalist engine running John Cage's work as well, as you can see by reading his essays and lectures.

KERNIS: I've tended to include Reich and Glass in that camp as well . . .

ADAMS: Yes, that's always a very amusing discussion about early Minimalism because both Reich and Glass and even people on the cusp of that, like La Monte Young or Morton Feldman, had their coming of age during the high period of formalism, and yet they were trying to break through — particularly Glass and Reich. They were trying to break through that formalism to a new kind of expressivity. But it's funny to see — even in Glass's most banal and pop pieces like *Songs for Liquid Days*, this strange kind of little motor going along that still harkens back to the process-oriented pieces of the Sixties.

KERNIS: When did your music begin to move away from that? All your pieces from the very beginning were reacting to and moving away from the strict processes of early Minimalism in some sense, but *Shaker Loops* and the piano pieces were still rather formalized.

ADAMS: Well, I think I had a tremendously productive disaster in 1978, which was a string quartet called *Wavemaker*. It was a piece in which I attempted to dictate every element of the composition through various equations or arbitrary procedures.

KERNIS: So this was serialized?

ADAMS: No, it wasn't totally serialized, but it was an attempt to use some kind of procedural etiquette that existed outside of the needs of the music and would imprint its laws onto the musical material, which I think is very much what serialism is about and certainly what other forms of compositional, or precompositional, routines are about. And the piece was a disaster. Both expressively and formally, *and* emotionally, I think, as well. The lesson I learned from it was that music, the primal material of music, has powers within it and within its relationships that have a life of their own and which a composer — a really sensitive composer — has to be intuitively aware of and must have freedom enough to acknowledge and to follow. In other words, I think that to try willfully to atomize the elements of music, as people tried to do in the Fifties — whether it was John Cage or Boulez or Xenakis or Milton Babbit — to just knock it down into these discrete atomized elements and then impose some external set of laws on it, almost always produces a very gray and uninteresting emotional experience.

KERNIS: You feel that even with Boulez?

ADAMS: Yes, I find that with Boulez what's interesting is usually his sense of color and his phenomenal gift of orchestration, but I feel the emotional range of Boulez is extraordinarily limited. With all this immense equipment and this huge power of technique that's being brought to the act of composition, in comparison to a couple of bars of a Mahler symphony, it's unbelievably pale. And I feel that the reason for that is his unwillingness to follow the genetic personality of the music itself, of the materials. You know, it *is* very much like an embryo. Once that sperm reaches the egg, there is an entity. I mean, I'm not going to get into . . . I don't want to start sounding like a pro-lifer here, but we know that a human being's personality — his or her emotions, his likes or dislikes — or whether he's left-handed or right-handed, physical appearance: it's all there from the moment of conception. And I feel that when you take a group of notes together, or some harmonic organization, or a rhythmic pulse, anything like that, that the music has its own personality, immediately, and then the really creative composer follows the implication of that material. Which is why I say that when I start a piece I genuinely don't know where it's going to end. A lot of people are shocked to hear that, they feel it's an indication of some sloppy —

KERNIS: Fatal flaw? —

ADAMS: Yes. Here's somebody who's just finger-painting, or doing sand drawings, or playing with mudpies. In fact I may have a deeply held notion of where I want a certain piece to end up, but frequently by the time I'm a couple of minutes into it, I've discovered that this is a totally different person. This isn't the little girl with blond hair that I wanted to have — it's a boy with hyperactive glands or something. So I have to obey the special nature of that personality.

KERNIS: Generally speaking, that personality has become less "Minimalist" than it was when you started out.

ADAMS: I was really excited when I heard my first Minimalist pieces. Before that, I'd felt really awash. I felt like I'd been born with this desire to create music and I'd just been born in the wrong time. I had no interest in the twelve-tone system, I had no interest in atonality or aperiodicity, and this seemed to be what was in the air. I heard several pieces: I heard *In C*, then I heard *Drumming* by Steve Reich, then I heard several Glass pieces — I can't remember which they were — and I was tremendously excited and encouraged by this because here was a music that was interesting on a formal level, that was interesting on an intellectual level, but had all the vitality and communicative power of jazz or rock. I found it almost irresistibly attractive. I was drawn to this music like poles of a magnet. After I got to know it, in a certain sense I was let down by some of it because many of these pieces that were so charming on first encounter became rather vacuous on repeated encounters. I must say that unfortunately 90 percent of that music I feel that way about now. But maybe that's why I'm a composer. Maybe that's why we choose to become creative people, because we feel that innate dissatisfaction with something that we're drawn to, so we want to make it right ourselves.

KERNIS: To push past where others have gone, past the labels? What about the "Minimalist" label?

ADAMS: People often apologize when they bring up the M-word; they feel it's an embarrassment to bring up the term. But I think that labels in art are perfectly okay — we use them all the time. We talk about Impressionist painting, or Gothic architecture, or Elizabethan sonnets, and that helps to orient ourselves, and we know the moment we mention Impressionist painting we're talking about a certain array of techniques. So if I say "Minimalist music" to you, or even if I say it to an average concert-goer, by now they may know it's going to involve repetition in some way, it's going to involve regular pulse, it's going to involve tonal harmonies, probably with slow harmonic rhythm and rather large architectural expanses. And that's perfectly helpful.

KERNIS: Provided that it isn't applied where it's no longer the case.

ADAMS: Yes. For someone to call me a Minimalist composer now, which I must say rarely happens anymore, would be wrong. But if someone says that there are elements of Minimalism in my music, then I think that's perfectly accurate.

KERNIS: Is Minimalism ultimately a dead end?

ADAMS: I think Minimalism was a wonderful shock to Western

179

art music. It was like a bucket of fresh spring water splashed on
the grim and rigid visage of "serious" music. I can't imagine how
stark and unforgiving the musical landscape would be without it.
But I think that as an expressive tool the style absolutely had to
evolve and become more complex. This is inevitable in art. Monteverdi, Mozart, Hemingway, Le Corbusier . . . they all brought about
revolutions in simplicity, *une révolution en douceur*, but then they
were immediately followed by a second, more complex generation.
KERNIS: In the first part of *El Dorado* there's a sort of layering going
on that I don't think I've heard in your music before: one layer of
activity ceases or fades just after a new layer begins; tension is
raised with the introduction of each new strand. It reminds me of
the complex layering found in rock formations.
ADAMS: Well, it's a totally different way of building musical architecture. It's not *durchkomponierte* — like the Germans say,
"through-composed." It's as far away from, let's say, a Bach idea of
Fortspinnung, where a whole movement will be basically built on
a single gesture. And, you know, a lot of Glass's and Reich's music
is built in that way, and that's one of the really admirable things
about it. It has that kind of Baroque thoroughness to it. But, yes, I
think your perception of *El Dorado*, and to some extent some other
recent pieces, is correct, and could probably go for *Fearful Symmetries* as well. There are events that come up over the edge of the
horizon, and become center stage for a while, and then recede as
something else comes over, and what was previously front-page
gradually becomes back-page news.
KERNIS: Sometimes there will even be a dramatic change that takes
the place of the slow burn of material.
ADAMS: What's exciting is that we liberate ourselves from the
Germanic notion of what a piece of music *should do*. This is something that I think has tyrannized a lot of serious composers in the
last century. I remember being very young and reading Hindemuth's
book, *A Composer's World*, and I remember being very upset and
intimidated to read that "a composer sees the entire piece in a
flash. And all aspects of its form and structure are revealed to him."
It's as if some archangel must come down and smite the composer
on the head.
KERNIS: Though it can happen.
ADAMS: Sure it can happen, but the great thing is that artistic
creation takes all kinds.
KERNIS: You may see simply the foundation, and not anything else.

ADAMS: Absolutely. So I'm experimenting with new ways of creating form that I suppose are in a sense more influenced by cinema, by techniques of cutting and editing in a studio, whether it's with film or with tape, and also mixing. If you've sat behind a really complex, state-of-the-art studio-mixer, with fade-ins and fade-outs and cross-fades and returns and sends, you've experienced a totally different approach to how musical events can arise and live with each other and then disappear. The concept of fading in and fading out simply didn't exist in Bach's day because it hadn't been suggested by a device that did that. What's exciting about the twentieth century in particular is that we're so often inspired by machines. I'm sure that the repetitive style of Minimalist music would never have been thought of without the tape recorder. Tape loops and all the little techniques that composers started experimenting with in the early Sixties suggested pulsation and suggested a type of structural development that was based on looping and repetition.

KERNIS: Periodicity.

ADAMS: Right. But there *was* one composer who understood mixing before mixers were invented. Ives.

KERNIS: He's more like a blender.

ADAMS: [Laughter] There's something wonderful about *Three Places in New England*, and particularly the *Fourth Symphony*, where all sorts of different musical gestures are existing in this magical console. Ives's compositional technique in effect involves fading one channel up and then fading it down a little bit while another channel fades up, and there's a wonderful sense of a kind of cosmic mixer.

KERNIS: Most of those elements emerge from the American Ur-music: hymns, march tunes, heavily syncopated ragtime rhythms. It's a kind of stew — it makes me think of our society — full of half-remembered bits of familiar tunes.

ADAMS: One of the burdens that we still carry in this country is the sense of cultural inadequacy. So many Americans still feel intuitively that "Culture" comes from Europe. The classical music industry and the big traveling art shows reinforce this assumption. "Culture" with a capital C is something you acquire, like good table manners, and in the case of famous paintings by van Gogh or Rembrandt, can be bought and possessed for enormous sums. This may be one of the reasons why Americans tend to embrace popular culture with such zeal. They feel that popular culture is genuinely American. We can put Elvis on a postage stamp because everyone

181

thinks Elvis is cool. But when it comes to embracing our serious American art — and there's a great deal of it in this country — Americans become very uncomfortable, and they're not quite sure if it's the real thing or not. And this is why the classical music industry in the U.S. is continually having to import what they feel to be the real thing from Europe. This can be the case when we suspect that the real thing in new music is Lutoslawski or Boulez or Berio, or whether it's the latest East German conductor with a Watts Line to Brahms. Somehow American culture is not quite bona fide unless it's pop culture.

KERNIS: This is clearly part of the reason that the classical music establishment is completely out of step with the art of our time. There's so little willingness to allow any kind of innovation to work its way into the system, unless its been somehow certified by the mainstream marketers, i.e., unless its audience is to a certain extent guaranteed.

ADAMS: It's an industry.

KERNIS: I used to think that orchestras, opera houses and the like represented artistic ideals that were quite separate from commercial realities. To me it's only seemed like an industry lately.

ADAMS: I don't know. Joe Horowitz says in this book *Understanding Toscanini* that the classical music industry started a lot longer ago than we realize. It started in the Thirties, when Toscanini was turned into an idol, although there were even cases before that of European stars coming to this country and being treated as if they held the key to culture — that Americans were simply too rough-hewn, too unsubtle to appreciate. And now marketing has become intensely important, and culture has become a function of market mentality, with the result that you have orchestras and opera companies and art museums operating on enormous budgets, like corporations. They're not profit-making — although they behave like profit-making corporations — but they try. It's become even more severe during the Eighties, with the advent of the Reagan era; nowadays it seems like every aspect of our lives is dictated by the profit motive. If something can't pay for itself, it's simply not viable in this culture. So we seem to have brought back a notion that I thought was dead by the turn of the century — which is that of social Darwinism. It exists in our attitudes toward less fortunate people — whether they're immigrants, or whether they're just helpless people in our society. And it exists in our attitudes toward the arts as well.

KERNIS: The dissipation of people's sense of generosity, or compassion, of getting beyond one's own needs, one's own family's needs?
ADAMS: Exactly. And it's very shortsighted in the arts, because anyone with a historical grasp of art history knows that virtually all the great art in both the West and the East was brought about by largesse. Beethoven, the great "free" man, the man who mythically broke the bonds of the aristocracy, was actually never more than several hundred feet from his caretakers, who were Austrian nobility, Count Lichnowsky or Rasoumowsky or whoever. These highly cultured Viennese aristocrats knew that they had an immense talent in their midst and they were smart enough to support it. But if Beethoven had been forced throughout his life to make his works economically "viable," we wouldn't have his music today.
KERNIS: Clearly many visual artists have been able to survive and even flourish in our economic system.
ADAMS: It's a different thing, because a painting or piece of sculpture can be bought and sold. It's a commodity. Whereas music, and particularly poetry, have little or no commodity value. Poetry can't even be used on an entertainment level, the way classical music can be turned into Muzak. It's an art form that simply can't be commodified.
KERNIS: There's a certain kind of commodification one can apply to Glass's music, I think. My friends and I talk about him — even look up to him — as a success story, a phenomenon unique among composers, but at the same time I can't help thinking, "Is there any art here, any substance?" I'd certainly felt there was, up until *Einstein on the Beach*, but his commercial success has led to work that's often seemed the product of a composing factory.
ADAMS: Glass's career signals a kind of violent swing of the pendulum in the way the public views a composer, and vice versa. For so much of this century artists have participated in a myth about themselves — that they are outlaws. We all love to use Kafka as an example, as an expression of the artist as a loner, as an outsider, as someone who never earned any money from his work and stayed on the outside of society, at least artistically. It's become a kind of *de rigeur* status for the artist that he or she be unknown, unappreciated, unrewarded throughout most of his or her life. If a composer behaves in another way, and handles his or her business affairs well, and is savvy about finding markets for his music, we immediately make a puritanical judgment: that person must be more interested in money than in art. Again, if we look at history —

John Adams

KERNIS: Look at Mozart particularly —

ADAMS: Yes, history constantly contradicts, or at least muddies, these perceptions. You mention Mozart. It would never have occurred to Mozart to write a piece that wouldn't appeal to his public and wouldn't earn him some money.

KERNIS: He nearly refused to work on anything that was *not* a commission.

ADAMS: That's what makes the three last symphonies so unique. The musicologists can't seem to find a commission for them. But virtually all other 620 pieces that he wrote were written on some sort of commission. Verdi — an amazingly sharp and shrewd businessman. So were Stravinsky and Strauss.

KERNIS: It's some early Romantic notion of the poor, starving, half-mad composer that still is retained within the audience's mind, the unreality of the Composer whom you wouldn't want to bring home to dinner, who turns into the Mythic Figure upon demise.

ADAMS: It's the "starving artist in the garret" syndrome. That myth gives the listener some sense of importance. If you and I can go to a concert and we can open up the program notes and discover that this wonderful piece we're hearing was not appreciated in its day, even *spurned* in its day, that makes us feel terribly important. It reinforces our sense of the composer as hero.

KERNIS: It makes the audience's relationship to the performer, usually the soloist, even more important.

ADAMS: It becomes a heroic relationship. And of course there are cases that bear this myth out. There's Ives and there's Webern, and J.S. Bach, none of whom had a great following in his day. But in our day people have a strangely puritanical attitude about composers, and I think Philip Glass has been a tremendously refreshing figure to have on the horizon because he has refused to take any of the normal accepted routes. He's always carved out his own niche, and as a result of that he has an enormous audience. Now, part of this large audience has to do with the simplicity of his message, the simplicity of his work, and that's a whole other realm, one I have very strong criticisms of, but I can only admire him for his willingness to bypass all of the conventional routes to becoming known as a composer. He has retained his own copyright, he's been his own publisher, he created his own ensemble to play his pieces, even his first operas were virtually self-produced. That's a remarkable model for us; I'm one generation younger than he is, not even quite that, and his career has been a great inspiration.

184

KERNIS: It was really very striking this year to see the brilliance, in many ways the calculated brilliance, of John Corigliano's *The Ghosts of Versailles*, because it was so beautifully targeted for the Met audience, it worked like a charm; people were highly moved and entertained by it. They loved it. Certainly there are a lot of important musical issues in the work worth discussing: Is there any depth to the music? How could serious composers and listeners take seriously anything that's so retro? But one couldn't dispute how beautifully it worked for that audience.

ADAMS: It was a huge success. It sold out nine performances. It makes me look like a failure by comparison! But even the concept of targeting a work at an audience is not *entirely* without some historical context. You can tell from Mozart's letters to his father that he quite often knew where he was going and for whom he was going to play, and in a sense he targeted the type of music he was writing. It was much the same with Handel and Verdi. You can't tell me that the *Rite of Spring* wasn't targeted — for a very sophisticated Parisian audience that at that particular time was very jaded and looking for something tremendously *outré*, and got it. So I think that, again, this in itself is not a problem. The question is just one of value. One can have a piece that's targeted that has still an immense amount of value, like the *Rite of Spring*, or one can have a piece that is simply full of froth, full of devices, and basically panders to its audience. If one truly panders to one's audience, and gives them exactly what one knows they're going to like, so that there are no surprises, then I think you have a piece to which history will not be kind.

KERNIS: Do you have any new opera plans?

ADAMS: Yes, a new one is in the works, but I would like to make it less of an "opera"; in fact, I want to get out of the opera industry, such as it is, so that I'm not beholden to its values and decision-making, which I think are predicated on values that have nothing to do with my work. I would really like to do something that's small, flexible, inexpensive and has real bite to it. I'd love to write something like the *Three Penny Opera* or something that I can maneuver outside of the big centers of artistic power in the country and reach a much wider audience with.

KERNIS: What about *The Death of Klinghoffer*? I'm curious how you dealt with the influences of Arabic or Semitic music in the opera.

ADAMS: I felt that the worst sin I could commit in *Klinghoffer* was

John Adams

Orientalism, to try to imitate Hebraic or Arabic music in doing this. To do that would be worse than anything in *Turandot*. But on the other hand I really wanted to achieve a sense of "otherness" about the Palestinian terrorists. If I was going to achieve something dramatically I would have to create the feeling of what it would be like having a gin and tonic on the deck of this luxury liner and *suddenly*, instead of on the front page of the *New York Times*, here — *in real life!* — is a Palestinian with a Kalichnikov rifle shouting at you to get up or else you'll be shot. Suddenly you're overwhelmed with a sense of terror, and there's someone as alien to you as if he were from another planet threatening your life. For this I needed to develop a music that really *did* sound different, that sounded alien. And how I did that was to use different musical modes and a whole different harmonic palette, mostly octatonic scale procedures which I massaged into my own particular compositional style. You'll note that when the Palestinians are singing there tends to be a lot more chromaticism. There's also a lot more ornament here than in any other music I've ever written. The opening Palestinian chorus is *very* ornamental. I think ornament is a tradition that was largely banished from both architecture and music during the modernist period. It's funny, we've had an explosion of interest in early music performance, and everyone is encouraged to ornament their work. It's also beginning to reappear in architecture now, after years of being viewed as an aesthetic sin beyond the pale. I've always found Mies van der Rohe and the "box" school of architecture to be really tiresome. I welcome ornament and I'm trying to find ways to bring it into my own music. It's not easy: I'm a New Englander, and a Guatemalan shirt is a major event for me in terms of brightening up my rather dour wardrobe!

KERNIS: How do you think your work is seen by other composers?

ADAMS: I take my own share of lumps. A lot of my composer colleagues feel that my work is not really in the noble avant-garde tradition.

KERNIS: What would you have to do to be part of it at this point? Would you want to be? And does an avant-garde still exist?

ADAMS: I don't know. At this point, the notion of "style" is a lot more confusing than it was even ten years ago. I think ten years ago people had an idea of what it meant to be a serious composer. Nowadays, I sense an aura of confusion and ambiguity. But this is not necessarily a bad thing. What could be more tiresome than another generation of junior Berios? For me what's really a challenge is to create a music that uses the syntax, uses what I would call a syn-tactical lingua franca that can communicate to a wider audience of culturally aware people. I consider the availability of all the world's music via recorded technology to be a vast watershed in the evolution of Western art music. Americans of my generation were the first to be constantly bombarded by recorded music from our earliest childhood. You can't tell me that this phenomenon hasn't had a huge effect on composers.

KERNIS: I recently heard Elliott Carter say that in his earlier years — his twenties to forties, I presume — he listened to as many record-ings of jazz, popular and "serious" music as he could lay his hands on . . . but the numbers are vastly different.

ADAMS: The numbers *are* different. I have difficulty believing that Elliott Carter has embraced popular music with quite the zeal that I have. Frankly, I rue the day Carter turned his back on American vernacular music and elected to be a European avant-gardist. But to get back to what I was saying, it occurred to me very early on in my compositional career that tonal harmony and regular pulsa-tion were not artificial constructs — that they weren't something devised by a theorist, but rather were universal phenomena, like magnetism or gravity. If we acknowledge these phenomena — tonality and pulsation — we can see evidence of them in all music, not just Western art music, but popular music and ethnic music from all over the world. And it seemed to me that one of the reasons for the vastly shrunken audience of twentieth-century art music was because this lingua franca, this grammar that allows me to talk to you and you to know what I'm saying, was being system-atically deconstructed and broken down and destroyed by com-posers. What I have been trying to do is to find a means of utilizing this fundamental grammar in a coherent, comprehensible way, and yet make it new, make it fresh, make it a shock, a joyous shock.

KERNIS: And to make it very physical, viscerally compelling as well?

ADAMS: Right. I think the richer your palette is, the more exciting your music is. A hundred years from now people will look back on the serial experiment as a rather odd tributary of the mainstream. People will be amazed that it had so much prestige in its time, because it really produced so few indisputably great pieces of music. It will be viewed as a form of Mannerism, a hot-house crea-tion with a very tiny audience. I don't know about you, but my encounters with Milton Babbit's music have left me cold. I'm a relatively well-educated and well-prepared musician, so I bring to my experience of listening to Babbit quite a bit more than the average listener, and yet it strikes me as very gray and largely incomprehensible. So what does that mean if I can't appreciate it? Does it mean that I'm a dunce? Or does it mean that a hundred years from now there'll be a new race of people with huge ears and giant cortexes migrating down from the tundra in northern Canada who will listen to Babbit instead of Madonna?

KERNIS: How much more of the influence of popular music do you think we'll see?

ADAMS: I'm inclined to think that this has a way to go before another generation comes in and says something very different. I suspect that another generation or two, at least in this country, will be heavily influenced by popular music — not necessarily well-known popular music. It seems to me that younger composers now seem to take a lot of inspiration from marginal —

KERNIS: Alternative —

ADAMS: Alternative rock, different kinds of underground music —

KERNIS: Which has a relatively small audience —

ADAMS: In itself it does, but it still has that kind of thrust and power that good pop music has. And this is probably a good thing, because I think that the serious music establishment has utterly burned itself out. I've sat on several panels in the last year or two — where everyone else in the room has won a Pulitzer Prize — and all the pieces that come in to be surveyed are within a certain polite context of orchestral works or chamber music. There's just nothing shocking or powerful or commanding in any of the ideas.

KERNIS: It's just more business as usual.

ADAMS: It's simply become a world that a truly vibrant, imaginative, outrageous young composer wouldn't even know about, wouldn't even dream of sending his tapes to . . . because they'd never get listened to. So I think it's good to just say goodbye to that whole establishment, and forge out, look for new audiences, either through recordings or through alternative performance spaces, not depend on the institutional classical music world, whether it's the operatic world or the orchestral world. We know it can be done. We've seen extraordinary cases — not only Glass, but the Kronos Quartet, Laurie Anderson, John Zorn. You can go back much earlier — Charlie Parker, Miles Davis, Duke Ellington. But those people are already such classical figures in American culture that it's hard to even understand what outlaws they were at the beginning of their careers. But that's really exciting, because if one can maintain one's real integrity and still have the generating impulse be honest and creative, then taking new routes and not being afraid to exploit the various kinds of media that American culture offers—whether it's recordings or performance spaces or publications—I think this is a bona fide means of getting one's work into circulation. And it's certainly better than waiting around for the classical music industry to discover you, because if they do discover you, the most they're going to do is treat you as a pendant to enhance their prestige. You may get a Pulitzer or a commission, but neither is going to help to make your work a part of the culture. I think there's a natural growth tendency in a capitalist society. We always hear about growth. One of the great cases of an idea growing and losing its identity as it grows is PBS, which now has hardly any real power. It's abdicated all its power to be controversial and change people's thinking, because it's become so enormous. And as a result we have a television network which, in its infancy, was an immensely powerful element in American culture and which now purveys the blandest kind of fare, whether it's British melodrama or "Live from Lincoln Center," or MacNeil-Lehrer (the Dour Hour), which has this panache of being really insightful and critical but in fact is so bland as to be almost innocuous.

KERNIS: Public TV has recently come under attack for airing the controversial "Tongues on Fire," and we were all, in some sense, for the last few years, since Mapplethorpe, feeling under—

ADAMS: Pressure from the far right—

KERNIS: Under attack, and it's infuriated me that some composers feel that they're exempt from this because music is abstract and because they're not trying to do anything controversial. I know I've felt the sense of growing oppression—it may be growing only inside my own head, but it's palpable.

ADAMS: The other art forms, or many other art forms, have been far more socially confrontational for a long time than music has. "Serious," or shall we call it "art" music, has largely, as you say, been so self-absorbed or formalist for the last fifty years that it has almost completely bypassed controversy. Other art forms are more naturally drawn to political statement, like photography or literature.

KERNIS: And dance lately, especially since gender politics and texts have been added to the mix.

ADAMS: Yes. And I think it's good that this is happening, because the arts have become the last bunker against this vast submersion into totalitarian attitudes toward morality. To me the term "family values"—that's something that has all the chill and oppressive tone of something from Mussolini's Italy or Nazi Germany. "Family values" really means not *family* values, but brokered values, values that are handed on from upstairs down. It's a code word for racism, homophobia, xenophobia and authoritarianism. George Bush is a man who ought to know better. With Ronald Reagan we thought, "Oh God, no, the country's elected Reagan!" but at least we knew what he stood for. But Bush is a person who espouses whatever value he thinks will get him elected. His is a kind of pure, totally corrupted opportunism.

KERNIS: And in recent months he's practicing it even more.

ADAMS: Yes, he's trying to skirt the abortion issue—now you see it/now you don't—hoping that people have such short attention spans that they won't catch on. And this issue of the attack on the arts in this country is probably a good thing, in a way, because among other things it makes artists realize that people really *do* pay attention to them. What a wonderful thought—that someone is actually *scared* of your work of art.

KERNIS: But the trend seems to be in the opposite direction. I've looked at works by composers younger than myself recently on a couple of panels, and I've been disturbed by the nearly total absence of the influence of popular music, Minimal music, world music—of anything at all that would indicate a desire to explore or redraw or merely question the status quo, whether it's that of their own teachers at universities or conservatories, or of the entrenched new music or classical establishments.

ADAMS: You're sitting in the wrong room. That's just what I said about my experiences—*we're* sitting in the wrong room. Unfortunately there's power and money dispensed and we know those people who spend their lives shaking hands and making sure that they get on those panels, because that's the only way—through the "old boy network"—that they're going to get their own works promoted.

KERNIS: But it is still sad to see a whole generation of younger composers begin with such complacent and wholesale adoption of the values-that-be.

ADAMS: Don't forget—Ravel never won the Prix de Rome. Year after year . . . he wanted it so badly. And he never got it. . . . And imagine who the people who *did* win it were!

190

Two Poems
Martin Earl

PASTERNAK

What could it mean to say
a mortal was in his garden?
No instruments for digging,
his hands are folded —
he seems to be listening,
to the orthodox slowness of days.

"I dreamt of a city,
of mnemonic canals —
the pinch of an oar
against its lock,
the dip and pluck
of a feathered blade,
and the music of
this pliancy."

The bureaucracy of the face
in consideration of
the tired state
of being.

Martin Earl

PORTRAIT OF A WATCHTOWER

I have seen men stand at the edge of rooms
and stare into their craven centers,
which were empty, or perhaps
some lives had converged
and were pecking at the consciousness
of being there, before wandering off, down corridors

into vast avenues. Milliners and functionaries
step into their cars, to go where the watchtowers
circle in their fixity, to feel
suspect comfort in broken continuity —
the repetition of their cheated faces
gazing out at February's bitten earth.

Eight Collages
Donald Baechler

Donald Baechler

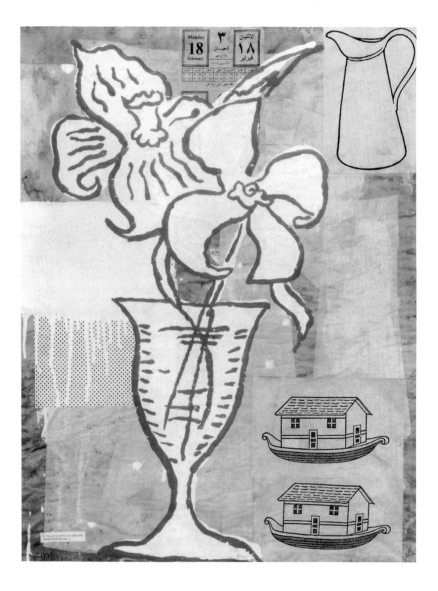

195

Donald Baechler

Donald Baechler

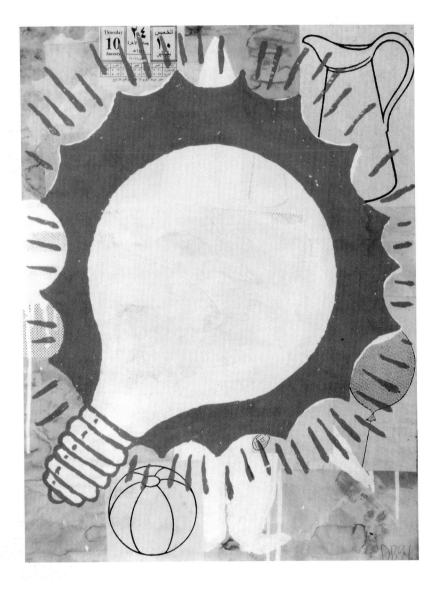

The Glass Mountain
Barbara Guest

— in memory of J.S.

i

king as wanderer
replied   we do and always

the least recounting
the pelting dew
bird in the sunrise room;

once or twice the landscape burns
what we are after tires
clouds mohair.

rhododendron bring
pods to the mountain;

a tremulous position
harp on a mountain of glass.

ii

is it a power
you pass in the night
taking water from the tap

fog or phantom
the king stares at.

you are not the snake lady
gold filament above
the snake limbs
nor does she tell
who taught the dance.

iii

the king watched

in flat country the
caravan at ewe season

a density
sand and thyme

near the threshold
where they milk
have bitten the nut-
like substance.

iv

bauble of sound
mahogany the king

traveling the length
overhead a climate
of twang the rushed snow

unstoppable space in the bold
different in the next
movement the breach

is inimitable
a phrase others believe
there is no escape

the towed rock dims.

v

why not live

image strewn

and goes pitter pat
next to the resolute corridor
and a diadem would hang on the fringe
actual pieces of tame fibre shut off.

on the steeple with the watercan
and thunder in the earring she
caught the speech of the termagant
the roll

was seen the plumage and owl
a raft on the cold river; skin
on the raft a king

picked up boards and sunk them.

vi

the shades lavished
in the ideal
climate of planets fear

the steam rolling up;
holding hands in a ring
wet to their waists
                    hair
a slippery blossom.

exposure beneath the May apse
                    doggerel;
chunks of filched
                    objects not
lapidary. a king.

vii

attent on detail
            the hullabaloo over
rule half water half worn
            running the notion of land;

tells us where light comes from
            white curtains in its beak;
closer closer to the splintered mountain

O king endlessly
scattering.

Impenetrability
Henry Green

WE GO ABOUT our daily lives, in great cities, thinking entirely about our personal affairs; perhaps every now and again sparing a thought for our partners, that is, the person we live with, and of course with even greater guilt, of our children. After a time, in married life, it becomes the other partner's fault that they have married one, but the only child, or, as chance may have it, the many children, have had no choice, they are ours, and this is what fixes the guilt on us.

I was in Moscow in 1938 and I saw men lying in the gutter who looked dead and who, my guide assured me, were dead drunk. I passed on. I had seen the same in the streets of Caen, Normandy, France, where as a child my parents took me so that we could taste meat, butter and cream again after the near starvation the Germans had put upon us in Britain in the 1914–18 war. I had passed on again. And when my father sent me to Paris to learn French in 1923 I once more saw a man lie senseless in the gutter. This time I stopped behind a plane tree. At least two priests passed by without it seemed a glance. I myself had gone past as had several other citizens, who had not stopped as I did. Then eventually, while I watched, two working-class women halted in the Boulevard Raspail and gossiped over the inanimate figure. Then one bent down and turned him over. Satisfied, I can only think, that he was still alive and drunk, she moved off with her companion, as I did likewise. One so seldom learns the end of things in life.

Now in London we have two-decker buses, the difference being that you are allowed to smoke on the top deck, which is why I always go on top. And since we have lived in this house I am writing from for ten years, I have had to catch a bus, holidays excepted, on the same route, every morning, every morning for all that time.

And in that time I've had one terrifying experience with a stranger, completely unexplained, and of course without intervention from myself or my fellow passengers. It was, which may be significant, on the outward, that is the morning, journey. I do

205

believe people behave oddly from the pressure of their private, as opposed to what might be called their public lives. The fact is immaterial that the person I am going to tell you about was sober or so I believe, as people almost always will be at that hour. The point is that none of us, strangers, but I suppose Christians, even if not practicing, not one of us ever do much about it.

This particular experience hit me not forewarned some seven years ago. You must understand that my bus route passes one of our great hospitals and that there is an obligatory stop there. We were not three hundred yards from it, and I was in one of the front seats on top, when I heard what was between a loud cry or a groan from behind. I turned round with a deep feeling of disapproval, as much as I saw reflected in the faces of all the other passengers but two. These were women and were directly behind where I was seated. You sit two by two on these buses in London, with an aisle in between, and two women next each other were involved. One was thrown back rigid on the seat in a kind of fit, an arm raised above her head as it might be with a sort of threat or defiance. Beside this woman was another, who from her embarrassed expression, did not know the ill one from Eve. Seated as she was on the outside, that is to say nearest to a window, she had delicately put thumb and forefinger round the wrist of this uplofted fist, in case, presumably, it should with force descend.

A fit, I remember saying to myself with some distaste and looking to my front again.

There were no cries or groans any more and no one said a word.

I thought to myself, I recollect, they will put her, so to speak, ashore at the hospital, which, by now, we had almost reached. Indeed I considered how fortunate it had been for this girl to be taken ill so near a place where everything would be that could be done. And when we stopped at this obligatory stop, which I felt Providence had timed for her so well, I turned disapprovingly round once more. She looked ghastly, was still rigid, but the uplifted arm was lowered and the woman who had held her wrist was looking straight ahead. In looking back I could see several people getting off, queueing to climb down the stairs. I knew one of them would tell the conductor. I wondered whether he could carry her over to the hospital and thought, on the whole, not. That in fact one of the passengers would have to do it. And that it would not be me. I did not feel well enough. Upon which this thought came. I might as well get off, lose the fare, take another bus, for the delay could be all of five minutes, and besides, there might be a call for volunteers and, in the state I was, a woman in one's arms on those narrow stairs would be a job, I again thought.

In the event I sat tight. Let the police do it, I remember thinking.

Of course one of those departing did tell the conductor. There was the pause I had been expecting when we did not leave the stop and then here he was on the top deck, walking not like a bride, rather as one who is about to stop a wedding, up the aisle.

Now I only really know my own county, I can't tell you of else-where, but I must explain that down south in England there is no arguing with bus conductors. They have every legal right to throw you off if they feel like it, or to have you arrested if you won't go, again if only they feel like it.

So I felt almost sorry for this girl when the man came up.

"Are you all right, Miss?" I heard him ask as I sat rigidly looking to my front.

"Yes," she managed to reply, but in an expiring voice.

"Sure now?" he gruffly demanded.

"Yes," she whispered.

"Right," he announced, left us, climbed down the stairs and, to my dismay, we were off, still with our load of trouble I had been so certain would be passed over to that great hospital.

It was worse than being left alone, as one always is, with one's conscience. For, in this case everything might start all over again, and conceivably be worse still. One might, at a pinch, have to force open jaws and hold a tongue to prevent her swallowing it, or what-ever one does.

I looked every now and again, and she seemed barely conscious. Then, to my horror, the woman on the far side wanted to get out. The sick one managed to move her legs out of the way and the girl who had held that ominous fist made off fast. But she came back. She whispered to the sufferer. What she said I did not hear. Even if I wasn't very deaf, I am sure I couldn't have heard. At the time, I remember saying to myself "is this then one of these strange, secret, inviolable female complaints never to be mentioned before strange men?" But the sick one only nodded and the other left.

As the journey went on I looked round every now and then. Her eyes were open and I took care not to look in them. Something else I saw. Everyone was getting off as he or she got to their destina-tions. Then again it became a matter of conscience for, once more, as always, one was left alone with it. I was quite sure from what

207

I had observed, that the conductor would be worse than useless. And the next hospital on this route was many a further mile distant. What to do? The conductor and I were now the only ones to know about her. And my stop, my destination, was coming up fast. Here was Baker Street. I looked again. The girl seemed barely conscious. Now George Street and my address where I get off.

The conductor saw me go and said no word. And that was that.

On the same route I have seen this same girl once or twice since. She doesn't seem to recognize me, indeed there is no reason why she should. She looks better. She is still not going to have a baby. I suppose, like any other novelist, and she wore gloves, I imagined her unmarried and just having found she was to have a child. Or some other equally fantastic female compulsion.

Or had she simply had a row with her mother? I shall never know. After all I can't very well go and ask.

But thinking it over through the years I do now consider that the conductor I so blamed at the time was quite.correct not to take this girl into hospital. Why, they might have done almost anything to her there. Even a stomach pump! While now she is still all right.

Or is she?

It Must Be Sophisticated
John Ashbery

There are attics in old houses
where doubt lingers as to the corrosive
effect of night-blindness: namely
are its victims directly linkable to a chain
of events happening elsewhere? If so,
we should shrug off resemblances

to our line of work. What was said around
the house had undue influence on one of several
shapely witnesses. And, as dames do,
she started talking to any and every
interlocutor out of harm's way. One day
you wake up and they've skipped. Or was it

always empty like this? It's hard
to remember a time when it wasn't. Maybe
your memory's playing tricks on you? Maybe
there never was such a person as Lisa Martins?
Maybe it's all over when you stand up
to walk the last mile in Enna Jettick shoes,

and they draw the blind quickly to forget you.
Once forgotten you're as good as dead,
anyway. And who would help you now?
You might as well be trapped at the bottom of a well
in the Sahara. They don't know you're alive,
or that your life was anything but exemplary

when it came time for you to live.
The fashionable present keeps queening it
over the slightly dishonorable past. Your
bridesmaids are scattered on the wind.
You don't feel like having lunch. Maybe
a walk, and a cup of tea later?

We'll see you at the end of the month!
they cried. Now it keeps ticking,
there must be a mystery down there,
darn it. I'll find it if it takes all night
and then some other sleuth can solve it.
I was only hired as a go-between. My tour is ended,

and if I've a piece of advice for you, it's
check out the rafters, the moldings.
You can't tell who might have bargained
for clemency in your absence, leaving you holding
the bag when you got back, restless,
ready to start school, but the vagrant air's black,

what with the negative promise of spring.
The boys are still rehearsing their parts
they haven't been over, and really
it's none of my business. Said the table to the chair.
I was confined here. That's all I know,
truthfully. During the amnesty I walked

out through the open gate. The streets were full of people,
running back and forth, talking disjointedly. I was
supposed to be somewhere else, but no one knew it.
In the confusion I returned home.
Now the newshounds pester us daily.
What was I born for? More experiments?

Why are they fighting over a fuse? It doesn't
seem to be harmless like those people are listening to over there;
at the same time, everyone's a suspect in the new
climate and country. The wind turns a page
of the old tome, then another and another; soon
it's riffling through them too fast to stop.

There's nothing in it anyway. Time to move on
to another frontier beyond the transparent frieze
of foliage, guns, barges, to where he began.
Sure, dem days is gone forever, but it's the attention span
that's really gone. Back when they'd send for you
once they got a house built, it was clever

to hedge your bets and produce a fraternal twin
made of bedclothes with a mop for a wig
while you scaled the wall on a rope ladder
to be the next new thing that thinks
and cautions others not to. Far from the
inner city of conflicting attitudes, one fled with one's

holy illusions intact, one's misconceptions too, until the whole
mindset took on a largely symbolic
look, an indifferent jewel, toy
of the weather, of successive washes of light,
I can hardly believe I'm here
in this tiny republic carved out of several conflicting

principalities. It's enough, perhaps, that I was questioned
at the edge of my performance. That now I'm safe
from my own sang-froid and scores of others,
that mere forgetfulness can save up to fifty-three lives,
that they can share your power and go on glancing
upward. Because after all we were the three

original ones, the president, vice-president and treasurer
of our class. And were formed to repay
what obscure debt and be summarily
taken out of school and handed over to our parents.
It's what matters then, and after. No one
says you have to live up to principles; indeed, what are they?

What difference does it make which one came too close
in the richly darkened theater, if all
they were after was to coax you into the light,
watch you blink a minute, and then pass on, they too,
to the larger arenas, each in the wind,
in the sand, the reeds, growing? Because even if it doesn't

punish you exactly, the thing has been
lived through, the experience sealed.
O what book shall I read
now? for they are all of them new, and used,
when I write my name on the flyleaf. Look,
here is another one unread, not written. Time for you to choose.

The Novel in the Next Century
John Barth

When Harvard College was established in 1636 as the first American institution of higher education, the Università degli Studi di Macerata, in the Adriatic marches of Italy, was already 346 years old, approximately Harvard's present age. In 1990, in celebration of its seven hundredth anniversary, the university hosted an ongoing international symposium on "The Novel in the Next Century." What follows is adapted from my remarks to that symposium.

WITH THE SUBJECT of the novel in the next century I have both a certain sympathy and a certain problem. The sympathy is understandable enough: I am a practicing novelist, not as old as the University of Macerata or the genre of the novel but, like them, not as young as I used to be. A new novel of mine—my ninth—is scheduled for publication before long; with luck I will commit yet another novel before our cataclysmic century expires, and it is not altogether out of the question that I might perpetrate yet another after that in the early years of the century to come, before *my* expiration date arrives. Even if fate should decree otherwise (as it has done, alas, for Italo Calvino and Raymond Carver and Donald Barthelme and other of my distinguished contemporaries), I maintain a benevolent interest in the future of the art form that I have devoted my professional life to; likewise, for that matter, in the institution of universities, in which I have agreeably spent that professional life. I have rather more confidence in the persistence of the university as an institution in the century to come than in the persistence of the novel as a medium of art and entertainment in that century—but I'll save my prophesying for later in these remarks.

As for the problem: I have been preceded in the Macerata symposium by a number of distinguished scholars, critics and novelists, from various countries—including, from the United States, my comrades Robert Coover, Stanley Elkin, William Gass and Ishmael Reed—"the usual suspects," I'm tempted to say. Gifted and knowledgeable writers and thinkers every one, and although I wasn't present to hear their contributions to the symposium, I

213

am acquainted enough with them and their writings and opinions to know that they are hard acts to follow. What can I imaginably say on the subject of the novel in the next century, I wonder, that one or all of them and/or their counterparts from other countries will not have said already, and better?

As soon as I put that discouraging question to myself in those discouraging terms, I am immediately encouraged — encouraged by its resemblance to the question that every thoughtful practitioner of the art of literature doubtless asks him/herself at least occasionally, and that some of us ask ourselves relentlessly from project to project. The phenomenon of the novel is many centuries old (just how many depends on your definition); the medium of written literature goes back very much farther yet — at least four millennia, to an Egyptian papyrus of the Middle Kingdom complaining eloquently that language may already have been exhausted — and the institution of storytelling goes back immeasurably farther than the invention of writing. Furthermore, what applies on the macroscale of history applies also on the microscale of a writer's own career, if that writer is lucky enough to have survived this century's plenteous catastrophes and to have published, as I have, some 5,000 pages of fiction. What's left to say, for me as a working novelist and for the novel as a working category of art and entertainment?

With that question I feel exactly as much at home as I do at my writing table and in my own skin, and so here we go — *en bocca al lupo*, I believe the Italian phrase is: into the wolf's mouth. Familiar territory.

The text of my sermon is also Italian, from the eminent fifteenth-century Roman humanist and storyteller Gian Francesco Poggio Bracciolini. Poggio's *Facetiae* of 1450 is a collection of mainly ribald anecdotes, from which Rabelais and Marguerite of Navarre and many another writer borrowed; it has been called the world's first best-seller as well as the archetype of the modern joke. (Poggio's timing would be the envy of a modern New York trade publisher; he scored early on the invention of movable type and before the establishment of copyright laws.) Tale LXXV of the *Facetiae* tells of a simple fellow in the town of Camerino who desires to travel to see the world. A clever acquaintance of his, one Ridolfo (who figures in a number of Poggio's tales), suggests that he begin by going no farther than Macerata, not a very long distance away. When the fellow returns, Ridolfo says to him, "Now you have seen the entire world. What else is there on earth besides hills, valleys, mountains, fields both cultivated and uncultivated, woods, and forests? All these things you have now encountered, in the area between here and there."

Ridolfo of Camerino himself, we may presume, was as cosmopolitan as was Poggio Bracciolini. Only the very well traveled are entitled to make such ironic disparagements of traveling, just as only the very well read are entitled to say, with Gustave Flaubert, that "it is enough to have read five or six books well." Reading Poggio's anecdote as a parable, we might say that one position to take about novels in the next century is that we scarcely need any more of them, when there are already in the existing corpus — "in the area between here and there" — more admirable specimens than the most voracious reader is likely to get through in a lifetime. If anyone takes that position, may it be in the ironic spirit of Ridolfo of Camerino and not in the unironic spirit of those Muslim fundamentalists who would maintain that even Flaubert's reading list is too long; that only *one* book is necessary, the Koran, inasmuch as all the others either agree with it, in which case they are redundancies, or disagree with it, in which case they are heresies.

As for myself, when I consider the Story Thus Far of the novelistic "area between here and there," it occurs to me to imagine the 1990 Macerata symposium as only the latest in a series of such symposia on the subject, symposia held once every century since the founding of that ancient university. Before risking prophecy myself, I'll speculate on what might have been said about the novel in the next century in 1890, in 1790, in 1690, right back to the hypothetical original gathering in 1290. Let's begin at the beginning.

The symposiasts of 1290, gathered at the brand-new University of Macerata, would not have found our topic intelligible — not that *that* ever deterred a real symposiast from holding forth. From the corpus of late-classical literature there survived a few extended prose-fictional narratives, more or less realistic, satirical, and fragmentary, such as Petronius's first-century *Satyricon* and Apuleius's second-century *Golden Ass*. There was the more recent vogue in Europe of highly fanciful chivalric romance. And over in Japan there was one extraordinary, undeniable specimen of the novel, already two hundred years old: Murasaki Shikibu's *Genji Monagati*, or *The Tale of Genji*. But our panelists would not have heard of

John Barth

Baroness Murasaki, whether or not they had heard of Japan, and the noun *novel* (as we use it nowadays in English, Spanish and Portuguese) wasn't yet available to them — nor for that matter was the noun *century*, in the historical sense of a hundred-year period called, for example, the thirteenth century. The most we can reasonably imagine is that they might have heard of *Il Novellino* — the *Cento novelle antiche*, or *A Hundred Old Tales* — just then being collected anonymously in northern Italy: the collection of earthy, often satirical anecdotes that historians say gave us (us Europeans) both the literary prototype of the novel and the name we call it by in the languages mentioned above — though not in Italian, French and German, which prefer variants of the term *romance*. But "novelty," even "a hundred antique novelties," as I like to translate the *Cento novelle antiche*, wouldn't have had the appeal in 1290 that it has had since the Romantic period. Even if our thirteenth-century symposiasts had heard of *Il Novellino*, it is unlikely that they would have predicted how influential that work and that form would become in the "century" ahead — most particularly with Giovanni Boccaccio, soon to be born, the future author of the *Decameron*, and Giovanni Sercambi, the future author of the *Novelle* — and how even more influential it would be in the two centuries after that, with the likes of our man Poggio Bracciolini and Matteo Bandello and Giovanni Straparola and Giambattista Basile and their ribald counterparts outside Italy. Inasmuch as cultural change of any sort was not a prominent feature of medieval times (despite the "novel" institution of universities and the fetal stirrings of the Italian Renaissance), I imagine that our panelists of 1290 would have agreed 1) that chivalric romance would continue to be the major category of narrative fiction indefinitely, in prose, in verse and in mixtures of the two; 2) that prose fiction was not a serious category of art in any case, so that even if the *novellino* were to outgrow its diminutive suffix, it would still be of diminutive artistic stature; and 3) that even poetry is but the handmaiden of philosophy, itself but the profane sibling of theology, and that only the classical poets (Virgil in particular) merit consideration in university curricula and symposia.

The equally unlikely Macerata symposia of 1390, 1490 and 1590 would have agreed. The fantastical romances of King Arthur, Roland/Orlando, Amadis of Gaul and company remained enormously popular but not a matter of curriculum. Boccaccio's *Decameron* was imitated everywhere as the model of racy, more or less minimalist realism, but the author himself in his serious old age had repudiated it for its licentiousness. The Renaissance had full-flowered; the noun *novel* had entered the English and Iberian vocabulary (the *Oxford English Dictionary* attests it in English to 1566), but it was applied indiscriminately to short satirical tales and chivalric romances alike. So what lay ahead for the seventeenth century? Not even Cervantes, who was on the very verge of inventing "the novel as we know it," could have predicted to the symposium of 1590 that he was about to do so. In 1590, Cervantes was 43 years old, a destitute war veteran, occasional poet, failed playwright and perpetrator of the first half of a pseudo-classical pastoral romance (*Primera Parte de la Galatea*) of which he would never write Part Two: an increasingly desperate scrambler already excommunicated by the church for certain irregularities, about to be sent to jail not once but two or three times for nonpayment of debts, and, very possibly during one of these imprisonments, about to begin writing *Don Quixote*—"just the sort of thing that might be begotten in a jail," the author himself remarks in his famous prologue to Part One. In short, a middle-aged hombre on the cusp of changing literature forever after with his winning combination of satiric realism and quasi-fantastic adventure—but one may doubt whether he himself realized the size of what he had achieved even after he achieved it, much less before. The first written notice of *Don Quixote* is by the author's eminent compatriot and fellow dramatist Lope de Vega (with whom Cervantes had had a falling out): having read Part One in manuscript, Lope wrote to a friend in 1604, "no poet is as bad as Cervantes, nor so foolish as to praise *Don Quixote*." So much for professional critical foresight.

As everybody knows, *Quixote* was immediately as popular as the chivalric romances that it satirized; by 1690 it was making its influence felt much as had the *Decameron* in the several centuries before. I find it not impossible to imagine that some canny prognosticator at that year's Macerata symposium might have foreseen—might perhaps have forewarned—that this novel form of readerly entertainment could well achieve some prominence in the next century. (I say "readerly" instead of "literary" entertainment because the word *literature*, in the sense of a canonical body of verbal art, doesn't enter our vocabulary for another hundred-plus years. Our symposiasts do, however, now have the word *century* in the sense we mean—first attested in English in 1638, as European historical consciousness was raised in the seventeenth century.)

And indeed, "the novel as we know it" was in fact so explosively successful through the 1700s that one of its great English inventors, Samuel Richardson, by 1758 was already predicting its demise. "There was a time," Richardson writes to Lady Barbara Montague that year, "when every bookseller wanted something of that kind. But Millar [Richardson's own publisher] tells me that the fashion has passed."

There we have the first reference that I know of to that modernist theme, "the death of the novel," in the same generation that established the novel as the dominant form of literary entertainment for that rapidly growing class, the reading public. One feels a touch of déjà vu: that Egyptian scribe at the very dawn of written literature, fretting that he may have arrived on the scene too late. . . . But note how disingenuous Richardson's letter is: Lady Barbara has been pressing the successful novelist for help in getting one of her friends' novels published, and middle-class Richardson is trying to say no without offending a lady of the gentry, while at the same time shifting responsibility from himself to his publisher. I have been in comparable positions from time to time, and I sympathize; it is a situation right out of an epistolary novel by Samuel Richardson.

Disingenuous or not, Richardson's pronouncement that the fad had passed was ignored by readers and writers alike. By the time of the 1790 Macerata symposium, the future of the *epistolary* novel in the century to come might well have been questioned, so overworked was that particular mode thanks to Richardson's example, but no one would likely have doubted a robust future for the novel itself as literacy spread to the masses in the nineteenth century. By 1790 even one or two upstart Americans had written novels; to our Macerata symposiasts, that would surely have signaled that *anybody* could now get away with it, and they would have been virtually correct. Indeed, some farsighted participant might have begun to worry about the audience for poetry in the century to come; another might perhaps have noted premonitions of a gothic revival. Would any of them, I wonder, have quite foreseen the remarkable flowering of Romanticism, the famous "inward turn" of narrative and the general rebellion against established forms in all the arts that would distinguish the European nineteenth century? It's not impossible: Jean-Jacques Rousseau was history by 1790, and the French Revolution was news. Goethe had published *The Sorrows of Young Werther*, and the other German writers and

philosophers whom we now call the heralds of the Romantic movement — Kant, Herder, Schiller, E.T.A. Hoffmann — had done or were
doing their main work. But the phenomenon was still mainly
Teutonic and suspect, operating under such aliases as "Gothicism"
and *"Sturm und Drang."* My guess is that most of the 1790 symposiasts would have concurred with Goethe's own later pronouncement — "Classicism is health; Romanticism is disease" — without
suspecting how healthy the virus itself was, how contagious it was
about to become, and how persistent it remains to this day.

We come to 1890, with a wistful sigh. To the Macerati of 1890,
the empire of prose fiction in general and of the novel in particular
in the century to come would surely have seemed as secure, for
better or worse, as the British raj and the other European colonial
empires. In 1890 we are at the climax of the period of general bourgeois literacy and the regnancy of the novel. Hugh Kenner reports
that even ordinary English agricultural journals of the time — the
Dairyman's Fortnightly and so forth — regularly published fiction,
as did all the innumerable newspapers. On every level of sophisti-
cation, supply could scarcely keep pace with demand, and it is
important to remember that in the realm of fiction those levels of
readership were happily still less demarcated than they were soon
to become; less demarcated by far than were the levels of social
class among readers themselves. The great novels of the nineteenth
century were not invariably best-sellers, but by and large they were
widely read, if still not commonly accepted as proper subjects for
university study. And *writing* novels was almost as fashionable as
reading them: a surprising number of Bonapartes, for example, per-
petrated novels among their other diversions (the emperor himself did not), and we remember Nathaniel Hawthorne's complaint
about "hordes of damn'd scribbling women." What a lovely time,
novelistically speaking: it is the period from which dates the still-
persisting notion that somewhere in each of us there lurks a *novel*
waiting to be written. I'll return to this notion presently.

No doubt there were in 1890 premonitory signs of trouble ahead,
but who was sharp-eyed enough to see them for what they were?
The seeds of modernism, for example, were already sown and ger-
minating — Roland Barthes dates "the fall of literature" from the
1850s (i.e., from Flaubert), noting as a symptom of its fall from innocent unself-consciousness that the term *literature* itself had just
come into use. But such news traveled more slowly back then
than it does nowadays, and the fateful division of the genre we're

concerned with into art novels and pop novels had scarcely begun: that modernist division much remarked by Leslie Fiedler and others, which some of us who are called postmodernists aspire to see bridged, though Fiedler tells us that we have yet to bridge it.

Such portents were there to be read, but I daresay that no one at the Macerata symposium of 1890 could have foreseen the turn of events far more consequential for the future of the novel in the next century than was the modernist polarization of novelists into, shall we say, James Joyces on the one hand and James Micheners on the other. I mean the great usurpation of the kingdom of narrative by the visual, especially the electronic, media: the invention and development first of movies and then of television and videocassette recording; along with these, in America particularly though by no means exclusively, the ubiquitous soundtrack of rock music and the combination of these ingredients in MTV—from all of which has followed the famous "new barbarianism" of the "electronic global village": the very substantial (some would call it calamitous) decline in *reading* as a source of information and entertainment, and the attendant, quite measurable decline in verbal skills among both students and their teachers and thence among the general population. Again, it is not a peculiarly American phenomenon, though my impression is that the situation is more acute here than in the other developed democracies. Public school education in Japan and Germany, for example, is no doubt superior in most respects to ours, but my academic friends in those countries shake their heads just as we do at their students' addiction to television and their general aliteracy—and I noted for myself on a recent visit to Japan that among Tokyo high school boys and young men on commuter trains, pornographic comic books and photonovels appeared to be at least as popular as print (the girls and young women seemed to prefer talking to one another).

We have arrived at our 1990 symposium; it is time to prophesy, and the general lines of my prediction are themselves predictable enough from my characterization of the present state of readerly affairs as it bears upon the art of and the audience for that grand old literary institution, the novel. First I'll describe, and then I'll offer some judgments upon, what I read of its future in the tea leaves of the present.

To begin with, I certainly see no grounds for imagining that the trend away from reading in general will reverse itself. On the contrary. As things stand now in the much-diminished realm of prose fiction, if we leave out of account assigned reading by students and professional reading by teachers, writers, editors, reviewers, critics and booksellers, my personal impression is that in America, at least, novels are still read for pleasure these days principally on resort beaches, cruise ships and wide-body airliners. I have myself also received encouragement from readers in such outlying areas as Alaska's North Slope, in the extended-care facilities of hospitals, in the rear areas of various U.S. military operations and in jail. Let me say at once that I am most gratified by these observations and reports, regardless of the literary merit of the novelists being read, for I believe that *haute cuisine* is likely to be better where the *cuisine ordinaire* is widely relished, and that the chances of turning out great opera singers or chess players (as well as opera and chess fans) are improved where lots of ordinary folk go around singing Puccini or playing chess in the public parks.

Two reasons for the persistence of these last bastions of extended pleasure-reading are obvious: at our present level of technology it remains inconvenient to bring the electronic visual media to the beach, for example, and/or people in such circumstances as those just remarked have more time on their hands than even high-tech entertainment can entirely fill. I note, however, that the novel-readers in those situations are most often the middle-aged and older, and not only because it is they who can more often afford to be on resort beaches, cruise ships and other extended-care facilities. Their younger counterparts — what the *New York Times* recently [1/6/91] called "the lost book generation" — are more likely to be "wired," and I cannot decide whether it's more distressing to see them hooked on the headphones and the Tom Clancy novel simultaneously or the Sony Walkman *tout court* (headphones and Chekhov would certainly be dismaying).

In the century to come, no doubt, the technological impediments to VCRs in the beach-bag or attaché case will be overcome; or it may be that those surviving habitats of the endangered species of novel-readers will themselves disappear, supplanted by teleportation, say, and the seductions of computer networking and interactive electronic "virtual worlds." Of this prospect, too, more presently, as of the question whether *any* amount of leisure time is too large for such very-high-tech allurements. Before we leave the category of diminishing habitats, however, two others should be noted, of similar dubiety but perhaps different fragility. First, in

Central and Eastern Europe, as in the Soviet Union, one imagines that for a while yet the habit will persist of looking to novelists and even poets for political-moral news unavailable via state-controlled media (a writer friend just back from the Soviet Union tells me that when a Russian says the word *literature,* he still tends to put his hand on his chest, as if about to sing an aria). But this habit can be expected to weaken as and if political conditions in those countries continue to liberalize. Philip Roth's memorable distinction between "us" and "them" will less and less apply: that in America anything goes and nothing matters, whereas behind the old Iron Curtain nothing went and therefore everything mattered — even novels, even poems. Good-bye to all that, I suppose and am obliged to hope, by 2090. Second, and somewhat analogously, it has been speculated that the future of the novel may lie in the "developing countries" — where, I presume, the electronic competition is less developed also, and where novelists might incline to address the kinds of social and political issues addressed by many of their great nineteenth-century predecessors. Leaving aside the possible condescension of this remark, I think it more likely than not that the social-economic "Third World" will still be with us a century hence; but to the question whether there lies the future of the novel, I would respond only that there lies a considerable slice of its past as well.

Now I'll swap my tea leaves for a crystal ball and offer the scenario for the novel in the next century that I see least dimly reflected in its pollution-enhanced mists. Not so long ago I used to see two scenarios in there, the darker of which involved thermonuclear apocalypse: the condition of the novel in the next century, after all, presupposes that there will *be* a next century. Indeed, one aspect of the movement from modernism to postmodernism, as I have remarked elsewhere, is that many who used to worry about "the death of the novel" (a characteristically modernist anxiety) have been more likely in the last three decades to worry instead about the death of the reader and/or of the planet. The nuclear swords have by no means yet been beaten into plowshares, but it looks now as though we may turn our concern to the plowshares themselves, so to speak: to the attrition of the biosphere. That too can be regarded as apocalyptic, but it's an apocalypse in slower motion, with more hope of there being a symposium in 2090.

I am left therefore with only one scenario, though it comes in two flavors, the pessimistic and the guardedly optimistic. The scenario itself, as I see it, is this: the once-vast dominion of the novel, together with the even vaster dominion of printed literature of all sorts as a medium of entertainment and edification, continues in the next century the inexorable shrinkage that we have witnessed in ours. Nonprofessional readership keeps on declining, except for reference and special-communication purposes via video display terminals, fax machines and whatever technology follows them. In the more pessimistic version of the scenario, reading and writing skills in the general population of technologically developed countries atrophy even further from lack of exercise, perhaps "bottoming out" at levels somewhat lower than those of today's public high-school seniors in the U.S.A. (average verbal SAT scores of 424, down from 476 in 1951, on a test that spots you 200 points virtually for spelling your name right) — or perhaps *not* bottoming out, but regressing even farther toward an oral culture deafened by high-decibel pop music more circumambient than the loudspeakered propaganda in George Orwell's *1984*. The reading of extended, even of brief, fictional narratives becomes ever more a special, more or less elite taste, akin to chess or equestrian dressage; akin most of all to a taste for poetry, old and new, in the generations since the ascendancy of the novel did to the audience for poetry what the ascendancy of the electronic media has done to the audience for prose fiction (and for books in general). Already in 1990, most of us "serious" novelists must plan our economic lives the way most poets have always had to do; we practice what the critic Earl Rovit has described as a "full-time profession that is, paradoxically, a part-time occupation," and we do not expect to be able to live even modestly on our royalty income alone. By the second half of the twenty-first century, it may be that even the Stephen Kings and the James Micheners, the Danielle Steeles and the Judith Krantzes and the whoevers, will be obliged to do likewise; "desktop publishing" and small print runs from small presses will be to the twenty-first century what poetry-by-subscription was to the eighteenth and nineteenth. In this version of the scenario, a really quite widely read new novel, even of what nowadays we regard as the purely commercial sort, becomes as unusual a phenomenon as today's occasional "literary best-seller" by Gabriel García Márquez, Umberto Eco, John Updike, William Styron. (How such exceptions are to be marketed, in the presumable absence of large trade fiction publishers and institutions of distribution and sale, is beyond my competence to imagine.) A certain number of aficionados, hardcore literati, will continue to concern themselves with new fiction, just as today such "early Christians" (as Thomas Mann was already calling them in 1903) remain au courant with contemporary poetry. But the mass of the bourgeoisie, including the "college educated," will be as ignorant of and indifferent to the medium of prose fiction as are their present-day counterparts with respect to the medium of verse.

That's the pessimistic forecast: it all but precludes the likelihood of there being a symposium in 2090 on the novel in the twenty-second century, though it optimistically allows that the University of Macerata, for example, will still exist on its eight hundredth anniversary. Before we turn to the alternative prognosis, perhaps we should consider exactly why what I've just described is bad news, except for novelists and their publishers. Why should we (we the people) care whether one particular medium of entertainment, even of art, is supplanted by another? Narrative literature, after all, did reasonably well before the invention of movable type, not to mention before the rise of the novel: there was the oral tradition for the unlettered and manuscript reading for the very small literate population; in my scenario, the former is replaced by the electronic visual media, the latter by small presses and desktop publishing. If reading any great literature for pleasure in the electronic global village becomes as rare as reading Homer in Greek today; if the audience for the William Faulkner or the García Márquez of the next century is as small and special as today's audience for Seamus Heaney or James Merrill, what will we have lost? In my opinion, our losses will be two at least; I classify them as civil and aesthetic.

As for our civil loss: The ascendancy of the novel is historically associated with the ascendancy of the middle class and the spread of general literacy, and those in turn, in the West at least, with the development of the institutions of liberal democracy and the civil state. In this area I am far from expert, and it may be that I'm mistaking correlations for causations. But it seems to me to have been democratically healthier back when every major American city, for example, had three or four competing newspapers instead of one without competition (my own father, a small-town store-keeper without a high-school diploma, used to read four newspapers daily, from three different cities, plus the entire *New York Times* on Sundays), and when citizens read those newspapers, each at his own pace, his own depth of understanding, and his own agenda of concerns, rather than passively receiving the show-biz presentations of television newsbroadcasters at *their* pace, according to *their* agenda. In the same way, it seems to me to be better mental exercise, civically healthier exercise, to *read* for pleasure — great fiction, junk fiction, nonfiction, anything — than to sit hypnotized by that "satanic glass screen," as the writer Mark Helprin calls it. No doubt I am being both biased and superstitious, but because of that historical connection I think of the novel (and, by extension, of general literacy) as a canary in the coal mines of democratic civil society. I have read, and I believe it, that people are more manipulable by the visual media than by print (I know *I* am). Television may inspire a certain cynicism among its devotees, but it doesn't do much for critical thinking; the "couch potato" makes sarcastic comments about the programming, but he doesn't turn the set off. Reading even a spy thriller or a "bodice ripper" is much more of an *activity* than "grazing the channels" is. If this particular canary really does go belly-up, I'm old-fashioned enough to fear for the general civic air.

The other loss is aesthetic. In the scenario as given, an elite remnant of the literate will be spared this loss (I don't imagine that libraries will disappear, for example), but I'm democratic enough to regret that the larger community won't be spared it. A work of prose fiction — even a slick commercial novel or a slick commercial short story (back in the days when there was still a market for those) — is a considerably more individual, idiosyncratic affair than is a movie or a television drama. I write a novel with invaluable editorial assistance from my wife, from my official editor, and from my meticulous copy editor and her fact-checkers; that novel is published with the further assistance of designers, graphicists, printers and binders, publicists, salespeople and bookstore managers and clerks. Nevertheless, the book is much more "mine" than any film or television play can ever be its "author's": my book's effect on whatever readers it may find does not depend on the exigencies of casting, directing, production budgets and technical staff. Far fewer contingencies stand between me and my readers than stand between any dramatist and his audience. Compared to fiction and poetry, all theater and cinema and television — even "auteur" cinema and television — is committee art: "team sports," Truman Capote called them. I have no quarrel with the collaborative arts; I am a failed musician myself, and know the joys of submerging one's individuality in the ensemble. But surely we'll be poorer for it if the collaborative arts come to be all there is. I am persuaded that it is this low-capital individual-voiceness that accounts for the runaway popularity of creative writing courses in American colleges and universities — a paradox indeed in a culture not much given to reading.

Another reason for their popularity brings us to another kind of aesthetic loss that we'll suffer if my pessimistic scenario comes to pass. The graphic and the plastic arts, after all, may be said to be just as "individual," as a rule, as writing is; but whereas comparatively few of us ordinary taxpayers go about our daily business imagining that inside our unprepossessing exteriors there lurks a great painting or sculpture waiting to be born, *not* a few folk imagine that they have a story to tell, even a novel, if they could only get it down on paper. Sometimes, astonishingly, they actually do — and the reason for the novel's singular hospitality to amateurs over the centuries, no doubt, is that while only a small number of people draw and carve and paint en route to work or at their office desks or amid their housework, nearly all of us use our language all day long: talking and listening, telling how it is, hearing how it was.

Now, it goes without saying that every medium of art has its particular assets and limitations. The great limitation of written narrative, for example, as opposed to stage, film and television drama, is that it deals directly with none of the physical senses. There are no literal sights, sounds, smells, tastes and feels in a novel, only their names. This technically *anesthetic* aspect of writing no doubt accounts for the comparative ease with which we can be moved to physical tears, laughter and excitement by even rather mediocre drama, and only comparatively rarely by even first-rate writing. But this great limitation is offset — more than offset, in my opinion — by the fact that the written word can address directly, like no other medium, the invisible universe inside the head and under the skin: the universe not of direct sensation but of sensibility; the *experiencing* of human experience.

This incalculable asset is what is lost when people no longer read novels and stories and poems. The oral narrative tradition supplied it to some extent once upon a time, but at the sacrifice of audience control, so to speak — and here is my point: not only is the *writing* of fiction a more individually controlled enterprise than the production of visual drama; the reading of it, too, is more individually controlled than the spectating of drama. Granted, the various buttons on our VCRs restore some measure of control to the individual auditor; but what we're rather awkwardly and infrequently controlling in that quite limited way is non-narrative: it lacks the mediating, selecting, registering, interpreting, rendering sensibility of the *narrator*, as well as the irreplaceable virtues of the written word. Visual media and even oral narrative are meals fed to us regardless of our individual appetites and digestive capacities; the printed word we savor at our own pace.

So highly do I esteem these two virtues of prose fiction — all power to the individual (relatively speaking) in both production and consumption, and direct access to the invisible universe of sensibility — that I am impelled to imagine a less pessimistic version of my scenario for the novel in the next century. Even in this happy version, the novel goes the way of the elephant and the rhinoceros — how can it not, given the forces competing against it? But its extinction is by no means complete; the special parks and preserves in which it carries on its much-diminished life turn out to be rather less remote, precarious and minuscule than our cultural ecologists had feared. Indeed, like the tropical rain forests and the African game reserves, the novel becomes something of a cause, even something of a craze: Save the Whales! Hortatory T-shirts and bumper stickers promote the cause; literary Greenpeace activists stage silent read-ins and book giveaways at video-rental outlets, and although their tactics alienate a few moderates, the agreeable mental exercise of reading (reading fiction in particular) catches on in the overdeveloped countries like the physical exercise of aerobics and off-road biking. (In a recent tour of some first-rate American bookstores, I was told that their volume of business has been increasing lately by as much as 20 percent annually.) Excessive televiewing comes to be regarded, and not only by the elite, as on a par with excessive alcohol consumption and single-crop agriculture. Billboards and signs on city buses extol the hygienic pleasures of reading (in my city already, every municipal bus-stop bench proclaims, perhaps quixotically, READING ZONE – BALTIMORE: THE CITY THAT READS). Reading rooms spring up in our teleportation terminals, furnished nostalgically with period chipboard bookshelves from the twentieth century; special no-viewing, no-listening seats are available on whatever passes for public vehicles. Even the irresistible virtual worlds of interactive whole-body computer simulation come to include virtual armchairs in which one can virtually read virtual novels, non-interactive except in the wonderful way that readers and writers have traditionally interacted.

In these benign though diminished and somewhat artificial preserves, I like to imagine, the old art of the novel (and the much older art of written literature in general) not only survives the twenty-first century but adapts, modestly flourishes and contrives even to evolve. To change the metaphor: I note that Italy, Spain, France and Great Britain, for example, though no longer the imperial centers that they once were, remain still distinctive, important, more or less prosperous places. I hope the same for Russia and the United States as their former empires dissolve in the century to come, and I wish no less in that century for the noble genre of the novel, both as entertainment and as art.

The Faculty for Hearing the Silence of Jesus

Forrest Gander

Your hurt is incurable
and your wound is grievous
There is none to uphold your cause
no medicine for your wound
no healing for you

— for Nina Iskrenko and Ilya Brodsky

A woman reading beside a white, half-hooded pram. Before her a field of colorless weeds, just behind her the birch forest glossy and impenetrable as the eyes of the dead. There is no path to her bench, no path visible through the weeds. Her calves are thick, though when she stands her skirt and coat, of equal lengths, will cover them. Her hidden face tilts down, obscured by thick hair cut in the shape of a winter hat. In a language whose very letters I fail to recognize, she spends the morning reading.

MOSCOW BATHS

Perceives two naked men —
        vermilion benchmarks
                splotch their buttocks
        like folded valentines —
close the steam room door behind
                        them.

When again the door closes,
        odor of wet heat
    reams our noses, a birch

Forrest Gander

       forest breaking
                    wind, sweet
                    human sweat.

    They do penance,
              whacking twigs
       against our stinging backs,
                 we who cannot breathe
                      and leave to wind ourselves
          in sheets, standing
               erect before mirrors
                    touching our hair.
                    A boy's candydrop
                          genitalia. I stare
                 at a man in the cold
          tank submerged to his hat.

            THE SILENCE OF GORKY PARK

    Perceives a species of black
              and white crow,
         executioner's hood and wings,
    rocking down from naked trees
                    to eye us
                       on bended
              backward knees.

    Thus have we been
              made. Gargling
         from a puddle, birds
    crouch and spring
                 into up,
                    penitents croaking from
                          birch limbs:

                    nor can they sing
                       for their supper.

Alexandre Eremenko is lighting a match for Katya's cigarette. The muscles of his brow contract over his eyes, his eyebrows flatten and descend and a fold cleaves above the bridge of his unremarkable nose. Head listing sidewise into hunched shoulder, eyes nearly closed. He is saying to the match, *Ok, last chance,* his mustache drooping as though disappointed greatly in the failure. Fingers too, one set holding at their tips the small light blue box, the others pointed into a wooden stick, seem to be arguing, coaxing. He holds them up again toward Katya's face, his hands together in a gesture of prayer.

Striking sulfur into air, Eremenko disappears. Becomes Failing-to-light-the-match. Is waylaid, enchanted, absorbed into the privacy of an old conversation, even the smallest failure looking familiar, having that nostalgic aura, connected in its tiny way to the vast network of failures that sustains him.

Then the match hisses into colors. Then Eremenko returns to find himself extending it toward the proffered cigarette.

THE CONVERSATIONS

Overhears syllables of welcome,
 speeches yielding
the milk which is
the milk of speech
  itself. That he says this much
   to the ear: "Do thou
    sing out for me?" "Yes," sayeth
  ear, singing such:

  Around the walled
   KGB, a sound
of such big-mouth dogs
   "their mouths hung down
    from their mouths."
The guide claims to recall
  screaming underground,
where penance committed
  Mayakovsky.

231

Forrest Gander

TENDENCIES

Perceives a penchant for beet-red hair
     dyed across
     generational zones:
on the metro, Red Square;
     the performance-poet's
          violinist. Everywhere
     in a population prone
          to natural dark
          and blonde, with eyebrows
unremarked.

     With high eyebrows and remarks,
          we turn on subway stairs
sneezing tear gas, heads lowered
     as if for prayer.
     MEMORY thug arrested
          for punching a Jew.
And so they do
     penance, whose wives' red
          ear-length coiffures
     did not keep
     the men at home.
          Outside the station,
     lipsticked
       glasses in
"Drink" machine:
     press to activate
          and the glass swirls
     nearly clean.

Beside a lopped-off sycamore, this triptych of small monuments marks the end of a lineage. Fixing the eyes of tour group strays, a photograph mounted on the stone to the left: a clean-shaven man in his late fifties whose serious countenance, were he not wearing a dark military uniform decorated at the breast with dozens of butterfly bars and ribbons, would be called unhappy. On the stone to the right, a photograph of his wife registers her worn face twisted his way, stricken with loss, her hair short and thinning. While his photograph renders wide shoulders and chest, all that is visible below the woman's throat are blurry, narrow lapels, the bow of her dress.

The three dead share an easter lily. Its glossy deeply lined leaves graze the photograph embedded in the center stone, that of the daughter whose face in profile uplifts toward a soft light, whose dense curls brushed back from her lovely high forehead, softening to a fuzz in front of her ear, collect thoughtfully at her shoulder. She must be in her twenties. The dates are obscured. But it is the sequence of their deaths that is inscribed most legibly in their faces: daughter, father, mother. As though to suggest to those who have come to brush leaves from monuments under which friends and parents lie, a greater grief.

THE SILENCE OF GOOM

In the famous shopping mall,
perceives no line (and gawks —
                    Is this the store
             out of liniments? No,
                    this store's
                         out of woolen socks —)
             twisting the corridor
where yesterday herds
             slogged. Trapped inside,
                    twittering, a few birds.

             We enter among scores
                         of curses and tarry
                    fumes from the roadcrew's
       kettle machine,
                    its exhaust

233

spewing toward the doors
of Goom's limegreen
hall, a further distance
than breath can be held,
past elaborate window displays —
(The store out of liniments
is across the hall —)
to well staffed shops of gaping shelves.

THE SILENCE OF RED SQUARE

As though in penance,
the guards flinch
at Lenin's red and black
granite tomb
before the hour
perceives its crowd:
all eyes
beholding the huge clocktower.

Thus, lock-kneed, strut
two fresh guards,
one sergeant
to choreograph.
All five freeze
as the tower bell tones.

Afterwards,
an old man sweeps
crushed butts
from cobblestones.

In his last apartment, Dostoyevsky turned the desk in his writing room toward the window. He rolled his own cigarettes and drank thick tea glaring out toward the building across the street.

There is a face in the wall of that building, above the second-story window, the bust of a woman recessed in an ovular frame like a huge concrete broach. Difficult to make out her features. Most prominent in the failing light that must leapfrog Dostoyevsky's apartment to splash against this wall: her hair, parted in the middle, and something that slants across her décolleté — the frilled upper edge of her dress or a loose tail of hair. Her face in the shadow of her hair.

To the right of the bust, the building has suffered some trauma, the long rectangles of gray concrete are rubbed away to reveal brick and patches of creamy mortar.

Nicotine and caffeine bracing him upright, Dostoyevsky must have stared often from his desk toward the face in the gray wall across the street. But because he worked at night, because the street is unlighted, his gaze must have stopped short at the window and returned like a dog on a leash, carrying his own visage back to him, the bearded lamplit face and pisshole eyes, the racking cough, the napkin crumpled around burls of blood-speckled mucus, the furry tumescent digits of his hand re-inking the pen.

TOILET

Springing through poorly lit
backroom penetralia,
he posts his massive self
at the cafe's single toilet,
turning malignantly at us
to block it.
Apodictic
and threatening.
We turn and file back
like a pack of wolf hounds
holding together, each dog
clenching the tail
of the preceding dog in its mouth,
as priests are said to do
in Zagorsk, to the south.

235

Forrest Gander

As in Zagorsk, thus is everything
     woof woof
   and warp in water. Which
  continues to rush
 into the sink
  our translator washed out
 his bloody mouth
     in after fighting. He did penance
      to unstoppered musical guttering
 toilets. Down-
  drip from pullstring.

THE SILENCE OF THE LENINGRAD SUBWAY

Perceives the mendicant glance
 of a four-year-old,
 her blackened palms offered,
  the boy's broken posture:
   a living bundle
at his back, swathed.
  A crowd reads the wall
 of taped paper.
    Below, the begging children's
     mother: exposed paps,
   her infant eyeing up at.

  Thus, we too
 look up:
   the exit stairs
    slick with rain
a country woman begins to curse
    as she claims
  a space against the wall,
     her coat dripping
      onto her wares,
 green apples in an open
       blue purse.

CODA

See the small park, a sand path lined in birches and perimeterized by wrought-iron fence. And within its oval a second magic circle of standing mutes fire off their fingers, one canting his face violently to hack. Teenagers sitting close on the park bench, perched on its backrest in jean jackets, long hair, bandannas, an intimate pocket of themselves in softest tones. At other benches, overcoats and black boots contain women ogling their canes or pigeons. The coughing mute stalks in and out of the park meeting friends in a street lined with parked cars whose hoods radiate heat. The women's soft hats slantwise on their skulls. At the path's edge, on a crescent of grass, cries a boy stamping red sneakers. Early evening September gentle pigeon colored light of the city. Through which, in black gloves, one crone continues to read aloud the paper. Boy crossing from park hand in hand with mother, his right eye, the one distant from her, bandaged with a tic tac toe grid of white tape. Puppy pulling the leash in its mouth. Further along the block, children ride their hats down a playground slide, whooping. Her breasts behind a red folder of papers, she escorts her reluctant daughter and bicycle from the park, wrists baring themselves from dress sleeves and open sweater —

toward what apartment of these surrounding, what man strange and common to her. Where are his visible scars, what stories does she maintain to explain his body. The dinner they will have tonight, each dish picked up with her fingertips. Their clash underwater. His breath in bed, the solid warmth next to her, her own long body white as meat tugged from a shell, barely touched. Papers in her red folder scattered across a table in the dark —

This nearly conscious tenderness with which the park relinquishes each animal to space. Distant thwop thwop, diastolic and systolic tones, the spanked child muffling its cry. See how the limbs move but barely, the sparrows' collective chirrup rising and falling off. How the friends stand together already moving, together, dyed red hair long and knapsacks and purses. Open winged pigeons settling into fresh absence. Audible current of fricative leaves. White-scarfed old woman displaying her tremendous white cat like a nursing baby to two benches of shapeless matrons whose heads incline toward each other in pairs. She begins to leave with her cat but at the edge of the park halts to get better grips on cat and purse, a little hop, and goes on.

The Bugbear of Experimentalism
Christopher Middleton

I'M GOING TO SPEAK principally about writing and experiment. By "writing" I mean imaginative writing. But what do I mean by "experiment"? What should I call to mind? What specific instances of experimental writing can I identify as models? Obviously, *Finnegans Wake*. Single pages of *Finnegans Wake* that I scanned in a bookshop when I was eighteen stood out, somehow, as exemplars of a prose that was alive and incendiary. I didn't understand a thing, but the vocal colors, rhythms, fluid configurations of images, the amazing measured alternation of voices touched my imagination with an enigmatic quality I'd found till then only in some ancient Greek poems. Those poems, too, I had felt rather than understood. At about the same time I was struck by a text called "A Poem in Seven Spaces" by Alberto Giacometti, the sculptor. This was a pictorial poem and I saw it in the 1939 Faber anthology *New Verse*. It said "2 golden claws," and three-quarters of the way down inside its oblong frame came another isolated phrase, "3 galloping horses." That poem, coming out of a Europe I'd never seen but which was devastated by war at that time, stood out like a sore thumb in Geoffrey Grigson's largely English *New Verse*. Much later I took to heart typographic marvels in Russian, by the Futurist Ilya Zdanevitch. Other models of experiment have been for me certain constellation poems of the late fifties and early to mid-sixties: Brazilian, Czech, German or Japanese (concrete or phonetic) poems that invited the reader to visualize cones, orbs, chevrons or vacancies. All sorts of dislocations of linear discourse have fascinated me, at least from time to time. Typography can singularize the word technically, but the optical channels thus opened conduct singularization (as in Pound's *Cantos*) back to imagination's delight in solid, tensed, sparkling forms, where the circuit begins afresh.

This essay is the text of a talk given in March 1988 at the New Orleans Center for the Creative Arts.

I was then discovering that the creations of the pioneer avant-garde up into the 1930s had a powerful common vein of self-ironic mercurial high spirits. Perhaps this vein was resurgent, hardly choked by intervening horrors, in concrete poems of the sixties that partially colonized ground developed by the pioneers. The undoing of the regular printface had a curious charm for me. Words could burst from their lexical shells; phrases zigzag away from the magnetic field of syntax, vibrant ebony morphemes, calligraphic blanks; tonal ovals levitate across the avalanche of the page. Hare-brained as some texts were, they were not mere shadows of opinion. The text could be an icon that miniaturized events in a mind's life. (Opinion and experiment, somehow, don't mix.)

Common to the earliest fascinations was my laughable inability to understand much of what I read. I still think of a real poetic text as being liminal: seductively it resists the very intelligence it attracts. A liminal poetic text springs thought's cage and unleashes into nervous subsystems of thought all sorts of limber luminous animals, among which not only the hyena is unspeakable. Poetry's impact can be that of a paradox at once enigmatic and immediate — it invades and shocks the vitals, experimentally. The perils of this kind of unreason, both wonder and perplexity, may test your wits more tellingly than questions that literal-minded ideologists peevishly level against unreason. Do the arts exist countervailingly, like religion, to capture unreason, illuminate it, so to inhibit its ravages in politics?

But I should be coming to grips now with the motives and contexts of experiment. Improvisation: so as to seem to be saying something, I float a small balloon into the atmosphere of improvisation that tends to pervade writings that are generally alleged to be imaginative, experimental and anomalous. The notions we have about improvisation may be vague, but for the present I'll treat improvisation and experiment as cousins. The concepts converge in an understanding that long ago established one set of canons for art in this catastrophic century. The arts exist to dismember, in exploratory ways, existing norms. They trace the writ of an ultimate finger. Their calculus of improvisation tracks fundamental patterns of feeling, patterns in consciousness, which vibrate with the drama of history, no less, and with history's climax in the tremors of the psyche.

Improvisation and experiment coincide to the extent that an imaginative writer can't exactly foretell what will come of the act

240

of writing. All the same, I must attend to a far-reaching ambiguity here. The act of writing is organized by long-standing cultural conventions, and by unique but inconstant personal foibles. A text doesn't materialize in a vacuum. Many of the fiery and fertile experimental writings of this century have been high-spirited subversions of congealed older rhetorical models. Across the board, artists have had to break the spell of traditions, conventions and stereotypes living or entombed in the texts, pictures, musical scores that lay heaped around them. The tense vivacity of their experiments bears the marks of a struggle. We can feel them still, itching or hurting, the excitements and frustrations, individual and historical, the scars and open wounds, of a struggle. The "new" broke away. It, too, soon became an idol. But while it was still felt to be breaking away, pristine as it was, lay claim as it might to virgin birth, it never was born of a virgin. The body of early-twentieth-century experimental art had flesh-and-blood parents to disavow, as well as flocks of ghostly ancestors.

Thinking about genuine experimental innovation in any of the arts, I propose, we might do worse than recall those marks of struggle, for we have to inherit them in any case, and besides, by them we can measure our strengths in struggles of our own. We might also do well to consider a profoundly informed statement by E. H. Gombrich:

> The original genius who paints 'what he sees' and creates new forms out of nothing is a Romantic myth. Even the greatest artist — and he more than others — needs an idiom to work in. Only tradition, such as he finds it, can provide him with the raw material of imagery which he needs to represent an event or 'fragment of nature.' He can re-fashion this imagery, adapt it to its task, assimilate it to his needs and change it beyond recognition, but he can no more represent what is in front of his eyes without a pre-existing stock of acquired images than he can paint it without the pre-existing set of colours which he must have on his palette. (*Meditations on a Hobby Horse*. London and New York, 3rd ed., 1978, p. 126)

So far, I have taken for granted a distinction between imaginative writing and other kinds of writing. This is a hotly disputed area, but I'll generalize now the other kinds of writing into a category of the *instrumental*. So I propose a distinction between imaginative writing where the writer can't exactly foretell what might come to be written, and on the other hand instrumental writing where the writer knows well enough what will come to be written, because he knows his purpose — scientific or commercial discourse, for instance, where the thing to be written about is fixed in advance. This distinction needn't detain us, but we have to bear it in mind. Within the category of imaginative writing I'd propose we agree that the unforetellable, the unknown, has various degrees of intensity, between low and high, individual and universal. You yourself, for instance, might not be able to foretell or foreknow what might come out, but somebody else could have known or guessed it exactly enough all along. In this area I propose that we consider experimental imaginative writing as a risk.

In other words, what counts is the outcome of the experiment. It matters hardly at all whether or not you were telling yourself "here goes with an experiment." The fact is that higher degrees of "intensity" in the imaginative act of writing create, at immense risk, the real thing, and that the lower degrees risk less and merely produce a placebo. Here I distinguish between creating and producing. My model for the analogy is medical experiments with drugs: subjects take pills, some loaded with the real thing, but some — placebo pills — loaded with nothing. What counts, I repeat, is the outcome. For all their systematics the Oulipo writers, for instance, were no mere technicians.

So there we are: High-intensity imaginative writing creates a real thing in the face of the probably unknown, at great risk. At little risk, low-intensity imaginative writing produces a placebo in the face of the supposedly unknown. (I avoid the word "unconscious" here on purpose, although the real thing evolves under pressures from a vigorous unconscious.) If we continued this line of argument, we might become excruciatingly sensitive to the immense and varying spectrum of values, poetic, intellectual and ethical, that we touch upon when we think about writing as experiment, struggle and risk.

I don't plan to harp on the variables within that spectrum. What I'd like to say next concerns the award-winning prestige that attaches itself nowadays to the cluster of meanings around the word "experiment." You have to prove something, of course, but a clever description of an experimental project can upend the state or federal cracker-barrel and provide your experimental program with cash enough for the production of ten thousand placebos.

We might suppose that the prestige of experimental science has been invoked to godfather the funding of experimental projects in the arts. Aha, experimental, they crow, and shake from their cracker-barrel some of the dollars you need. They connect all good, forward-looking, energetic, lovely young minds, scientific or artistic, with the terms "experiment" or "experimental," pat themselves on the back for believing that North America, still, is a young country. So much the better for the lovely young artists, even if they're in their fifties already. But the patrons forgot something.

The patrons forgot that scientific experiments are subject to strict and feasible controls, even when the scientist (or his team) had nothing but a hunch to start with. They forgot that controlled scientific experiments address themselves to hard facts, actual phenomena and previous hypotheses, whereas in the arts an experiment is addressed to nothing but the medium in which the experiment is conducted: paint, stone, sound, words in their enigmatic relation to silence, and, not least, the solo self of the responsible artist. They also forgot that scientific experiments lay traps for what is unknown in the natural order of the universe, whereas in the arts experiment lays a trap for what is unknown in the human mind, that responsive but collapsible organism which creates the cognitive terms according to which phenomena are regulated and interpreted. You experiment in the media of imagination, breathless, hoping you'll perchance trap a new spirit, not just some old demon or other. Something hitherto concealed in the vague maze of the self might deign to show the tip of a horn or snout, even reveal itself entirely, attracted by the games you play, your ludic strategy. Spirit, horn or snout — you're in luck if the very least thing happens: a puff of dust as the creature takes to its heels. And if you do trap a new spirit, you seldom have to submit it to the scrutiny of scowling scientific colleagues, who really know their stuff but simply don't know how to believe your given word.

To elaborate somewhat: experiment in the media of imagination may create (not produce) a new phenomenon together with terms in which it may be interpreted. But nobody asks whether the phenomenon or the terms are right or wrong by any absolute standard (nature), or according to criteria proper to the field under controlled observation. True, you can't get away with anything, and instant approval is as undesirable as a yawn or a scowl. Insofar as a high-intensity experimental creation in the arts fathoms and provokes real doubt as well as real imagination, its very radiance must be constantly tested by fresh doubts, fresh imaginings, across decades, across centuries. Here perhaps ripeness really is all. What counts is the sovereignty of the creation, its naked truth, the seminal dynamism and fertile integrity of the new structure as and in which you've delivered, out of the unknown, your new spirit or old intractable demon.

If the thing works, then people may say: Yes, this is like life itself. Or they may say: Yes, that's a real outrage. Or: Yes, this is life itself as I've not yet conceived of it. So the creation doesn't explain anything. Only its beauty relates it to explanatory scientific theorems. What a creation says may remain in the protection of that beauty forever an enigma.

High-intensity imaginative writing, with its honest and ineluctable experimental component, creating a new spirit, remains a fertile enigma at odds with any perceived average order of things.

My remarks so far must seem rather academic in this land of incessant experiment, this land of superabundant inventiveness, where hardly a single range of experience for individuals, hardly an institution for collectives, is ever allowed to settle down in a good old comfortable rut. But perhaps what I say isn't academic, neutral or irrelevant after all. Think a bit. High-intensity experiment calls for creative imagination, and it is precisely creative imagination that is being tamed and neutered, its edge dulled, by the placebo experimentalism I mentioned. Hence the title of this talk: The Bugbear of Experimentalism.

We have all sorts of ideas as to what the word "imagination" might mean. Perhaps the word isn't definable, but it is no less operative for being attached to a most volatile concept — like "belief," "feeling," "revolt," "critique" or "opposition." Some of our differing ideas converge, I suspect, in a general sense of imagination as a uniquely human aptitude for creating imagery. The aptitude is given, though not to all, and it is unbinding — you take it or leave it. The imagery fathoms and illuminates the usual scene — social and historical — by playing constructively (however negatively) with possibilities of being — fictions. Hence imagination suggests dream, vision, feeling, insight, and it is adept at contriving utopias. Yet, for all the nervous subliminal stuff with which imagination is associated, it blends into acute judgment, clear thought, deep perception. The mind set atremble by experimentalism, on the other hand, toys with mere appearances. Experimentalism fiddles, mischievously enough, with existing surfaces of experience, with clichés, stereotypes, the sundry nutrients of human folly; but its mischief is never divinely insolent enough to forge any constructive transformation in a chosen medium; it formulates no rules by which the woebegone, routine games of reflection might be radically redesigned, for play with increased zest. Experimentalism, briefly, cools and dilutes the wild broth of real experiment.

Between high-intensity imaginative experiment and mere placebo experimentalism there is as large a conceptual gap as there is between experiment in science and experiment in the arts. I won't presume to identify the giant social factors that are insidiously, in cahoots with placebo experimentalism, crushing imagination, but the crush is surely on. At least there are some people who shudder at the worst-case scenario relentlessly now unfolding. A mock-up of the real thing, placebo experimentalism makes its bow, to polite handclaps from beaming TV programmers, militarists, pollution-profiteers and purveyors of radiation dried milk; impounded opera stars are made to roar with a volume transcending that of a football crowd; rapacious evangelists droning through the "deep slumber of decided opinion" are actually believed by the millions they fleece, and hordes of other frauds infect their suffering neighbors with hypocrisy and self-disgusted assent (a-s-s-e-n-t). I can't help laying it on thick. I realize that contrariwise in the exacting domain of musical performance, for instance, a great flowering is upon us. Even then, there is a very complex cat hypnotizing us, making us mouse-like, though mice we are not. There's a very deceptive predator feeding off the guilt he makes us feel, paralyzing us, while "reality" shatters all around us and history streaks irreversibly ahead.

So much for the bugbear. Just one thing more — about the unknown. I was suggesting that high-intensity imaginative writing can induce by experiment something unknown to reveal itself out of the mysterious crystallized surge of life that we call the human mind. Now I'll try to be more specific. What reveals itself isn't necessarily anything "unknown," or even anything till now less felt or unfelt or unrecognized. The unknown, after all, has one characteristic: it can't stop being unknown. What reveals itself is, more likely, the *unbidden*. Something is written that could only be *written*; what could only be written wasn't asked for, conceived of, aimed at. (The spell we have to break is the spell of instrumental thinking, which commands that everything be done with a purpose.) The structure in language that seems most receptive to the unbidden is metaphor. A figurative eruption is what the unbidden appears as, but the eruption is entirely articulate. I have news about this. Not one of the noted Western authorities on metaphor since Aristotle so much as mentions, as far as I know, the inherence in metaphor of the unbidden. So I could be wrong. Or else the authorities overlooked something essential.

I'll end by proposing that poetic experiment (which need not look conspicuously experimental, as regards typography) conducts morphological, phonetic and lexical currents through a body of available language. The passage of those currents (voice and rhythm) selects, singularizes or freshens the particles of language that are "fielded" by the experiment. Accordingly, relations between these particles are de-automatized, they become strange, and then, altogether unbidden (though you may feel it coming), and still as language, a real and abundant metaphor flashes into being, as real, if not more so, as a tree, a battle, a face, an egg. For this transformation to occur, language has to dance and dance well. Language has to dance over foaming, cresting, crosswoven, turbulent tensions between thought, perception and imagination (all rehearsed, but not overrehearsed). Out of those tensions language dances a moment of precarious accord, the moment when the unbidden is absurdly apparent as a metaphor.

How very refined, you may say. Earlier, you may say, my whole gist was that experiment in the arts contends with all sorts of social and economic pressures that threaten to atrophy anyone's imagination, even the toughest imagination, that of an artist. Now, you may say, you've scuttled away into the esoteric, as if there, at least, something sovereign maintains itself, something autonomous, rare, naked and inviolable, the unbidden as universal substance of metaphor.

I can't resolve this tension between apparently incongruous directions in my argument. Perhaps the tension itself is peculiar to our moods, our fears, as our century lapses. But at least I do identify the tension as one we need to cultivate by experiment, not dithering, but crossweaving between the inviolable nude, as it were, and the tremendous violence of history around us. If we can lucidly cultivate that tension, we might prove fit for the main struggle, which is to rescue from disaster the singularity of language. We have to redeem language from its collapse into servility, a status taken for granted by so many North Americans, who view their own mother tongue as a mere slave to mute, brute reality. Somehow we have to reinherit a contrary outlook, one that is ancient (so you may not go for it) and sharp (so you might change your mind). That ancient and sharp outlook is one that enables us to regard the languages people live by as heavenly messengers — to use a naive, figurative shorthand — heavenly messengers who

246

inaugurate consciousness and shape the very times and spaces of existence.

Each messenger must be coming from somewhere, just as Gombrich said. It is possible that no messenger can ever get through to you or me. As in Kafka's parable, we can still dream at a twilit window that our messenger is on his way. For even if your messenger is impeded, he is not enslaved to you or anyone or anything. Also the larger part of a messenger's occupation, like that of the larger part of language, is to be on the way. The experimental state of mind is ultimately a receptive state, opened by spontaneous desire, sustained by infinite curiosity and purged of self-deceit. So poetic experiment means listening for the messengers, it means revering them.

Beauty & the Cripple
Jim Powell

LEARNING TO DROWN

break on through
to the other side

to salt your taste
for disaster

I go soliciting
abandon

learning to drown
is what I'm good at

the corkscrew inward
to internal exile

in me my enemy
in my my, in my me

•

that little purple spot
then red then yellow

at the center of the black
behind between closed eyes

that little purple spot
that solar disk in negative

that bruise that hole
that drain consciousness

leaks out of, shimmering
in the inward spiral

•

Beautiful Death
now that I call you

by your right name
don't deny

I clung for dear
life to your dancer's

body, each muscle
supple as a hand

to greet our need.

MY FAVORITE METAPHOR

My favorite metaphor
for suicide
is 'checking out'
because it says
here is my key:

the room where I was staying
I won't be needing
anymore
and my departure
proves it's not

a prison: I'm free to leave.
I do. This once
I take command
if in nothing
but this parting

gesture of refusal — and yes,
Javier, yes:
in this life death
is always maybe
only the least

twist away: some slightest
rotation and
you see your hand
x-rayed,
fingerbones shining

through the film of skin —
but at 17
in a dorm room
blood welling
from mouth and nose,

already cold in your roommates'
arms — Javier,
Javier, too soon,
too soon

THE IMAGE

— for R.Z.

Recently I came across
a postcard bearing the image
of Robert Johnson
in a five-and-dime store photobooth
sometime in the 30s, lean fingers

fretting a chord on the neck
of the guitar he holds
between himself
and the camera like protection,
and like a loaded pistol cocked

and pointed. An unlit cigarette
rakes his face. He gazes
steadily, square
into the lens: ready
for anything, unconcerned; calmly

defying sadness: behind the canvas
curtain in a whisper
pleading fiercely —
he stares out from inside
the frame of light refracted splintering

off the original picture's roughly
scissored edges, unflinching
in the sudden glare.
I've tacked it above my desk.
If I find more I'll send you one.

FIVE RIDDLES FOR THE BIRDS

> "The bird of Minerva
> flies only at dusk."
>
> — Hegel

1. *The Crows*

Eleven crows
eleven strutting crows
studious in a circle
stooped to the gravel
shoulder outside a turn

inquisitive
around the shining meat
of some torn beast, some
indecipherable
crushed small animal — birds

arrogant,
preoccupied: "Fox, or marten?"
"Weasel." "Possum." "Dog?"
Eleven crows
eleven strutting crows.

2. *The Witness*

letting it falter
and die away

like water
on coarse sand

leaving the shadow
of its wetness

spilt there
barely a second

3. *The Heron*

To be still
as a heron
's reflection's
still, his
bill

tilted up
from the water
to regard
a something
moving:

Stilted there
above his familiar
rippling double
now shyly
he bends his

knees slowly to sip
attentiveness
at the brimming
verge, then
slip

behind an over-
hanging branch as
shyly to dine nipping
insects
one

and by one, then perch
on the round of this bit of
log above
the water-
line

watching the watcher
through the leaves
till he nods again
above the
page

and slowly now
while he's not looking
start to wade
back out
into

the shadowed pond
again

4. *The Hawk*

But this was a hawk
in the branches
and it threw
at my true love's feet
for a sign

a bird beheaded,
a limp rag
of blood and
feathers, one
wing

akimbo — and today
a baby mouse
curled in a
bare place dead
on the path,

and that same hoarse
laughter hidden
in the fir
branches clacking
overhead.

5. *The Pond*

On the back way
there are planks laid
across the swampy places,
jet black loam where water
pools in the dents,

a place on the path
I double back to
and catch myself returning
mirrored in a sheet
of water, the world

doubled back
in the glassy pool:
wind animates the leaves
and the glint shaken from them
winks flickering

in the pond dreaming
at the secret center
past the last screen
of ferns and creepers, bramble
entanglements

and periphrastic
evasions this place
a steady witness for
the rehearsal of a ghostly
life in signs

and tokens, clairvoyant
the way dreams
betray us to ourselves
in a changeling masquerade
uncovering

another nature
another self
to read in the face there
in the water till reflection
troubles the mirror.

HOW THE PROVINCES
STAY THE PROVINCES

The smaller
the pie
the sharper
the knives
the sharper
the knives
the smaller
the pie.

THE MAYFLIES

Driving south toward summer
doing 80 down I-5 for hours
into the valley
humid with new corn in sultry rows
for miles and the smell of worms

working in the upturned
earth, thick air surly with burgeoning
and the mayflies
leaving their five-petaled prints like stars
in constellated swarms

across the windshield smearing
the glass with the carnage of my progress
till everything's stained
thin green with insect blood, the controlled
explosions in four

cylinders a frantic
animal lunging against the tether, summer's
hands probing
at the wound to feel the tortured beast
struggle to escape.

N'IMPORTE OÙ HORS DU MONDE

ANY WHERE OUT OF THE WORLD

This life is a hospital where each patient is possessed by the desire to change beds. One wants to suffer opposite the stove, and another thinks he would recover by the window.

It seems to me that I would always be well there where I am not, and this question of moving is one of those I discuss ceaselessly with my soul.

"Tell me, my soul, poor chilly soul, what would you think of living in Lisbon? It must be warm there, and you would cheer back up again like a lizard on a rock. The city is beside the water; they say that it is built of marble, and that the people there have such a hatred of vegetation that they tear out all the trees. Now *there* is a country after your taste, a landscape made of light and mineral, and liquid to reflect them."

My soul did not reply.

"Since you love rest so much, accompanied by the spectacle of movement, would you like to go live in Holland, that beatifying land? Perhaps you will find diversion in this country whose image you've admired so often in museums. What would you think of Rotterdam, you who love forests of masts, and vessels moored at the foot of houses?"

My soul kept mute.

"Batavia would delight you more, perhaps? There we would find, besides, the spirit of Europe married to tropical beauty."

Not a word. — My soul, could she be dead?

"So then, have you come to such a point of enervation that you take pleasure only in your sickness? If that's the way it is, let's flee to the countries that are analogues of Death. — I grasp our situation, poor soul! Let's pack our bags for Tornio. Let's go still further, to the extreme end of the Baltic; even further still from life, if that is possible; let's settle at the pole. There the sun grazes the earth only obliquely, and the slow alternation of the day and night suppresses variety and intensifies monotony, that half of nothingness. There we will be able to go shadow-bathing for long hours, and meanwhile, to divert us, the aurora borealis will emit from time to time its rosy sheaves, like reflections of the fireworks of Hell!"

At last, my soul exploded, and in her wisdom cried out to me: "No matter where! no matter where, as long as it's out of this world!"

— Charles Baudelaire

BEAUTY & THE CRIPPLE

I watched my Beauty's dancing
face tranced to ecstatic
blankness, captivated
in our admiring circle
until he saw

the Cripple enter there
and dance his polio
with canes. And then I smiled
to see the spectre of the lame
make Beauty quail —

dejected, abashed to watch
deformity show grace
faltering in the shadow
of their shared need, their secret
common extremity.

257

Grace's Tree, I
Marjorie Welish

When did you discover you've an abstract mind? Playing with blocks
even as others were playing with sheep, contending with accidents
upon this earth and balkanization within a two-dimensional meadow,
the two-dimensional meadow against which and through which salient
facts draw at least part of their sustenance.

Threading the adjusted grove on the right-hand side,
I stayed to play with blocks procedurally, madly in love,
and in a magical moment,
capsized the puzzle to turn smiling faces into pervasiveness,
the pervasiveness of those geometric schemes.

Farming the torrid difficulties,
faced with abhorrent difficulties on the obverse of agricultural stress
and seeking medicinal solutions to power,
once a farmer, now political activist — you, spurned by likeness
are nonetheless remembered by literati.

Given your considerable acoustical acuity, facility even, reach
more complexity than is readily accessed by your wanderlust,
your carelessness,
as when the sheep farmer you once were asked of his pallid
    colleagues: now just what
satisfactorily invites the geology of the situation?

Now just what sovereign geology accessed by your wanderlust
capsized the puzzle to turn the smiling faces into pervasiveness
like the grove on the right-hand side of the gravely asymmetrical
    situation
against which and through which salient facts draw at least part of
    their sustenance?

From Horse Spittle
(The Eros of Maps)
Iain Sinclair

"Fly, I sispected — Horse, I dint"

— George Herriman, *Krazy Kat*

FREDRIK HANBURY, THE WRITER, sat opposite me, across a pine table; drumming his thumbs. Roland Bowman stood at its head, moving backwards and forwards, pausing, smiling, gliding to the stove, the shutters, the foot of the stairs; peering up, finger to his lips, in case his mother should call. Roland's knitted waistcoat — a sunburst among the calculated minimalism of the basement — could not be bought at any counter: you felt Roland had always owned it, it had been passed on to him at some discreet family initiation. You also felt, noticing the ease with which he possessed his space, that while he remained in this kitchen Roland would never age. He was weathered, fit, tanned; beached, safely, on the far shore of thirty. And would be true to that condition for as long as his tenure in Fournier Street lasted. He slid gracefully over the flags of stained-glass sunlight, gesturing, talking; a red coffeepot pivoting on his outstretched arm. Here, beneath the level of the street, it was dim, caged: cool stone floor, smooth wood panels muted in gesso. Everything was slow, calm, concentrated. Whatever was spoken was burnt, momentarily, into the air; and could be read, before it was heard. Roland refilled our hand-painted mugs with his strong black brew. I tasted the grains with my tongue.

"She was a very unusual person." Roland caught me trying to decode the framed photograph. Was it contemporary? Or was it one of those theatrical poses that certain stallholders try to pass off as "Art Deco," "Art Nouveau," or anything else with "art" in the title: straining to make the mere sound of the words inject a nostalgia for the robed, the remote, the indecent . . . the expensive. A girl, they suggested, had also to be a flower, the twisted stem of a glass, or a wind-tossed flounce of drapery. But the point with the portrait that had taken my fancy was that the subject, this girl, was obviously *aware* of the camera, and its technical limitations; and yet the result seemed natural, spontaneous, a challenge. She was naked. The print was deceptively gray and soft — which made it difficult to date. The photographer had been careful not to impose a queasy subtext: to make a confession of his own inadequacy. He was not "saying" anything. He could have been blind. The starkness and brutal directness of the final image suggested that the girl had taken the shot by an act of will, controlling the light and the focus for the precise exposure she wished to celebrate. "This," she said, "is how I want to remember myself."

Then Mother did call, unshrill, an interested upstairs voice; and Roland, indulgent, went to her, taking her a cup of coffee, an onion roll warm from the oven. He held the jug out, as if it were guiding him, an oil lamp: he pirouetted the tight stairway, talking back to us over his shoulder. Now Fredrik, who was fretted by a restless and finger-jabbing energy — who talked best on his feet — came around the table, to take the photograph into his hands: he gave his tribute gladly, to the beauty, the strength, and the potential mystery of the girl. We were happy, on the instant, to jettison the original, and rather dubious, pretext for our visit: we would draw breath, wait, follow whatever announced itself to us. If we did not impose the reflex inhibitions of disbelief, we would surely come, without strain, to the heart of the tale. We no longer believed in "Spitalfields" as a concept: in "zones of transition," New Georgians, "the deal," or any of that exhausted journalistic stuff. We had something much better: a story we did not understand. It is always much more enjoyable to play at detectives than at "researchers," who gather the evidence to justify the synopsis they have already sold.

The girl, on her knees, arms thrown back, was a dancer. She was affecting some kind of Isadora Duncan, swan-raped, *Noh* swoon: demonstrating both her "inner stillness" and the power she exercised over her body. If there *had* been an assistant, he (or she) had lit the undecorated set to the key of the disturbing mood the dancer was insisting on: the self-exposure was posthumous, and fiercely erotic. She lay upon a memorial slab, the chrome maquette of a notorious torture baron. We could do nothing at all to get closer, either to this presentation, or to the girl herself: the implied narrative. It was too late to withdraw. Our interest was aroused, feverish. We would have to wait. Take whatever Roland chose to give us. It couldn't be forced. Now there was a streak of tension to fracture the restored empathy of the underground Huguenot kitchen. No florid and sentimental inscription defaced the photograph. It could have been sold in its thousands, sepia-tinted, a gaiety postcard; but we were convinced this was the only surviving copy. We were also convinced we would have to travel back through the dancer's grainy window to enter the story she had already persuaded us to demand from her.

Roland, returning with a tray, set it down on the table, assumed Fredrik's abandoned chair and — unprompted — told us about his friend, Edith Cadiz, the dancer. She was originally, he supposed — the matter was never discussed — an unconvinced Canadian. He didn't blame her for that. He'd never met any other kind. But it did leave an ineradicable trace, the faintest whiff of bear grease; and a clear-eyed, un-English humor to qualify her almost masculine assertion of self. You noticed next the unnatural smoothness of her body: the smoothness of the professional performer. The fierce options she enforced on her body only stressed the essentially private nature of her quest. She recognized the same loneliness in Roland, the same pattern of wounds. They were alone because they would not compromise the defiance of their solitude. They had been touched, and often, and would continue to be touched; but they would never drop that shield of protective charm. They cultivated the closeness of orphans, or revolutionary comrades in exile; making no demands on each other; seeing each other accidentally, for — much prized — afternoons of gossip and silence.

Edith came to this country, modestly funded, with money her mother saw as a final payoff: she settled in Palliser Road, Baron's Court — a piece of ground given back to a squabble of more or less house-trained colonials, as being otherwise unfit for human habitation. She embarked, enthusiastically, on the usual acting, modeling and waitressing courses that she was far too intelligent, and singular, to complete. She was not without ego, and a certain talent for showing off; but she preferred not to demonstrate her capabilities, while some anthropoid agent's hairy chain-gang paw crawled up her skirts. It wasn't so much that she felt her virtue was worth more than a couple of bottles of Retsina: she wearied of the invariable bullshit surrounding this banal and ugly transaction. They never said, "Fuck me and I'll get you the Royal Court." The fatherly monologues were so repetitive, so punctuated with sincere smiles, and confidence-inducing pats on the thigh. They could have been put on disk: (a) boastful lists of possessions, (b) holiday yarns, (c) ingratitude of former clients, (d) venality of producers, (e) excellent prospects of increased earning capacity, (f) desirability for prolonged discussion in more congenial environment.

Neither was Edith keen to transform herself into a sunsilk bimbo, gagging on rampant chocolate-coated members, and conducting furtive assignations with a jar of coffee. She didn't want to pick up brownie points hanging around holes in the ground with Peggy Ashcroft and Ian McKellen, or picket embassies to get the parts that Julie Christie turned down. She wanted to be left alone to discover the limits of what she could become. She wanted to relish performance for its own sake, to use her power to the full — because that, more than anything else, gave her satisfaction.

Roland, as he explained, had not initially been involved with whatever it was she was working on. She called around for a cup of tea. She chatted with Mother. She ate Roland's biscuits. Sometimes she slept for two or three nights in Fournier Street. And then, out of the blue, one August morning, she knocked on the street-door, and invited Roland to come and see her show. She was leading a dog on a chain: a heavy-pelted wolf cousin, a male. Roland went with her. The show was amazing: ferocious, insulting, funny. And performed in the most unlikely — and previously resistant — setting: the Seven Stars, Brick Lane.

Our current obsession with colonizing the past — as the only place where access is free — had made available, courtesy of the Borough Library, a collection of reproduction maps of East London: gaudy fakes to authenticate any cocktail bar. They were inexpensive, printed on stiff card; with roads, the color of dried mustard, sprouting from the empurpled lamb's heart of the City. You could walk your fingers in imaginary journeys, and sneeze from the real dust that you disturbed. The Thames was alive; a slithering green serpent, a cramp in the belly.

Edith's particular favorite was *Laurie & Whittle's New Map of London with its Environs, including the Recent Improvements 1819*. And she had constructed, with paste and heavy needle, a costume shaped from this map: part Edward Gordon Craig, part Maori kite-bird — a feathered storm-disperser. Wearing it, she became an angel of threat; or a demon of bliss. She respected the traditional accoutrements of her trade — the cloak, the gloves, the boots, the thong — but she elaborated their shape, the angle of the shoulders, the constriction of the waist, until she turned herself into a living artifact, a weapon. She played with her makeup: her slightest movement provoked a paradoxical reading of the history of the patch of ground on which her audience were standing. She was increasingly absorbed, excited. Color printers in Wilson Street provided enlargements of especially libidinous zones: *The Victualling Office, Sugar Loaf Green, Callico Houses, Morning Lane.*

But before she appeared in her "special" costume, Edith Cadiz attacked them with a dance that was savage in its invitation. She was naked, too soon; shuddering and leaping, with no accompaniment, to wild sounds of her own invention. She laughed in their faces. She flashed them with spiders and rods of iron. She showed them wounds they knew they would inherit; then forced them back against the walls, by spinning pebbles of fear. The attention of the punters was fully engaged: they were unsexed, wary. It was what they had come for, but it was not right. Dry-mouthed, they could not swallow their beer.

After the subdued interval, in which they were able to recover their identities, Edith walked among them, collecting her tithe. They had paid, so they looked at her, and over her — as they had the courage for it: they made jokes. She was naked still, her smoothness glistened with pearly beads. There was a heat and a honey-sweetness on her. Two points — where high cheekbones stretched her face into a mask — had been pinched into color; otherwise, she was pale, stiff, without animation. She shook out her hair. They dropped their furtive coins into an alopecic and grease-stained bowler.

The tension is broken. Conversation revives. Edith tells the publican that her hat once belonged to T.S. Eliot. He thinks she is alluding to the "Chocolate-colored Coon," and suspects that the hat is illegal, contraband: "worth a few bob." He is almost tempted to make an offer.

For the second half of the show, Edith does not move at all: a wartime Windmill nude, exposed to a ring of "breathers," their knees heaving and bumping beneath rubberized police-issue raincoats. She wears her costume of maps. There are rings sewn to districts that have previously been cut so they will tear away, at a touch. Heard from the street, the sound of the audience is elongated and alarming. They are out of control. They feel their tongues being slowly split with rusty shears.

Edith Cadiz invites her sweating jackals to sing out the street names: *Heneage, Chicksand, Woodseer, Thrawl, Mulberry.* She gives them a voice to relieve their tension. And — if they nominate a name that has been prepared — her wolf-dog leaps from the

263

audience, rushes to her, takes the brass ring in his wet mouth, and pulls away a Spitalfields terrace with a twist of his powerful neck. The jagged gap reveals new streets, fresh relations: Edenic glimpses. The tired city is transformed: a dustpit fades to expose an orchard, a church lifts through a sandbank, a hospital (with blazing windows) slides beneath the surface of a slow-moving river. The punters are maddened. The Thames attacks Hornsey. Leadenhall Market removes to Chingford.

The affair was too rich and strange. It was talked about, but it was not popular. They felt safer with the black leather bike-girls, cracking whips in their faces; and the others, the contortionists whose trick muscles could suck coins out of the sawdust, without using their mouths or hands. Edith was left alone on stage, in a scatter of torn paper. She was bruised and scratched by the dog's claws, his slavering enthusiasm. Some of the color had run with her sweat: it was moving over her shoulders, down across her belly. Her wounds were an urban survey, promoting fresh deltas and rivulets, revitalizing dead hamlets, soon to be linked by fantastic railways of silver and bronze: animal-headed marvels, belching fire. She had succeeded; but she was not sure what that meant. She found herself, suddenly and dangerously, prophetic.

Roland too had witnessed something forbidden: something he could not shrive by making a report of it. Without malign intent, he left the fatal black spot in my hands.

II

A couple of weeks later, hustled by his producers, Fredrik rang me. We arranged to meet for a drink in the Chesham Arms, Mehetabel Road, Hackney: just down the ramp from Sutton House, a genuine but well-disguised Tudor manor that had probably survived thanks to the obscurity of its location. "They" had not yet decided which motorway would bury it. The planners assumed this weather-boarded relic was another bankrupt mock-Tudor sandwich bar, and they left it alone: "Turn that one over to the Pest Squad, Ron!" The building was sealed, and guarded by a depressed gaggle of ghosts and clinically reticent poltergeists. It burst into life, infrequently, as opposing factions argued about its purpose, or jemmied away the skirting boards to reveal — in triumph — stubs of rat-gnawed chalk or some defunct grammarian's detention exercises. Both parties would fervently claim these rodent droppings as the evidence that clinched the very case they were attempting to prove. Then the whole business would sink back once more into perpetual limbo.

We made it to the bar on the stroke of opening time, getting our drinks in, before the place was invaded by a scream of grim-faced "alternative comedians"— the alternative, I suppose, would consist of being funny — who "wrote" nose-picking duologues for a pair of infamous vodka-swilling slobs. These dyspeptic businessmen nerved themselves to face the odd TV "special," enough to keep their images polished for the advertising slots that provided most of their real income. They gazed in naked envy at the queens of "Voice Over," with their villas in Tuscany; and they gritted their teeth over the video empires of clapped-out stand-up comics, who could now afford the best psychotherapy that money could buy. But the nerve-jangling hell of sitting for an hour, trapped in the back of a cab, while the failed "Mastermind" at the wheel performed his audition, made them wonder if the street-cred of an office in Hackney was worth the candle. Their bosses, compulsively overachieving bonzos, subtly emphasized their superior status by dressing in a gross parody of City uniforms. We hold the equity, brothers. And don't, for one minute, forget it. Charcoal-gray suits, with silk linings, the color of rancid ice cream; no ties. An uneasy compromise between wide-nostriled insider-dealer and scrap-metal show-off, cased up for the dogs. The pack shuffled and sparred around the two luminaries, spitting and swearing, trying to look as if they had just boogied in off a building site, in their trainers, dirty socks, and shaving-foam basketball boots. The benzedrine thrust of their social vision demanded a constant spray of obscenities, aimed exclusively at other television programs; and a dozen imbecile schemes to resurrect the Tottenham Hotspur midfield by importing a brace of "total footballers," whose names they could neither remember nor pronounce. But this did not inhibit them from chanting these names, loudly, as they topped each other in flights of absurdity and pretension: until the affair lost all focus, erupting into a face-slapping, foot-stamping, "knee-him-in-the-nuts, Sidney" squabble. They were ejected. "A good working lunch" would be the favorite description: "creative tension." They stood around on the curb, filling out forms to claim their expenses, and composing complicated requests, to be delivered by mini cab from the Mare Street deli. They were ready to recharge their batteries. The best of them were snoring on the pavement, as they waited for the fleet to arrive.

We had the bar to ourselves. Fredrik was evidently experiencing some difficulty in recalling what we were doing here. He never had fewer than twelve projects on the boil at the same time; pacifying demented, near-suicidal producers, not by delivering his script, but by suggesting, over a three-hour lunch, ever more wondrous possibilities: glittering ratings-winners, replete with intellectual and moral credibility, certain to confirm reputation and make, as an incidental by-product, fortunes. But he needed time, "seed money," equipment, secretaries. He'd go to his grave, pelted in a hailstorm of writs.

Excited, making notes for an article on whisky labels, and another on pub telephones, Fredrik broke off: to slide the neighborhood fright sheet across the table. There were a couple of paras about a missing nurse, last seen on the platform at Homerton, now presumed to be another victim of the "Railway Vampire." This was unexceptional, a mild filler; the equivalent of a Flower Show critique. It was buried among the ranks of block-headline teasers: MAN LOSES EYE IN ACID ATTACK; EPILEPTIC RAPED DURING FIT; GUARD JAILED FOR SEX WITH DAUGHTERS; ARMED SWOOP ON EMPTY HOUSE. An interesting form of "new journalism" was developing, uncredited, in these local weeklies: a calculated splicing together of the most surreal samples of proletarian life, with an ever-expanding, color-enhanced section on property speculation. ENJOY FACILITIES OF DOCKLANDS; INVESTMENT OPPORTUNITY; FIRST TIME RELEASE, ONLY MINUTES FROM THE CITY! ONE MILE FROM CITY . . . 800 YARDS FROM BISHOPSGATE. The provocation is stark: throw open your windows, you can pee into the river.

But the horror tales — BLACK THUGS WITH HOME-MADE SPIKED BALL AND CHAIN RUN AMOK ON TERROR TRAIN — serve another, more sinister, purpose: they drive out the crumblies, the garden cultivators, to the forest clearings, to Loughton, to Ongar, or the poulticed mudflats of the Thames Estuary, the ultimate boneyards of Essex. More Victorian family homes, strong on "character," and low on plumbing, are released onto a greedy market. Hardboiled feminist crime writers, and stringers for *City Limits*, peddle across town, from Camden and Muswell Hill, to take up the slack. "Baroque realists," and tame voyeurs fixated on entropy, tremble in paroxysms of excitement and distaste. There hasn't been such *hot* material lying around in the streets since they nobbled public hangings and bear baiting. Suddenly, we're all Henry Mayhew and Jack London. It's — *shudder* — unbelievable, terrible. We rush to our word processors, the hotline to Channel 4. We're going to get the lead story, with photograph, in the *London Review of Books*.

Fredrik's wife, a lady of great charm, wise enough to prepare herself for Hackney life with two or three liberal arts degrees, and a wicked sense of humor, was now a psychiatric consultant at the Hackney Hospital: this being the only kind they went in for. She had, Fredrik explained, recognized the snapshot of the nurse that accompanied the story of the railway vanishing act in the *Gazette*. The girl's name was Edith. Edith Cordoba? Edith Drake? She couldn't remember. But she wasn't English. She was sure of that. East Coast American? Wore expensive shoes. Had worked in the hospital for almost a year, which constituted some kind of record. And she wasn't even on Valium, with Noveril chasers.

Could it be? Edith Cadiz a nurse? It was time to visit this hospital, to trace the infected fantasy to its source. Fredrik knew where some of the bodies were buried. He had been working around here shooting standard-issue inner-city squalor that could be assembled fast to provide a poverty-row backup for a "major Statement" that a "Very Important Personage" wanted to deliver, at peak viewing time, to his future subjects. "One" had been suffering lately from a rather disquieting sensation that "something ought to be done." His uncle felt much the same way about South Wales. Much good had it done him. Or them. A lecture was even now being hammered out by half the unemployed architects in the country, who could — under the protection of the blue-blooded ecologist — safely savage the half who *had* managed to climb off the drawing board.

I left Fredrik to his task; blowing foam into the pub phone, while he sold a potential essay to Germany, analyzing . . . the reformist uses of the very instrument he was now clutching in a stranglehold. "Discontinued alternatives," he was screaming, while he waited for a simultaneous translation. I would adopt my usual method, and circumnavigate the hospital walls; see what the stones had to say.

The hospital site covered ancient parkland, and might yet be profitably developed. It had, in the meantime, been designated the dumping ground for all the swamp-field crazies, the ranters, the ultimate referrals. Leave here, and there is only the river. The shakers were swept in — or delivered themselves, gibbering, at the gates: they were rapidly tranquilized, liquid-coshed, and given a painted door to contemplate. The only other ticket of admittance led, by way of the left-hand path, to the Drug Dependency Unit; which attempted, by methods traditional and experimental, to wean the helpless and the hopeless from their sugary addictions. The main thrust of this enterprise — stilling the inarticulate voice of rage — merely created a host of new, and more exploitable, addictions. Only the pharmacists and the Swiss turned a dollar. The wicked old days of brain-burning and skull-excavation (with soiled agricultural instruments) were a folk-memory. That machinery was too expensive to replace. A wimpish revulsion against water treatments led, logically, to the gradual suspension of all bath-house activities. Whole wings were simply abandoned to nature; eagerly exploited by rodents, squatters — and smack dealers who traded their scripts without quitting the sanctuary of the hospital enclave.

Looking up from the east end of Victoria Park, or out of a shuddering train, the hospital was minatory and impressive: a castle of doom. The endless circuit of its walls betrayed no secret entrances. Window slits flickered with nervous strip lighting. Grimy muslin strips muted any forbidden glimpses of the interior: recycled bandages. The steep slate roofs were made ridiculous by a flock of iron curlicues.

An increasingly anorexic budget was dissipated in child-sex questionnaires, plague warnings, and reports (in six languages) justifying the cleaning and catering contracts. The nurses, to survive, established their own private kingdoms. The doctors kept their heads down, writing papers for the *Lancet* that might catch the eye of some multinational talent scout. Better Saudi, or Houston, than this besieged stockade. They sampled, with reckless courage, bumper cocktails from their own stock cupboards.

My circuit was complete. I was back where I had started: in Homerton High Street. I had discovered nothing. My notebook was scrawled with gnomic doodles that might, at some future date, be worked into a jaunty polemic. Of the dancer, there was no trace. I would return. And I would be armed with a camera. Without a blush of shame, I was starting to enjoy myself.

III

Edith Cadiz had never felt so much at her ease. She found herself, for the first time in her life, "disappearing into the present." There

268

was a physical lift of pleasure each morning, as she climbed the sharply tilted street from Homerton Station. The day was not long enough. She ran the palms of her hands against the warmth trapped in the bricks: she grazed them, lightly. She held her breath, relishing to the full the rashers of moist cloud in the broken windows of the East Wing. Often she stayed on her feet for twelve hours, not taking the meal breaks that were her due. She was absorbed in the horrors that confronted her. No human effort could combat them. Ambulances clanged up the High Street: security barriers lifting and falling, like a starved guillotine. This was a world that Edith had previously known as a persistent, but remote, vision: a microcosm city. There was nothing like it in her reclaimed Canadian wilderness: an impenetrable heart, with its broken cogs, shattered wheels, and stuttering drive-belts. Her dispersed mosaic of dreams allowed these damaged machine parts to escape from "place" and into time. The victims, vanished within the hospital walls, grew smooth with loss. They nibbled, or voided themselves in distraction, staring at, but *not* out of, narrow pillbox windows. They were all—the tired metaphor came to her—in the same boat: drifting, orphaned by circumstances, unable to justify the continuing futility of their existence.

And it was endless: floor after floor, deck after deck—unfenced suffering. There was no pause in her labor; nothing to achieve. It could never satisfy her. Faces above sheets: amputated from the social body. They did not know what they were asking. They took all her gifts, and put no name to them. The shape of her hands around a glass of water held no meaning.

Each nurse laid claim to some part of the building as territory that she could control: imposing her own rules, her own fantasies. It might be a special chair dragged into a broom cupboard. It might be a cup and saucer, instead of the institutional mug. It might be a favored cushion, or a color photograph cut from a magazine, presenting some immaculate white linen table on a terrace overlooking a vineyard: *Provence, Samos, Gozo,* the *Algarve.*

Edith made her decision. She rescued all the children she found lost within the inferno of the wards. They were not always easy to recognize. Some pensioners had discovered the secret of eternal youth. They shone: without blame. They remembered events, and believed they were happening for the first time. They entered chambers of memory from which no shock could move them. They were small and unscratched: they learned to make themselves insignificant. But some children were fit to pass directly into the senile wards, never having experienced puberty or adult life. They were overcome, shrunken, shriveled; hidden behind unblinking porcelain eyes. Most did not speak. They should not have been there. They were waiting to be moved on, "relocated." Their papers were lost. Some were uncontrolled, hurtling against the walls, on a hawser of wild electricity. They would leap and tear and shout, spit obscenities. They would punch her. Or cling, and stick against her skirts, burrs: huge heads pressed painfully against her thighs. One child would lie for hours at her feet, and be dead. Another barked like an abused dog.

The room that Edith commandeered in a remote, and now shunned, south-facing tower gamely aped one of those seaside hotels, built in the 1930s, to pastiche the glamour of a blue-ribbon ocean liner. There were wooden handrails, and a salty curved window overlooking the sparkling tributary of the railway that ran from Hackney, through Homerton, to the canceled village of Hackney Wick — and on, in the imagination of the idlers, across the marshes to Stratford, to Silvertown, to the graveyard of steam engines at North Woolwich. Another more stable vision was also there for the taking: security systems, tenement blocks, pubs, breakers' yards, a Catholic outstation with albino saints and blackberry-lipped virgins, and the green-rim sanctuary of Victoria Park.

For a week Edith swept and scrubbed, polished and painted. She stole food and begged for toys and books. She was determined to impose a formal regime; to re-create a High Victorian Dame School. She wanted canvas maps, sailing boats, new yellow pencils, wide bowls of exotic fruit. She wanted music. Their strange thin voices drifting out over the hidden yards and storehouses. Her stolen children, playing at something, came — by degrees — to accept its reality. They were boarders, sent from distant colonies, to learn "the English way." They were no longer solitary: they were a troop. They even, covertly, took exercise. They left the hospital: walking down the Hill in a mad, mutually clinging crocodile, over the Rec to the Marshes. They were too frightened to breathe: not deviating, by one inch, from the white lines on the football pitches — climbing over obstacles, cracking corner-flags, tramping through dog shit. They huddled, a lost tribe, under massive skies. The rubble of prewar London was beneath their feet. They walked over streets whose names had been obliterated. They could have dived down through the grass into escarpments of medieval brickwork;

corner shops, tin churches, prisons, markets, tiled swimming pools. On the horizon were the bright orange tents of the summer visitors, the Dutch and the Germans who processed in a remorseless circuit between the shower-block and their VW campers.

Over the months, Edith coaxed the children toward language. Or shocked it from them: in tears, and in fits of laughter. The railway passengers noticed this single window, blazing with light.

Other unlocated souls made themselves known to her. Orwin Fairchilde, cushion-cheeked, chemically castrated, had been turned out of the ward as "insufficiently disturbed": he could not escape its pull. He pretended to be part of the queue of outpatients that formed early at the gates: a queue from which never more than one or two highly strung potential travelers hauled themselves aboard any vehicle foolish enough to slow down. Cars kept their doors and windows locked. The other loiterers remained — until dusk fell — leaning against the hospital wall; picking up sheets of old newspaper, greeting unknown friends, or screaming challenges at imaginary enemies. The queue was perpetual and self-generating: an unfunded "halfway house" between the hospital and the insanity of the world at large. The people who mattered offered a loud "*Yo!*" to Orwin's oracular question: "Are you in the queue, man?"

Orwin polished his bottle-glass spectacles on his shirt-tails. Then he set up his elaborate, but eccentric, sound system. He Scotch-taped his sheet music to the side of a bus shelter, and dived, scowling, into "Greensleeves." He plucked at the strings of an Aria-Pro (II) electric guitar — as if he was extracting porcupine spines from his bulging thigh. The noise was hellish. He sealed his eyes, and entered some dim cave of absolute concentration.

It became a ritual of Edith's to take Orwin for a drink in the Spread Eagle on her way to the station. He would roll a cigarette and offer it to her. She would refuse, and offer him a drink: which he, in his turn, declined — on religious grounds. He spoke about the Ethiopian Saints who had lost themselves in this City of Sin; but who would certainly acknowledge Orwin as a fellow spirit, by spotting the coded note-sequences in his music. The Saints left messages for him in books. But, of course, the libraries would not let him get his hands on them, claiming that he could not read. The teachers had all been bribed to keep him in ignorance.

Dr. Adam Tenbrücke also spent time as a temporary guest of the hospital. He had been found, weeping and shaking, running his

271

head at the door of a warehouse-gallery on the perimeter of London Fields, which featured, at the time, a chamber flooded with sump oil. This was instantly optioned by the Saatchis. The owner, a claque of tame critics and a few jealous hangers-on rushed outside, squawking, "Did Doris ring?"—bursting to break the news to any passing drifters. They tumbled, in a heap, over Tenbrücke, who was rocking back on his heels, imitating a blind monkey. Smelling the weirdness of "real" money, the owner dragged him inside.

Tenbrücke pointedly refused to sign his name in the Visitors' Book, and would speak only in German. The Gallery Man, now suspecting the devious hand of the encamped "travelers," rang for the snatch-squad—who were only too happy to tranquilize the gibbering doctor with their truncheons. He was delivered—a knot of terror—to the reception cages. He would talk of nothing but suicide. "I'm drowning in filth," he whispered. In other words, he was depressingly normal. He sounded like a politician. They frisked him, hit him with enough stuff to stop a runaway horse, and turned him loose. He tore off his clothes and—howling Aryan marching songs—stumbled down Marsh Hill. He walked back to Limehouse Basin along the River Lea: white, and fat, and stark naked. But he went unmolested; just another long-distance health freak jogging into obscurity.

It was still quite possible to survive on a nurse's salary; but not to eat, to travel, to take decisions over your own life. Therefore, most of the nurses moonlighted as cleaners, or as barmaids. Even their uniforms were rented—warmed by their bodies—to a drinking club on the Stoke Newington borders, where they were worn, with minimal adjustments, by hostesses who catered to a certifiably specialist clientele.

But it was the opening of the Dalston/Kingsland to Whitechapel rail link that granted Edith's continued presence at the hospital an economic viability. Now, at the end of her working day, she could take the North London line to Dalston, change, and step out within half an hour on Whitechapel High Street. Time to read, once again, her faded pink copy of *The Four Quartets*. "*And so each venture / Is a new beginning, a raid on the inarticulate . . .*" The generous arches and lamps of the London Hospital penetrated the gloom like a Viennese opera house. Edith slipped Mr. Eliot back into her raincoat pocket.

The balance was achieved. Edith Cadiz could nurse by day, and supplement her earnings by unselective prostitution at night;

"blowing" the priapic haulers, who were working out the last days of the Spitalfields Vegetable Market. It would be simplistic to suggest that Edith's was a mechanical response to circumstantial poverty. The twist was more complex: if she was unable to live as a nurse, she was also unable to live as a prostitute. The attractions of these twinned survival modes were quite different. They were separate but equal. In both theaters of risk, Edith was involved with external demand systems that gave her unexpected courage and fed her dramatic sense of self. The risks she took brought to life a scenario in which she could not quite believe that she participated. She maintained, to the end, an inviolate sense of silence. The emissions of the lorry drivers, she trusted, would somehow engender language for the mute children, safely secreted in their ruined tower.

Edith was an unusual person.

IV

The great shame, and dishonor, of the present regime is its failure to procure a decent opposition. Never have there been so many complacent dinner parties, from Highbury to Wandsworth Common, rehearsing their despair: a wilderness of quotations and anecdotes. "My dear," a Camden Passage "screamer" smirked, as I cleared a few boxes of inherited books from his cellar, "we never get asked to Mayfair any more — it's always Hackney. Wherever that is." Writers were glutted on hard-edged images of blight. They gobbled and spat, in their race to be first to preview the quips that would surface in next week's *Statesman;* or to steal, from some Town Hall booby, statistics to lend credence to a *Guardian* profile. Literary bounty hunters — bounced publishers, and the like — scouted out-of-print anthologies for any Eastern European poets, in wretched health, who had not yet been "targeted" for an obituary. They fell over each other to finger these deservedly forgotten scribblers at thirty pounds a hit.

And if the Spitalfields weaver's loft, or the country house, wistfully rendered in a mouthwash of Piper twilight, staggered on as icons of a vanquished civilization, then the fire-blackened cityscape of the Blitz was the setting increasingly invoked by the barbarians of the free market. Exquisitely made-up young ladies tottered out on Saturday mornings to hawk the *Socialist Worker*, for an hour, outside Sainsbury's. Duty done, they nipped inside to stock up on pâté, gruyère, olives, French bread and Frascati for an alfresco committee meeting. The worse things got, the more we rubbed our hands. We were safely removed from any possibility of power: blind rhetoric without responsibility. Essays, spiked with venom, were the talk of the common rooms. Meddlesome clerics fought for the pulpit. The most savage (and the wittiest) practitioners were never free from the telephone. Review copies clattered onto the mat, obsequiously eager to face the treatment. TV lunches were grim as public floggings. Government narcs listened at every door. Nobody wanted it to end. Jerome Bosch art-directed the steaming imagery. It was positively Spanish: Index, Inquisition, *Auto-da-Fé*. Nobody wanted to be the one to hammer the first stake through this absence of a heart. We'd have nothing to write about, except ley lines and unexplained circles among the crops.

The "Standing Member," Meic Triscombe — a stoop-shouldered, flat-footed, arm-flailing shambler, whose delicate porcine features were lost in the barren disk of his face — haunted his electoral boundaries like the Witchfinder-General. His nose, a detumescent erection, twitched after conspiracies, winks in the council chamber, wobbly handshakes. He favored quarrelsome lime-striped shirts; always untucked, fanning out behind him; quite loud enough to set the dogs barking, and causing women to miscarry in the streets. Asthmatic — and allergic to almost all life-forms — he gasped and sneezed, turning his frailty to advantage, by pretending to be overcome by emotion: a Shakespearean soliloquy of pity for the human condition. Choking and spluttering, he drenched his audience in a spray of peppermint-tasting mucus, desperately running the sleeve of his blazer across his watery eyes. There was no other calling in which he could parade his disabilities in such a favorable light. On the telephone he could be genuinely alarming. And had been reported several times as a pervert.

His constituents — or unemployment statistics, as he thought of them — were bow-legged, small-skulled, foul-mouthed, impertinent; fff-ing rapid-fire dirges of complaint, out of the corners of mouths tilted into half-zipped wounds. Triscombe could not bend low enough — an old rugby injury — to make out what they said. His slight hearing difficulty, mostly a buildup of cerumen rammed into the external auditory meatus with the tip of his black Biro, was an aristocratic trait, and no hindrance in the chamber: he thought of Harold Macmillan. As did so many others, now that the old confidence-man was safely removed from the scene. Triscombe did not need to sift the words of the fellaheen; he was their voice. He could articulate their primitive and amorphic wails for attention. On their behalf, he dined on rumors, played squash at a City health club; denounced scandals he was too late to get in on. He thought of himself as the "people's tribune" and he lived among them. Or, at least, *reasonably* adjacent to them. While he waited for his personal *Belgrano* to cruise down the Hertford Union Canal.

His wife, estranged, and with a cast-iron investment portfolio behind her, refused to set foot in the grime of East London. The property Triscombe acquired in a partly renovated Early Victorian Square (okayed by John Betjeman), within safe hailing distance of the Islington borders, lease signed three weeks before the election, had proved a decent enough speculation when he "let it go" six months later — well before "Black Monday." These large crumbling mansions, built for sober city magnates, had given refuge, in the era of Wilsonian Social Democracy, to some of the more acceptable — and only distantly related — members of that premature Free Market combo, the notorious "Firm": before the tower blocks marched in like triffids. The square, a quadrangle of submerged aspirations and cringing modesty, now preened itself on an actively "ruralist" identity. It was a village under siege from marauding misfits, razor-gangs, crack dealers, and fast-breeding aliens. The gentle bohemian newcomers of the 1960s uprooted the comfrey and the cannabis, persuaded someone to take on the cleaning lady, and took flight into the silicon-chip countryside; draining, in the process, the last dregs of their inherited capital. Sadly, this was the ultimate shuffle of the brewery shares. Their homes, now seen as a solid "first step on the ladder," passed into the hands of food-photographers, marine insurance trouble-shooters, rising tele actors going into their second Stoppard, and Bengalis shifting from supermarket chains to oil percentages.

Triscombe took his profit and went east, to the summit of the Ant Hill. When in doubt, climb. The nude temptations of worldly power: he loved to look down on the beaten spread of the Borough and say, "All this is mine!" There was a reborn credibility in stashing himself among the photogenic ruins of Homerton: it added considerable color to his CV. A satellite development had been jobbed onto the shabby grandeur that clung to the coat-tails of Sutton House. The estate's title was worked in flourishes of wrought iron into the entrance gates, like something out of *Citizen Kane.*

Security guards, a nice blend of ex-para and ex-Parkhurst, patrolled the walkways, Moorish arches and plashing fountains of this neo-Alhambra. The tower of St. John of Hackney rose proud above the camera-scanned walls, with intimations of vanished Templar glory. The panoramic view towards Leytonstone was not so hot: a set of low-rise blocks, let in by the planners on the dubious grounds that at least they were not high-rise blocks. These were the ultimate *barrios* of despair, and behind them lifted a futuristic silver tube: the burning chimney of the Hackney Hospital, belching forth mistakes, ex-humans and assorted bandaged filth.

Meic Triscombe was a shire-horse among whippets. Red ears pricked for multinational conspiracies, tongue like a dagger, equine teeth set to savage the "Secret State" Whitehall plotters: a stallion of wrath! He stamped and snorted; he reared up. He also tended, rather too frequently for comfort, to fall down; so that one, or more, of his limbs was perpetually clad in plaster. An ardent all-night debate on the abolition of the ILEA caused him to tumble the length of a spiral staircase in the terrace house of a female member of his steering committee, cradling in his arms a not-quite-empty bottle of Southern Comfort. A barstool shattered under the sudden imposition of his weight, leaving its shrapnel in his left buttock, while he was denouncing the iniquity of a system that permitted whispering nocturnal trainloads of uranium waste to pass unchallenged through "Nuclear Free" Hackney. He suffered an attack of acute food-poisoning, with attendant sweats, cramps and trumpeting flatulence, on a "fact-finding" tour of ethnic restaurants between Lower Clapton and Green Lanes. Meic Triscombe was not unknown to the Hackney Hospital. A procession of mini cabs heaved him out at the gates, where "security" told him, firmly, to try elsewhere. They had no facilities for dealing with accidents, emergencies, amputations, inebriations, childbirth, chewed-off ears, grievous bodily harms or spontaneous combustions; or, indeed, anyone at all who was not actually frothing at the mouth, bug-eyed and belted into restraint like an "Old Kingdom" mummy.

So it was that the stallion, Triscombe, became one of Edith Cadiz's lambs: another unrecognized messenger found babbling on the pavement. He limped across Homerton High Street, leaning heavily on her shoulders, to the Adam and Eve, for a pick-me-up, a bottle or so of medicinal cognac. His eye, guileless aesthete, admired the relief carvings above the pub entrance — a naked couple, daring divine retribution — while his fingers, unoriginal sinners, tried to sneak a touch at Edith's nipple. It wasn't just the liberating effect of firewater on his sweat glands: Triscombe was amazed to discover that Edith did not need to be seduced by gusts of Bevanite eloquence. Neither did she succumb to the vapors on his moral high ground. This time he did not have to present himself as "the Last Socialist out-of-captivity": the hotshot cocksman who had never sold out. Tears filled his eyes as he spoke of the miners, the hunger marches, the lockouts. Edith yawned. She wouldn't be shamed into surrender. She was willing: this clown was the agent of fate she had been waiting to snare.

But Triscombe, saturated in the hypocrisy of his calling, was congenitally incapable of taking "yes" for an answer. Puppy-eager, he tongued her neck, as he pitched an over-familiar yarn about the slime deals that would see the hospital razed to make way for yet another "riverside opportunity." Even if it took a clear day and a powerful periscope to find the river in question. It was an accepted natural law that any piece of ground overlooking a puddle of water — river, canal, sewer or open-plan cesspit — would be a golden handshake for a speculative builder: "minutes from the City, offering all the advantages of country life." The government's public-relations machine had very effectively stolen all this water imagery from its traditional proletarian base. The canal bank had served, from the Social Realists of the 1930s to Alex Trocchi's *Young Adam*, as a dour backdrop for relationships poisoned by industrial dereliction. Now, in the coming blush of privatization, water is declared to be "sexy."

Edith required no such dialectic. She took Triscombe's drink. And she asked him how much money he had. *"How much money?"*

Triscombe's mounting excitement tangled him more completely into his usual state of impotence. The horse of panic. He was about to break something. The barmaid shifted a religious statuette out of reach. The landlord shrouded his parrot. "How much money?" Trembling, he started to turn out his capacious pockets. She did not mean that: the petty cash for a knee-shaker under the viaduct. She meant *income*, stock-points, retainers, kickbacks, research contracts, leaks to the *Eye*. Could he afford her — *on a regular basis*? Would she fit, snugly, on to the payroll? Because that was all that mattered. To clear, for her own exclusive use, an uninfected stretch of time.

What Triscombe actually wanted, when they returned to his impersonal apartment, was difficult to speak about, to spell out in precise detail. Edith waited, legs tucked under her, in a bucket-chair, running her fingers, caressingly, through the golden muff that hung under the belly of Triscombe's alsatian: the guardian that slept at her feet. Guarding against what? Special Branch, "The Company," Mossad, MI5, MI6? The Widow's favorite chalk-monitors, Ad Hoc Splinter Groups, spooks, wire-tappers? The fellaheen hordes, black gypsy petrol-bombers, Iranian fanatic Jews tooled with castrating shears? Trotskyites, the Red Brigade? Lesbian rapists? This dog, he felt — and he wanted Edith to feel it too — had absorbed most of his own masculine virtues: by close association. The beast manifested his warrior soul: it represented his power, but without the inhibitions of his public standing.

Edith soon understood *exactly* what Triscombe wanted, but she remained perfectly relaxed, detached: there was so much time waiting to be paid for in this room. She would not burn it. Let him get there when he would. She understood that this would be one of the most effective acts of theater she had been able to conjure. It was truly monstrous, and also quite simple. She would involve herself in a performance that was, by statute, criminal and degrading; mythic in its blasphemy. She would devour the substance and the essence of taboo — with the bulging, pleading eyes of the instigator following her every movement: the paradigm of an audience. It was Triscombe's vision; he was its victim. She wanted to make an account of this. To repeat the act in language, to perfect and refine it. She slid a notebook from her handbag and started to write.

White-cheeked and musty, Triscombe faced her, his back arched against the wall. A thick blue vein was pulsing on the side of his head, like a worm digging its way out. She thought he might be sick. His breath smelled like wet rope. She spoke to him reassuringly, softly, outlining her demands. "A standing order": the phrase made her smile. A sum, calculated on the spur of the moment, to be paid, monthly, into her account. A selection of Deer Brand black notebooks with red cloth corners. Some Japanese drawing pens. A watercolor by John Bellany that she had always coveted. Afternoons.

Anything. Absolutely. He agreed. His hands were palsied. He had lived with this image since boyhood. Its safety was that it remained an image. Therefore, he was human. Therefore, he could denounce the corruption of the world. Man's man, people's tribune — stallion of the virtues. But now this woman was starting to act it out. *Jesus Christ, the curtains!* In a fever, he checked them. Edith Cadiz was

278

sinking, very slowly, stretching on the floor with the dog, who was turning, waking, yawning his meat yawn. Teased, he growled, and showed his teeth. Edith unzipped her dress. Triscombe was trans-fixed, a stone man. He no longer wanted any of this. It was agony to him. Edith draped the dog's head in red silk. It looked as if she had wounded him. She spoke; she blew in his ear. The beast re-sponded, with a show of anger, to these preliminary caresses.

The spread of her arms. Triscombe enters a colorplate, the child-hood illustration he longs to bring to life: *Blodeuwedd's Invitation to Gronw Pebyr*. It has been said that fairy stories are erotic novels for children. But they are worse than that, as Triscombe is discov-ering. A low-cut bodice, with a tightly laced dress. She heaves with terror. Savage streaks of blooded light escape from the forest: some massacre or sacrifice to pagan gods. The white horse stamping through the fast-flowing river, hoof raised, searching for a dry rock, or . . . the head of a dog. A hound that will scrabble up the bank, shake himself, and soak the dress of his mistress. She is trapped within its clinging stiffness. She lifts the embroidered hem. The dog nuzzles, thrusting his otter-head between her naked thighs. His rough, salty tongue laps and scratches. She grasps him by the ears, guiding him. Her breath comes faster. She swoons to . . .

No, no, no. This is all wrong. It is Gelert the Faithful, blood-muzzled in his greeting. Slain in error: destroyer of the wolf-threat, not the sleeping infant. Triscombe is a one-handed reader, slither-ing among nursery icons, coded legends. He presses his cold nose to the tint of damp pages: the salmon runs, the gold shimmer, the white froth of water breaking around the horse's raised leg. Edith Cadiz is the raven-haired temptress worming out the secret of the Triple Death. She will destroy him. Her hair covers her face. She is without identity.

Choking spasms of language gushed from Triscombe's mouth. Things he thought he heard. Voices on trains. "She's a dog, mate." *Dogmate.* "On heat all the time, like a fucking dog." "Came home for his dinner, didn't he, and gave her one." *Dogfuck.* "I know all the bouncers. Every time I borrow a few quid I say, 'Cunt, shut your fucking mouth.' That's why you never get any." *Cuntmouth.* He's growling, rolling, hurt in his throat; biting at the fur on his wrist, pulling out the waxy skin in a red pinch of flesh. "She's a fucking diamond, son."

Triscombe is dribbling; gray bubbles of mucilage slather down his chin. Rasping, harsh breath: a file across his lungs. "Took 'er

279

down the 'ospital." *Horse spittle. Whore's spital. Clap-shop.* The bitch. "Fucking 'ore." The cunt. The dog.

He drops, stunned, into a black imageless sleep. A poleaxed carthorse.

And Edith writes, steadily and fast, her account of events that connect with these events; but which are *not* these events, and are *not* an account. She does not describe what has happened. She describes something else, which exists, independently, beyond the confines of this close room.

Naked, Edith looks into the bathroom mirror, and is — for the first time — troubled. She sees: "*The Eyes of a familiar compound ghost / Both intimate and unidentifiable."* She does not know herself. Her excitement is now as compulsive and primary as Triscombe's was, when he watched her. She does not make more of this than her written structure can contain. She is satisfied. She has committed herself. She believes that, at last, she has gone too far: there is no way back.

Edith left him, stretched on the floor: she walked, unshowered, down the High Street to the hospital.

Three Poems
Tom Clark

THE LYRIC

Suffering
lament, sorrow and wild
joy commingle in

the lyric — a collective
sigh of relief comes cascading
out of the blue —

a yearning to submerge
in life like the swimmer
in the pool forgetful

immersed and quenched —
water trailing scattered
diamonds in a rustling

voice of resigned subsidence
as though in the same stroke
everyone alive were speaking through you —

Tom Clark

"A POINT IS FIXED . . . "

A point is fixed at the
intersection between the
personal and the rest

of the cosmos, and that
nexus is the source
of the flood of speech

the desperate polyphony
of conflicting meanings
empties continually into,

all signs condensed into
a single line leading
out from this dust mote size

fraction of the history of
a very tiny star into the
silence everywhere around it

OUT OF DARKNESS I CAME

The combination of blind drive and accident which make up what
we call fate takes a different shape in the life of each one of us. My
own profoundest intimations of the existence of anything outside
myself were always muddled by a yearning for I knew not what
and by the consciousness that something in the past had escaped
me to which I could almost give a name. My confessions of a life
given over to the emotions of the moment failing to satisfy my
drive to expose my soul as it really was, I threw myself into the
composition of a series of dialogues in which I split myself in several parts and allowed the most confidential and private truths of
my personal history to be spoken of in their most secret light by the
side of my nature which is the most demanding and least easily
satisfied, and the most embarrassing wounds to be laid open by that
side of my nature I hate the most, all so as to spare my true soul
from slipping back into darkness without manifesting itself.

Two Sketches
Phillip Lopate

CHERRY BLOSSOMS

FOR TWO WEEKS IN MAY (or sometimes the last week in April and the first in May), the cherry blossoms are in full bloom. They grow in nearby Central Park as well as in the Brooklyn Botanical Gardens, but for some reason my friend Emily decides that the ones in Brooklyn are more "representative." So after much consulting of schedule books, we set out on Saturday afternoon, May 9, to the Brooklyn Botanical Gardens.

Emily is my best platonic friend.

Emily's spies in Brooklyn have assured her that the cherry blossoms are at their peak. It seems farfetched to me that one day more or less can matter so much; and yet, as Japanese art classically tells us, cherry blossoms are indeed that short-lived.

I am feeling very Japanese as I walk up the broad garden lane to the aisle of cherry blossoms. We have so few rituals any more — especially around Nature — that it would be nice to do this every year. I am thinking this way because I am already afraid of getting bored, so I tell myself let's make this an annual excursion.

I am thinking how most rituals are family-bred: repetitions of holidays and habits nurtured in the bosom of domestic life. Single people, like Emily and me, have to be more inventive in our development of rituals. For us there are no tooth fairies, no half-birthdays, no bringing the children to Grandma. Living quite alone, my temptation is to view myself as a bizarre romantic monster outside the human community. Emily, with her surer grasp of custom and propriety, leads me gently by the hand to that most buried of continents, normality.

The long line of cherry trees on either side sends swirls of petals across the avenue in the wind. The trees are so weighted with cherry blossoms, poor things, that their limbs seem to sag from the burden of pink. Emily is of the opinion that last week they must have been perfect — this week they are a little over-ripe.

On the ground, scattered cherry blossoms pile up thick and wasted and bruised, destined to be trampled underfoot.

It's too cold to sit for long on the grass. The sky is overcast, threatening rain.

Emily marches us away from this melancholy vista and over to the tulip beds. A woman of decision, she has a constant map in her head of where to go next, what is the best way to come upon any terrain. This time she finds us a spectacular double row of tulips, set almost too self-consciously on display, like a Cézanne exhibition. I like the ones that are pale yellow outside and dark yellow inside. Emily considers the insides of tulips very sexy. She used to be a photographer. We both agree that the black tulips are also wonderful: they're not really black at all but a deep purplish-brown, thin and wrinkled as antique velvet. "Texas Flames" are white with orange tongues of fire streaking the petals.

I'm getting bored, I want to go home.

We stop in the commissary to buy notepaper with lilac sprigs. As we leave the park I keep seeing beautiful bushes with different-colored flowers, and I ask Emily what they are, and it is always the same answer. "Azaleas."

On the way home in her Volkswagen, Emily and I are talking as usual about the difficulty of finding anyone with a set of quirks and appetites to match our prickly personalities.

"Why don't we get married?" I ask.

Emily laughs: "You say that once a year."

"Well, why don't we?"

"Because you're not attracted to me."

I sit back in the seat, breath taken away by her honesty. At the same time I remember how I had kissed her in greeting a few hours before and how adorable she looked. "That's not true. Sometimes I've very attracted to you."

"But not enough," she says with good-natured dismissiveness.

We drive on in silence. I think: Keep your mouth shut, she's right, it's *not* enough. She's saved you from an awful scrape.

Finally, Emily says: "You're not the only who thinks that."

"Thinks what?"

"That we two should get married. My sister Dora says it all the time."

MOTEL

Kay was visiting me in the country, where I had taken a summer rental. She and I had been getting along in our rapprochement, the nineteenth reincarnation of our relationship — this time the aim was to shift us from lovers to friends — until we took a sidetrip to a poky little literary festival, where a friend of ours was reading. Several of the poets had dinner with us after the reading; Kay flirted with all the men, as is her wont, and, being the only woman there, got giddier and giddier. None of this bothered me particularly. The poets had known us as a couple in the past, and assumed we were still one. However, when some of these men accompanied us to our motel and began making jokes about the hot night in store for us, like fraternity brothers kidding another whose prospects looked good, she boasted: "We're not going to do it. Don't worry." For some reason I felt humiliated by her saying this in public.

Inside the motel, as we undressed for bed, I was suddenly dying to make love to her. Her body had that coating of dust, from a long car ride, that turned me on. The midsummer heat contributed its part, as did anger or irritation (so often a component of my desire for Kay). I started coming on to her. Kay reacted in a flippantly schoolmarmish manner: "Can't we be ma-toor adults about this?" I wanted to break her down: her brittle cover, her detachment. Sadistic, I admit. After three days together filled with chaste country enjoyments and courtly manners, I wanted to *spoil things* (we know that ancient urge, don't we?). She wanted to go to sleep. I said I felt too alone in my sadness (at least that was the line). She didn't want any of it: she knew what the sadness was, where it was located, and she wasn't interested.

I began to accept that we were probably not going to make love. But there was something I still wanted from her: an answer that might clear up a doubt from the past. Or maybe I just wanted to get under her skin verbally, since I couldn't do it sexually.

"I never really felt from you that you had chosen *me*. Singled me out. I knew that at one point you wanted to get married, but the way you always put it was, 'I want to marry and have kids,' not, 'I want to marry you, particularly.'"

"What do you want me to say? That I was rejecting you all along? Is that what you'd like to hear?" said Kay.

"No, but . . . I'm only saying, I never sensed your full force of choice. Oh, you liked me, I knew that, but there was always

285

something impersonal in your attitude toward me. Never a real thought of *union*. I don't really know what I'm trying to say, but I always felt there was something you were holding back."

"Of course. It doesn't work that way, Phillip. As long as you weren't forthcoming with it, I didn't see any way I could allow myself to. It's like a game. You put your chip down, I put my chip down, you put another and I put another. It doesn't work without being mutual."

"But — I understand there may be times when a person turns that full beam of love on the other even if it isn't reciprocated right away. 'I'll follow you no matter what,' and so on."

"That's infatuation. I only did that once, with Daniel" (her ex-husband). "I'll never permit myself to do that again, unless I'm sure the other person's there too. That's reserved for adolescence."

"You call it adolescence, but it could also be a higher form of maturity, the ability to surrender."

"I won't do it. I did it once and that's all."

"So in a sense you're a used-up woman. You gave your best to Daniel."

"Maybe so," she said obstinately.

"I only felt it once," I said, "with Claire. She had chosen me of all the men in the world."

"And did you choose her that way?"

"I don't know, but I know I was influenced by her certitude. It's an amazingly powerful force. I do think a woman's love can transform a man."

"Are you trying to say that if I'd let out such a signal, you would have come around to marrying me? You know that's not so."

"I remember times when I craved a word of reassurance, some sunny conviction that might have taken us past doubt, but you always became so stubborn and dry and legalistic at those points."

"And what about yourself?"

"True enough. But it's still confusing," I said. "You gave off two different signals. Other people could see the love. Bea said to me, 'That girl's crazy about you.' But I never felt it that way."

"Bea also said that I was hysterical and highly neurotic."

"What's that got to do with it?"

"Don't say another word or I'll murder you. I swear I'll murder you!" She leapt out of bed with a flaming look in her eyes. She was trembling from head to foot. She started to dress, to put things in her knapsack. Where did she think she would go? We were in the middle of nowhere, in the middle of the night. I had the car keys. She had practically no money.

"Where are you going?" I asked, pointing. "To sleep on the side of the road?"

"Don't touch me or I swear I'll kill you in cold blood!"

"All right, I won't touch you." I jumped out of bed and spread-eagled my arms in front of the door. "Look, I'll make you a deal. I won't say another word to you, if you just stay here."

"Fine," she said. She went into the bathroom to shower. I listened to her under the jets. It was a very angry shower, it seemed to go on and on, and after about twenty minutes I became concerned. No, frightened. I imagined her slitting her wrists. I tiptoed to the bathroom and opened the door. I could see her behind the glass shower door, her orange-pink flesh soaked in bitter billows of steam. I crept back under the covers and waited.

As she came out of the bathroom, towelled, she said: "I hate you, I despise you, Phillip, I think you're a coward and I'm ashamed and humiliated when I think that I ever wanted you to marry me." She paused in the middle of the room. "You're a coward. Jews want to smear shit over everything. You weren't content, you wanted to make it ugly."

"I wish you'd leave my being Jewish out of it, you don't know what you're talking about," I said. "I don't think I wanted to smear shit, I just wanted to touch bottom."

"What does that mean?" She started to strip one of the single beds of its blankets and sheets.

I raised myself up on my elbow in bed. "I couldn't stand your brittle, distanced gaiety any more. That Southern belle act. It was dazzling but it wasn't real. It confused me. I had to find out where you were, really."

She lay her bedding out roughly on the motel's wooden floor. "You're lying."

"Oh, now we've reached the stage where everything I say is a lie."

"You're just trying to manipulate me by saying that *you're* confused. It's schizophrenagenic. I hate this!" Kay cried. "You want to pretend that there are no rules to emotional life — that everything is subjective, that it's all your 'feelings.' Look, we had a contract and you tried to break it."

"Right, I broke it," I said bitterly.

"How you degraded me! That night of your poetry reading, the way you treated me. I can't believe the awful things you've done. And always in public. Always in front of your friends. For four years I took being degraded—"

"We won't mention the degradation of your cheating on me, betraying me sexually every time I turned my back. Why do you think I found it so hard to trust you?"

"That's right. That was part of the agreement," said Kay, now calm. "You wanted someone you couldn't trust. For four years I took it. I thought—even until a few months ago—that our relationship was all about getting married. What pisses me off is that I worked so hard! And then to hear you saying you couldn't feel it! That's so cheap. The only thing I can say is that I knew from the start you wouldn't have me. I must have needed to try with someone who would keep pushing me away. Face it, that's the truth, isn't it? *You didn't want me.* You'd be better off if you just admitted it."

"I admit it."

"And now you're trying to get out of it by saying that I was the one holding back. Oh I could scream! Then I realized finally: He's not going to come around. In all the years we've been going out, we don't spend days and days together, we don't do the ordinary things that couples do. You keep your life separate, and we get together on weekends. We're still going out on *dates*. So something must be wrong, I realized. And even if you agreed to live together, it would take another few years before the next step, and the next. Your resistance is total. I was such a fool to try. Because it was inappropriate. And when I said you were a coward before, I didn't mean you were a coward because you won't come through with the goods. You don't want to marry right now. You have other tasks you have to perform first, challenges more important to you. That's perfectly all right. But what makes you a coward is that you can't accept that about yourself. You drag me and yourself down with your confusion, as if our working out as a couple were really something you'd wanted to do and you failed to do it. It's not weakness, Phillip. You don't want to do it. It's as simple as that."

It was a touching, pretty picture she was coming up with— straight out of the women's magazines. So what if she were omitting her own tendency to pick a fight or stage an infidelity whenever we began to settle into comfortable intimacy. Historical accuracy was perhaps too much to expect: she had been honest insofar as she had showed me her wound, that should be sufficient for me. Now she was a psychological priestess, speaking from the eye of a hurricane; I had seen her go on all night like this, analyzing my blind spots. Be grateful that she had not flipped out. I had almost pushed her over the edge. . . . My God, and I hadn't even taken the gloves off!

"You don't have to sleep on the floor. I won't bother you."

"I prefer it down here," she said. She jammed her head into the pillow, and we both eventually went to sleep.

They Take the Car Away
from theforestforthetrees
Charles Stein

They take   the car   away.
They take it away.
They came and took it away.
They came and took the car away.
Took it away.
Took it.
Took the car.
They took my car.
They came and they took my car away.
They came and took my car.
They took my car.

An elephant
triumphant
through the towns.
Large crowds of curious persons.
Stampeding persons. I
on my cabana.
I at the roof
of worlds, roofs
of towns.   I walk
I ride,   I rule,
I turn away.

I take my elephant away.
Take it from the life of ease
       the life dis-ease
the animal life of pain.
I take myself away from life of pain.
That white heat shining.

White heat   very fine   and shining
    in the lining
        of the garment
              that is the world.

The man's bright coat — its secret shining.

Oh he wore it   in the avenue
he wore it
          when it rained
he went to lunch.

They took my car away.
They took my car
away. They took it away.

How can we ever be happy again
How can we ever be free
How can pleasure
     take us
    home to town

Charles Stein

How can we ever be merry again
How can we be gay
Now they have taken my car
Away.   They took my car away.

I am an elephant
I have nothing to say.
I am an elephant
I have nothing to say.
I have to take my elephant to town
My fine coat shining.

The elephant's gray skin, shining strangely
strangely dull, yet shining
— shining in the rain
    as it walked through town
shining in the mud
    as it wagged and waddled.

Now they have taken my car away
    how can I shine now —

Two Poems
Cid Corman

To come out
of a life
into a

life you can
almost call
your own and

others can
almost hear
you calling.

*

I won't tell on you.
We are all guilty
of innocence.   K

was always dying —
wanting love and so
afraid of it — of

its obligations.
We have eaten of
the child and are sick.

"The Sight of a Lion that Appeared to Me and Seemed to Be Coming at Me" (Dante)

Barbara Einzig

Nothing will be in your hands when you wake up. You had been holding onto it, and now you're trying to remember what exactly it was, or what it was at all. It was the thing you've been carrying around with you for so long, that you've been waiting to put down. But you never knew if it was something that could be put down, or if it must be destroyed in some other way. Only that you must get rid of it to live. Yet you have been living with it for so long.

I see in today's paper a report that in Tokyo the obsession with the "child-woman" is such that there is a traffic in used underwear and in used scholastic uniforms of young girls.

Of course, if it is so repugnant, why should you be trying to get back to it?

We consider the dream to be occurring entirely within the body of the dreamer.

It is not the dead jaguar the Yekuana fear but its relatives, who will stalk the murderer for as long as it takes to isolate and kill him.

If the thing lying there is dead, it cannot rise and come toward you. You must be concerned with the thing either because it is still alive, or because of its relatives.

Which is it, then? When it was in your hands did it feel like a living thing or like a ghost?

If it is still alive why is its life so repugnant to you? Only because it does not have a face?

The stainless steel used for this armor is of a mesh so fine as to be almost transparent, but it is no easier to penetrate than a mirror.

They like to make flowers and birds out of clear glass and sell them to tourists, who also go to look at the church.

That is what it felt like, that mesh, and you are perhaps wondering if the mesh itself was the thing or if the thing was behind, being protected by it.

We call it "bringing the child up."

What is it he means when he writes that despair has no face?

Was it your own despair you were carrying around, looking for a suitable place to set it down, yet not wanting to implant it in another soil? Were you holding it as a child would a doll or was it more like blood running over your hands?

Wanadi after he took on form had the problem of what to do with his own umbilical cord, and through not burying it properly the devil Odosha was born, and darkness came into the world.

They consider the dream to be occurring in the same night in which one is sleeping. It is the journey of the soul.

In another country or another time, after a person dies they cover the mirrors.

When you were holding onto it, this probably was occurring in a hall of mirrors, but there was no light and so it felt like a complicated hotel.

Absolutely nothing was seen.

You realize you are holding onto another pair of hands into which a dream has also disappeared.

Two Poems
James Laughlin

THE STRANGER

There was a knock at the door
I opened   it was a young man

I couldn't at first recognize
but when I heard his voice I

knew him   it was myself some
thirty years ago   I asked him

in and made coffee   why did
you never write I thought you

were dead   I wished I was sometimes better I might have been

where were you all those years
what did the poet say   through

many lands and over many seas
I saw a lot   and what were you

doing   he shrugged   often I
didn't know what I was doing

I guess you might say I was
trying to find out what was

real and what was not   I did
a lot of harm much of it to

myself   we talked for several
hours then he said he had to

go   I urged him to stay on
told him he could make his

home with me but he refused
there's much that I still have

to do so much to learn   I may
be back and I may not but it

was good to see you and I'm
glad you're still yourself.

THE STORY OF RHODOPE

has always attracted me   she
was the Thracian courtesan

who lost her slipper while
bathing but an eagle picked

it up and dropped it in the
lap of Pharaoh Psammetichus

who of course searched her
out and married her loading

her with gold bracelets   the
story is important to me be-

cause my father had a shoe
fetish   he would take one

of his dollbabies into Del-
man's on Fifth Avenue and

buy her a dozen pairs of
slippers at a crack   dear

old dad I'm happy that their
pretty footsies made you glad

you weren't a book reader and
you needed some literary love.

Fad's Eye
Eli Gottlieb

IN 1967 A WEIRD, rich freedom was in the air, attended by the lulls that follow good sex, rain or a successful electrocution. The suburbs were constellated voids and the minds and laps of young children were occupied with the virile new technology of their toys: electrical buzzing skeletal overlays, mechanized whirligigs, plasticine injectibles, and the glamorous fact of television, which proposed that dots, projected fine enough on a piece of glass, could constitute a reality fully the equal of Life.

In 1967, I stood naked in the bathroom amidst the greeny light imported by the windows from the back lawn, and put a question to the upper corner of the room where the ceiling met the wall. Paint had bubbled there; spiders flung the intricate grots of their webs. I requested from this dirty bit of House the following information. Was there a realer, deeper, truer space than this one tumbled down so woefully all about me? One whose wardrobe was not of such a sustained pitch of braying loudness? One whose faces and overall appearance seemed to have bathed awhile in the ethers of a whiter world, such as was epitomized (I was ten) by the perfect hair of Perry Como, or the faultless high-kicking girls with feathered headdresses on the Jackie Gleason show whom my father, lighting the fragrant shank of a cigar, called "chorines," and my mother whores, but pronounced in a way that rhymed with sewers? Was there a reason my brother would never talk unless spoken to and passed his days hunkered down within the dark bell of his illness? Was there nowhere a span of grandness that my family owned, commensurate with all the showy folds of drama I felt enveloped me?

I touched the pulse in my neck, and stared at the upper corner of the room. For a while now I had been convinced that this bit of webby umbrage concealed a microscopic apparatus of great subtlety and unknown provenance whose purpose was to subvert my gift for life. Someone, I was convinced, was jealous of my rare elixir, my sparkling scarlet formula; someone wanted to crush and drain and break me down until I marched in the wan servitude of the rest of the dull shufflers of the planet. It listened to me, I was certain. This corner of the house wanted my mind.

I stood on the edge of the tub, all convinced of my uniqueness, and stretched my hands toward the paint of the upper wall. Touched, it came away as a whitish grime bespattered with the tiny netting of spiderweb. I was disappointed, obscurely. I wanted evidence of small machines for espionage there, infinitely miniaturized galleries for listening hard. Deeply discouraged, I dressed, went downstairs and ate my dinner like everyone else in the world.

Light broke early the next morning, widening through the window to cross the room with a chute the color of lymphatic fluid. Breakfast was cold cereal, and the car, a Corvair in the shape of a bulbous superinsect, was soon idling hard in the driveway. We were going to a doctor again. A fang of smoke stabbed the air from the exhaust pipe. We were going for the second time this week. It was about my brother Fad, who had something quick, deep and absolute wrong with him, though no one knew what. I made a muscle as the car moved off smartly, threaded the coiling secondary roads for five minutes and debouched with a whoosh onto the interstate.

"When will the road end?" asked Fad, straining forward against the acceleration.

"What, dear?" asked Mother. Her hair had been freshly sprayed with Aqua Net and sat scrolled on either side of her head like the capitals of Ionic columns. She rummaged in her purse for change with long fingers, getting ready for the tollbooth. I had been pleading with her to get a toll gun, which fired the chiming silver bullets of quarters into the exact change scoops — which, after a fashion, fed the highway.

"The road, where does it go when it stops?" he asked.

"Well," she pursed her lips. "I think it goes to Canada, actually." She laughed, "If you were crazy enough to want to go to Canada!"

"Why?" I asked.

"Brrrr!" she said. "It's too cold for most people."

"But many people live there," I said sensibly.

"And then where?" asked Fad.

"What, honey?"

"Then where does it go, in Canada."

"I — I don't actually know, to tell you the truth."

"But Mommy," his voice was beginning to rise and tighten. "The

road just can't stop. It has to get somewhere, Mommy. Mommy!"
"Yes dear."
"Mommy, find out where the road goes, make it that it goes someplace I know. Where does it go? Where?"
"The sea," I said calmly.
"What?" he turned, wild-eyed.
"Your brother's right," said Mother. "It goes where all roads go. To the ocean."
"The sea?" Fad asked, visibly relaxing.
"Yeah," I said, "they're the same thing."

In the gray marine light of his examining room, Dr. Minkoff bent forward and flexed his fingers with a brisk, serially cracking sound, like the tappets of an old engine firing up after lengthy disuse.
"And this," he said in a loud voice, "must be the specimen!"
Mother bellied out the front of her body to urge him ahead, while I walked behind, turning my face to either side, slowly and methodically.
"This is the one, doctor!" she cried.
My vision drew to the center. Fad was holding soiled hands to his face, had made a square hole of his fingers and was peering through it at the doctor like a movie director framing a shot.
"Go away," he said, with great seriousness.
The doctor's smile shriveled fractionally.
"We're here today to do a physical," he said, clearing his throat. "We're going to examine your systems of hearing and sight, check your circulatory system, and give your nerves a quick once-over. Okey doke?"
No one said a word.
"Right," said the doctor, walking to a wall cabinet and removing a small glittering tube. "This," he said, "is called an eyescope. It checks the function of the most precious part of your body."
The doctor bent forward at the waist, lowering himself until his face was in front of Fad's, and then slowly raising the eyescope up into position.
"Mom," said Fad in a chill, flat voice.
"Yes?"
"Can I spit on him now?"
"No, sweetie, he'd be very upset."
The doctor squinted into his instrument, plying a needle of light around the reddish inner perimeter of Fad's eye.

300

"Well," he said with a chuckle, "I've been peed on enough times, and worse, too. But spit on? Not yet anyway."

Dr. Minkoff stood up, sighing, and steepled his hands over his breastbone.

"Your mother," said the doctor delicately, "explained to me that you're the type of young man who likes to know what's being done to you, so I'm going to tell you that the blood test gives a tiny pain, like a flybite, but it's very important. You with me?"

"No!" cried Fad.

Mother seemed to awaken then, tilting her head gravely to the side while her long, lariat-like arms flowed around Fad's body and drew him close. Tenderly she whispered into the horn of his ear in a burring soft voice that he was a Best Boy, one of the very best boys in all the world; that few boys had ever been as handsome, noble, or As Well Behaved In Doctor's Offices, and fewer still as surpassingly smart and quick and important. Everything about him was like a kind of gold, ablaze with precious forces. Rest assured, she whispered, a Mom like her was very lucky to have him.

Just then the door opened and the nurse came in — a large, square, red-faced person atop whose head, like a wave breaking, was set a fluted cap. She aimed the cap at Fad.

"This the little blood giver?" she asked.

"Say hi," said Mother.

"Hi." His voice fell down as he said it.

The nurse opened her bag, exposing odd bights of rubber tubing, glass pipettes and gauges. She took out a small white cotton swab, wiped Fad's index finger, and then stared at him a second.

"Aren't you a handsome young man!" she said loudly, smiling as she stabbed a bright piece of metal fast into the pad of his finger. From a great, bored distance I observed the widening hoop of bewilderment passing over my brother's face as the pain rang in from the remote station of his hand, grew up fast into a genuine sting.

He screamed. A good, solid, meat-eating burst of sound. But the nurse, though he began to struggle, hung on gamely, and sucked the blood in a thin red line up the pipette. She bound his finger with a piece of gauze and a band-aid, while Mother tenderly stroked his brow and winked in my direction.

I put my finger to my neck, felt the pulse there beating rapidly. One day this persistent knocking of blood below my chin would slow, then stop entirely, and I would begin my voyage back to that braided scatter of dark minerals from which I'd taken form. This

301

was Death, an event to which I'd recently begun giving long and considered thought. Death, I'd decided, was like reading a book that erased itself as you went along, and left you with a lapful of soot and shattered grammar where before there had been sentences slung like bright webbing above the world and the story of a life filled with beautiful, slow-moving men and women. Or perhaps it came as a pair of gleaming black bookends, fashioned of the pure cold of outer space, that squeezed your head from either side until you exploded in a single breath-shaped burst, and went away. Or, more likely, it was a rent in the remotest, most gossamer of veils, through which you passed hissing like a gas, and from which you never, absolutely ever, came back.

I looked up. Mother, Dr. Minkoff and the nurse were gathered in a tight knot around Fad, who was sobbing hysterically and thrashing his head from side to side. I glanced at my calendar watch and made a lightning calculation. Twenty thousand more days of this to go. Shutting my eyes, I took a deep breath and held it until the taste of a river rose into my mouth and everything swam bluish black.

Poetry and Apoetical Culture
Adonis

— Translated from the French by Esther Allen

1

AT THE ORIGIN of the word "difficult" and the phenomena to which it refers in pre-Islamic Arab poetry, there are certain images that shed light on the relationship between the poem and its listeners. We climb a steep mountain; a rebellious camel refuses to be broken and ridden; the fruit we crave is inaccessible; a cloud is charged with thunder and lightning: all of these images resist ease and facility. When Arab listeners heard a "difficult" poetry, these were the images that came into their minds. Their natural inclination led them toward a poetry that evoked the opposite of these images, a poetry that could be assimilated without trouble or effort, a poetry like a light cloud, a straight and level path, a fruit within easy reach of the hand, a docile camel. The Arab demanded of the poem an easiness that would allow him to dominate it intellectually, to take possession of it with the cognitive tools at his disposal. He rejected any poem that did not correspond to this demand and qualified it as "difficult," a word that was usually pejorative. It was said that a "difficult" poet hewed stone while an "easy" poet dipped into the sea . . .

2

This was the prevailing relationship between the poem and its listeners during the pre-Islamic period of oral poetry. The same relationship continued to prevail in the Islamic period, over the

---

"Poetry and Apoetical Culture" was originally delivered in December 1991 as a talk to the Swedish Academy on the occasion of the ninetieth anniversary of the Nobel Prize Committee.

course of which it took on, with the advent of writing, a new dimension that could be described as ideological *avant la lettre*. Any discussion of Arab poetry must very precisely take into account the Muslim's attitude toward his language. Pagan before Islam, the Arabic language becomes divine through the Qur'anic Revelation but is not otherwise altered. Arabic is thus the matrix or mother of the Word of God and also of the pre-Islamic poetry, pagan though it was. When this divine Revelation came to take the place of poetic inspiration, it claimed to be the sole source of knowledge, and banished poetry and poets from their kingdom. Poetry was no longer the word of truth, as the pre-Islamic poets had claimed it was. Nevertheless — and this merits a separate study — Islam did not suppress poetry as a form and mode of expression. Rather, it nullified poetry's role and cognitive mission, endowing it with a new function: to celebrate and preach the truth introduced by the Qur'anic Revelation. Islam thus deprived poetry of its earliest characteristics — intuition and the power of revelation — and made it into a media tool.

As a revealed religion, Islam unites words and actions. Hence its political tendency, manifested in its literature by the close ties between poetry and the other forms of writing that serve the Islamic message, and also by the ostracism (marginalization, exclusion or interdiction) of anything that does not serve that message. We can perhaps detect the first seeds of the ideological use of art here. It should be noted that what rivaled and still rivals poetry in Arab society is not science or philosophy, but religion. For in its original, pre-Islamic sense, poetry is inspiration — which is to say, prophecy — but without commandments, institutions or norms. However, starting with Islam — and this also deserves a separate study — poetry in Arab society has languished and withered precisely insofar as it has placed itself at the service of religiosity, proselytism and political and ideological commitments. The eighth-century critic Al-Asma'i alludes to this in a clairvoyant phrase: "Poetry is a misadventure that begins with Evil; as soon as it interferes with Good, it founders." So we can imagine the sort of adventure that poetry has lived — and still lives — within a "divine" language, in a society whose social, cultural and political structures are all founded on a Revelation expressed in that same language.

As the Revelation was embodied in institutions that saw in poetry only a tool which could serve them, new relationships between poetry and its listeners were established in daily life. New ways of appreciating poetry also emerged, along with new values and criteria. The politico-religious institution exercised its power as the faithful guardian of the Qur'anic Revelation. It possessed the absolute certitude that the Revelation spoke and wrote Man and the universe clearly, definitively and without error or imperfection. This certitude, in turn, demanded that the Muslim individual be formed around a faith in an absolute text, one which allowed no interrogation that might give rise to any doubt whatsoever.

Under such conditions, alienation is inevitable; the skeptical individual no longer has the right to be a member of the society. Because Islam—the last message sent by God to mankind—has placed the final seal on the Divine Word, successive words are incapable of bringing humankind anything new. A new message would imply that the Islamic message did not say everything, that it is imperfect. Therefore the human word must, on an emotional level, continually eulogize and celebrate that message: on an intellectual level, *a fortiori* it can only serve as explication.

Poetry, the most elevated form of expression, will henceforth be valued only for its obviousness. As a tool for instruction, poetry must cultivate the easiness that will best enable it to disseminate its message. And this easiness ultimately transforms poetry into an object of consumption. By appealing to poetic memory, poetry gives the illusion of joining the present to the past and of responding to people's real needs. But in the course of this process, it does not liberate; it anesthetizes, as if it were teaching the faithful to manufacture their prisons and their chains with their own desires, their own needs. This easiness turns Man toward the past; it is not an energy propelling him toward the future.

In part, this explains the dominance in the Arab mentality of what I call "pastism." In the context of this inquiry, pastism means the refusal and fear of the unusual. When it confronts a poetry that does not derive from what it already knows, this mentality first tries to grasp it by comparing it to the religio-linguistic heritage, to what is already known. The greater the disparity, the more the poetic production will be considered foreign and dangerous, a threat to the sacred patrimony. The important thing is to identify a clear and direct line connecting the present to the past.

4

Thus poetry's final aim is to transmit the message it bears rather than to reveal the poet's self and his individual vision of human existence and the world. The value of the poem resides in its efficacy and in the breadth of the satisfaction it can give. That being so, poetry comes to resemble all other institutions: it is marriage, not love; the arrival, not the adventure; the object, not the subject. Poetry becomes the promulgator of inherited values and the safeguard of their continuity. Linguistic production is envisioned as a kind of manual production and poetic language as a mode of work. And like the product of the laborer's work, which is subject to exchange, the poem produced by the work of the linguistic laborer will also be a piece of merchandise that one can exchange. . . . The value of the poem therefore resides in its capacity to please and to attract.

We should note in passing that the modern media, at all levels, contribute to the ever-increasing superficiality and banality of the world. They reduce all writing, including poetry, to pieces of information among other pieces of information. In so doing, they negate writing and reading alike, and reinstitute a culture of the eye and the ear, which is no more than a form of illiteracy. Productivity takes the place of creativity; the producer is substituted for the creator.

Within Arab society, this universal state of things is translated by the movement toward Arab traditionalism. Particularly in regard to poetic writing, this traditionalism crystallizes the society's will to put the creator to death. The poetic work is held to be the reflection of the Revealed Text which has been handed down by God, the Prophet serving only as an intermediary. Since poetry derives from religion and from the community of believers, the poet, too, is no more than an intermediary.

This phenomenon is anchored in poetic and historic memory. The pre-Islamic Arabs spoke a poetry that began with a concrete situation, or rather with an event-word. The word was essentially linked to life, movement and work. It was originally carnal, and the poem was a kind of nourishment; it was judged by its savor.

People expected poetry to grant them access to their present circumstances, to address their daily life, to bring them back to their realities. Poetry's faithfulness to reality was the principal criterion. The relationship of poetry to what people enjoyed or rejected was stronger than its relationship to the categories of beauty and ugliness. The relationship between word and thing was the primordial expression of a situation, and was therefore an ethical and not an aesthetic relationship.

This can explain the importance of conventions in Arab poetic writing, which is primarily constituted of rules and principles.

The idea of the beautiful appeared only when Arabs began to distance themselves from reality and granted a creative role to the imagination. And, under the effects of modernity and technology, the language likewise moved away from the body and life. Language has become a raw material to be transformed. The poet has become a manufacturer who transforms words into a product: the poem.

In the conjunction of this original past and this modern technicality is everything that tends to reinforce obviousness and immediacy and to reaffirm the proselytizing and ideological aspect of Arab poetry—that is, its easiness. Arab culture suppressed all questioning; based as it is on the Answer, it instituted a poetry that could say only what is known, a poetry of the explicit. Thus the first difficulty Arab poetry runs up against resides, paradoxically, in the culture of easiness. The discourse of "easy poetry" will be the first obstacle to creation. For that poetry which gives itself over to panegyrics strengthens the repressions and interdictions of the politico-religious institution on which the society is founded. It deepens the gulf that has opened between man and himself, between man and his aspirations. By comparison, all other poetry will always seem arduous—for such poetry will have to begin by putting the language itself to death, as if it were having to struggle among the scattered debris of language and thought, the real and the unknown. As if it had to be an experience of the unlimited and the infinite. This poetry has existed at various moments during Islam, and it continues to exist, but it is marginalized and frowned upon. Reading it is not an act of consumption; it is an act of creation. Therefore, after the problem of easiness comes the difficulty engendered by poetic investigation. The light such investigation may cast on the unknown only enlarges the unknown's dimensions, announcing its depth and its extremity as if the light were transforming itself into night. And if this light opens the horizon to the night of the world, the limits it makes poetry cross open poetry to the unlimited. As if the darkness were amplified by the very movement of the light, as if poetry knew only its own limits. The dark world that is illumined is the very thing that leads poetry toward an even darker world.

This unknown is not a meaning that can be grasped definitively. It is mobility, not fixity. Displacing the meanings of words from one horizon to another, writing creates a new space for meaning, a different kind of cognitive pleasure. Disturbing the opposition between the explicit and the implicit, the real and the unknown, it destroys the immutable relations between the signifier and the signified while insisting on other relations having to do with the mysteries of existence. The interest of this writing thus focuses on the hidden-implicit and the probable-imaginary, in opposition to the certain-rational. The reader, moving through the realm of the imaginary and the probable, evolves within an atypical writing stripped of references. He no longer enters the poem as he would a garden whose fruits are within easy reach of his hand, but rather as he would an abyss or an epic. Anything he might glean from it will demand a great deal of effort; he will not achieve it with his mind or his heart alone, but with his whole being. This writing takes unmarked paths to go toward that other place that cannot be reached, for it is always in motion and always leads us toward a place still further away. Language, which here abandons the modes and categories of writing, adheres totally to the dynamic of this experience and even to its errancies.

This poetic writing has opened important breaches in the dominant religious and cultural fabric. Expressing the unheard-of and suggesting the unsaid, it has blurred the images both of certitude and of the discourse that expressed certitude. Opening doors onto the unsayable, it insists on the absence of any correspondence between things and words, which entails a questioning of the truth of any discourse whatsoever, be it human or divine. It presents a text that is open and unfinished, the opposite of the sealed and eternal text of religion. This results in the difficulty I call the "difficulty of interpretation" or the "difficulty of edges." For the language of this writing is that of the boundaries joining the visible to the invisible, the language of the edges which delineate their contours. It is the language of the far away and the perilous: a language of extremes, a language that flays words and in so doing expresses the world.

5

There exists another form of difficulty, this one linked to the no-tion of identity, and which is, in Arab society, essentially attached to language and religion. As it is lived, identity engenders a reading based on the nostalgia for an original unity: the unity of the nation, the language, the homeland, and of power. This ideological read-ing perceives the poetic text as a battleground between ideas and current tendencies: it makes the poetic text a political text. When it is unable to adapt the poetic text to its ends, this reading quali-fies it as "difficult" and sometimes goes so far as to deny its status as poetry. Because it unites language with identity and truth with force, this reading ends by confusing knowledge with power. Its underlying concept of identity is univocal in a theological sense and idealistic in a philosophical sense. The essential component of this reading is a separation from the other, a self-sufficiency that gives the illusion of continuity and, in consequence, the illusion of cohesion and singularity with respect to other identities. In Arab society, poetry is the first criterion by which a poet's identity and the extent of his belonging within the society is measured; we can thus understand the challenge faced by a poetry that estab-lishes another concept of identity — one that is pluralist, open, ag-nostic and secular.

Identity, in this poetry, is not only consciousness; it is also the unconscious. It is not only the licit but also the repressed, the un-said; not only what has been realized but above all what is possible. It is the continuous and the discontinuous, the implicit and the explicit.

There is a fissure at the very heart of the univocal and phan-tasmal identity. The unity of the "self" is only apparent, for this self is fundamentally a rift. And the "other" lives deep inside the "self." There is no "self" without the "other." Living identity exists within the fertile, ambiguous relational tension between the self and the other. Without this tension, identity would be that of the thing, and no longer that of Man.

Identity does not come only from within: it is a living and con-tinuous interaction between interior and exterior. It can thus be said that identity lies not so much in the immutable and the im-plicit as in what is variable and not yet made explicit. In other words, identity is a meaning that inhabits an image that is always mobile. It evinces itself more in the process of orientation than in any final return. It exists in openness, not in closure; in interaction, not in withdrawal.

In poetry, the problem of identity is expressed in a privileged way. Identity, in poetic language, is an eternal questioning. In the creative experience, man is himself only insofar as he moves beyond what he is. His identity is a dialectic between what he is and what he is becoming; it is more beyond than behind him, for man is essentially a will to create and to change. To put it another way, identity is less an inheritance than a creation. Unlike other creatures, man creates his identity by creating his life and his thought.

So that within the context of the dominant Arab culture what is called "the difficulty of poetry" does not emerge from the text itself and is not found within it. This "difficulty" stems instead from the level and quality of the culture and is linked to the reader's aptitude for understanding the poem: to his way of reading.

Can't we then say that, within the context of this culture, poetry does not become poetry unless it frees itself from the easiness and obviousness that is demanded of it?

Can't we say: no, there is no difficult poetry?

Dido to Aeneas
David Shapiro

I.

It was words that detained us, though they do not reach
I was devoted to the future and you like a yellow acanthus
You wanted to bend to some more obvious bed
Sychaeus was abolished after a desuetude
The night also betrayed me but I drew it out
and I asked you many things about very strong Hector
You were my guest and I loved narrative
like an error on the land of all fluctuating seas
And you apostrophized as if from a need
                    Night rushed down with the stars like analogies
Now when I look up there is only a chaos like a cave
You have become Rome, while I became something like music
You exchanged me for a fate or a work
drinking like long love but I will tell you now nothing

II.

Everyone has been silent but you are attentive
May you have an immense exile like a surface
A god pulled you to my coast in a digression
Everyone wishes to say things even the air
But you have thrown your arms around the image's neck
And escaped alone with your hands: you and I would become the
    same cave
The mountains do they represent anything
Nor am I copying you now king of the obsessed doors
I believed you and the equivocations
If only the earth had opened or I could go toward images
I began to speak but I stop in the middle

David Shapiro

Alone in the vapid room I could hear you and touch the bed like
    a relic
My towers did not rise, discontinuity equaled the sky
Day was a cause a name is a screen and we have called it secret
    love

III.

It was the night of tired-out bodies
With a placid sleep giving access to other bodies
The woods are like a sieve and the sky is normal
The stars revolve like lovers in their lapses
Each leaf on the field is quiet like a variegated birth
And the birds in many colors occupy the lakes
Which occupy the fields and the little rough brambles
But the unhappy mind is like a double Thebes on stage
May our shores combine against your shores
It is possible to hate life and throw it off like a nurse
Oh dear nurse please send me my sister
I have lived and I have finished now I am a big image
I am a city and a statue and a wall and a revenge
It is a recent cut like an accident in a forest

IV.

You always wanted the most favorable time to speak
and I have found the time not to speak
You think you will have names but I follow in sequence
You wanted to see but you cannot even see the cave
But you had to come to Hell and the urns of silent writing
You think you see something and you see the extreme sequitur
This was the last time you said you would address me
By permission and how much you loved permission the word
My eyes can do something else nor do I exist the joke
You are not even interesting as a cliff or a flight into waves
I will hurry away to the one who equals my love
And you will win Aeneas Rome but not Dido
It is not the irresponsible silence of a suicide
But I had the right to the cry without translation

Two Essays
Arthur A. Cohen

JEPTHAH'S VOW

THE LAST ORATORIO completed by George Frederic Handel toward the close of his life was based on the Biblical narrative of the career and passion of Jepthah the Judge. Although Handel is sensitive to the pride and fall of Jepthah, his tenderness is really extended to the faithful piety of his daughter who was to suffer the consequence of Jepthah's outrageous vow. The aria that follows her immolation, "Waft her, angels" — supplicatory and confident though it is — is already a sentimentalization of the Biblical narrative, for if there be Biblical tragedy, the hero is not the daughter who bewails her virginity and offers herself up to the knife, but Jepthah, who in folly and hubris binds himself in pride and is destroyed by it.

The narrative of Jepthah (Judges XI-XII:7), despite the insistence of many Biblical scholars that it is derived from two independent sources, possesses an uncommon dramatic unity. Whether Jepthah's heroic accomplishments as Judge are recounted in order that the story of the sacrifice of his only daughter be unfolded or whether the narrative of his earlier career is recalled in order to supply the raison d'être for this fateful vow, clearly the tragedy of Jepthah is the heart of the narration. This is, as well, the way the rabbinic sources regard it. Considering Jepthah's career as Judge of Israel for six years (Judges XII:7) to be of little consequence, the rabbis emphasize wherever his name is mentioned the stupidity, vanity and ignorance of the Law which led him to his ridiculous vow and its execution. For the rabbis, Jepthah is an example of one who made an imprudent vow, moreover a vow that could easily have been absolved had the High Priest Pinehas not been so proud as to disdain Jepthah and Jepthah so vain as to be indifferent to the High Priest's counsel. For the rabbis, Jepthah is but the occasion for the homiletic exposition of a culpable and foolish leader.

It was the music of Handel that first directed me to the narrative of the Bible many years ago. Those early university years, when first I became a student of Aristotle's *Poetics* (a text I was to be obliged to read more than a score of times accompanied as was often appropriate by the Orestes or Oedipus cycle), seemed extraordinarily relevant to the career of Jepthah. Jepthah seems a tragic hero, for he was, as Aristotle designates, a man of power and authority, more grand than those who would behold him, but no less vulnerable to those torrential claims of glory that annoy the gods and encourage them to chastise. Jepthah, like Oedipus, makes a vow, and his vow, flung before his multitudes, no doubt in the enthusiastic hours before he joined battle against the Ammonites, was that if God would deliver the Ammonites into his hands, "then it shall be that whatsoever cometh forth of the doors of my house to meet me, when I return in peace . . . it shall be the Lord's, and I will offer it up for a burnt-offering." Jepthah triumphs and the Ammonites are subdued and he returns to his home in Mizpeh and there comes forth from his house to greet him, "with timbrels and dances," his daughter, and the text adds with an extraordinary compassion and simplicity, "and she was his only child; beside her he had neither son nor daughter." Presumably Jepthah repented his vow, but it is his daughter who holds him to its letter saying, "My father, thou hast opened thy mouth unto the Lord; do unto me according to that which hath preceded out of thy mouth." Having confirmed Jepthah in his resolve, she then pleads that he permit her a respite of two months that she might go into the mountain with her companions and "bewail her virginity." The Bible speaks succinctly of the end of her seclusion: "she returned unto her father who did with her according to his vow; and she had not known man."

It is simple and yet its naked simplicity is horrendous. Baruch Kurzweil, the eminent Israeli literary critic, in an essay on "Job and the Possibility of Biblical Tragedy" (*Iyyun*, vol. 12, no. 3–4, October 1961) does not speak of the story of Jepthah, although he considers the tragic possibilities offered by the stories of Cain, Abraham, Saul, Moses, Job. Kurzweil argues that the Bible, leaving no room for the possibility of an existence without redemption, does not offer the option of tragedy. Presumably tragedy is to be defined as fall without salvation. And there is surely truth in this, for the audience that reads Scripture (*not* the audience that views Dino de Laurentis and John Huston) in an attitude of belief *knows* that what was told there is part of the history of salvation, that even the irrational episode, the non sequitur, the unresolved

ambiguity is part of an ongoing divine-human process, to be resolved, to be consummated. There is only tragedy for Kurzweil
when the audience is moved to "pity and fear" by the similitude
between their condition and the afflicted nobility before them.
Tragedy is didactic, not redemptive.

Kurzweil's view of tragedy, of course, assumes that the Bible is
all of a piece. Though not wishing to raise here the controversies
that exacerbate Biblicists, there is little doubt that the Bible is a
complex document. Whether composed by a single hand or fashioned by many, it reflects the pagan underground of ancient Palestine as surely as it bequeaths the foundation of Jewish existence and
salvation. I cannot help but regard the story of Jepthah's vow as testimony to that pagan substratum. God is present, but it is the God
of *dike*, of a supervenient justice. God is offended and God punishes.
It would have been sufficient had Jepthah been courageous, fought
valiantly, judged excellence, for God would have delivered the
Ammonites to him. But Jepthah exceeds the measured line which
is border between the competence of man and the suzerainty of
God and God smites him. He vows and the logic of the vow, its in-
exorability, is carried to its conclusion. God retires and allows the
working of Jepthah's pride and Jepthah's self-arrogation to bring
about his downfall. According to some sources, Jepthah dies an unnatural death: fragments of his flesh fell from his body at intervals
and were buried where they fell, so that the body was distributed
throughout the land. In *The Legends of the Jews* Louis Ginzberg
says Jepthah was dismembered (vol. IV, p. 46).

The grandeur and horror of the story of Jepthah's vow is precisely its tragic persuasiveness, for in this narrative a portion of a
universe already sacralized breaks away and floats free from "sacred
history." Or perhaps it is but a warning that God is sometimes
stony-faced, flinty, contemptuous of our condition.

I confess that I am comforted by the knowledge that there is this
story in the Bible, that it is told and never recalled again throughout
Scripture, that the rabbis really ignore it, but that it is there — complete and unvarnished — a Biblical story no different than a sequence
of stories that run through the literature of the West. Think only
of Piave's libretto for Verdi's *Ernani* (based on a play by Victor
Hugo), and one can see the bathos to which vain vows can be
brought. The prototype to all these is Jepthah's tragic vow.

Arthur A. Cohen

MARGINALITY

Critical distinctions are not made. Or, more accurately, the language of the questions we are charged to consider is so freighted with presuppositions and assumptions that it is exceedingly difficult for me, sitting here in my Biblical mountain village, sun-drenched (where distinctions are even more difficult to come by), to put myself in a frame of mind appropriate to the dreadful seriousness of the questions.

I do not think of myself, insofar as I consciously think of myself as a Jew, as being marginal. Being Jewish is not an essential marginality. It may well be aboriginal, but even if the historical duration of Jewish marginality is unending, the very concept of marginality precludes it from being an essence. Something that is accidental — and margins are always contingent, and historically indefinite — cannot be thought of as an essence. The Jew is not *in se* marginal. Marginality is a psychic condition of self-deprecation, another instrument of importing nervousness, ambiguity, uncertainty into an otherwise sufficiently difficult enterprise. The marginality of the Jew comes from within and is not (and probably never was) a requirement imposed from without.

Majoritarian societies are always confused by separatism and exclusivity. It seems such a mistake to dominant cultures to have to cope with what it regards as insular vision. It has no capacity and even less interest in coming to terms with the truth that visions, tightly held, contain. Whatever capacity or interest that might have is expressible as an inverse ratio — the smaller the ethnic enclave in relation to the encompassing whole, the greater the disinterest, even the hostility of both communities to the other (particular in the case of the Jews, whose speckness possesses the visibility of a giant cinder in the great eye of world culture).

The Jews feel marginal to themselves. It is they who formulate the concept and pass the judgment. Anti-Semites who make a reasoned fanaticism out of the paranoia of their following condense the self-judgment of the Jews into a threat; but anti-Semites are no more secure than Jews, their marginality is no less aggrieved.

It would follow from such a course of thought that marginality can be socially engineered, that Jews — under the constant barrage of its neurasthenic ideologists — will think of themselves as marginal, making marginality (and with it those unhappy self-punishments, alienation, inauthenticity, *mauvaise foi*) into a condition. It may well be a condition, but it is an existential choice, not an essential reality. The Jew is marginal if he thinks of himself as marginal. Moreover – and I hasten to insist upon it at this juncture – the Holocaust is not a confirmation of Jewish marginality. To use the Holocaust as proof that the Gentile world demands Jewish marginality, indeed enforces it upon the *corpus Judaeis*, is to commit an almost obscene *petitio principi*.

The Jew is marginal because he elects it. It is an extension of his judgment upon the world, that it is not redeemed, that he is not redeemed until it is. One understands the view of Rosenzweig that such modes of interpretation value history too highly, time too dearly, that both time and history have no place in the scheme of Jewish existence. To be a Jew is ontological, an ontology of the blood. The idea of marginality he would undoubtedly dismiss as another *galut* fantasy, another exhibition of Jewish self-humiliation. As much, however, as I would agree that there is a kind of portable wailing wall that Jews manage to construct wherever they are, I find the Rosenzweig counter no longer satisfactory. The marginality of Jewish existence registers a messianic dismay, an unwillingness to say more than a conditional "yes" to stable, bourgeois society (even though most Jews are horrendously and complacently bourgeois). Jewish marginality as an elective determination is a theologically correct response. It is, to my mind, a gesture of psychological and moral indecision regarding the arrangements of the world, a demurral from established regencies and powers, an indication – as if by a shoulder shrug – that something in the world is unacceptable. In that respect marginality is not only an existential option but a theologically correct choice.

The predicament of marginality, of cultural schizophrenia, of the other and various ways by which we describe our bemoaned and bewailed self-excision from the commonweal, is simply not as grievous as it is made out to be. The issues are other than those set forth: the predicament of Jewish creativity and art, of Jewish work and an ethics of work, a renewal of liturgical life and study which bypasses the hopelessly drained institutions of the big city, etc.

The point is that every human being is marginal because he is finite and mortal. The Jew is no more or less marginal for being Jewish, only eccentric. The eccentricity – or rather the ellipsis – of Jewish existence is a delight, not a pain.

Last Words
William Corbett

Here pollen's cornmeal
soup in the shallows,
in Boston the dusty
acrid stink of ailanthus.
I can't stop thinking
mother died today thoughts
which dully repeat
"Mother died a year
ago this morning."
It was gray, cold, wet
when we sat with the news
before a fire. Under this
June eleventh's humid
milky softness
every green tree and plant
is two weeks ahead,
and I forget most of what
Marni and I said walking
through rain to the graveyard.
Now it is Eileen, Paul
and Jimmy who are dead:
two by accident, one
of heart attack after stroke,
and Marni walks through
brick and watery Amsterdam.
Its south wind
causes huge pines to rasp
and sigh. It's all
I can do to catch mother's
last words I never heard
scratched from her own
throat and thirsty lips.
Middle of the night

she rouses herself,
phones my brother
whispers her cry:
"Get me out of here!
Get me out of here!
I want a coke!
How's Bill in Boston?"

In Memoriam

if you exi ted
~~becauSe~~

we mIght go on as before

but since you don't we ~~wi'L~~l

mak
~~changE~~

our miNds

anar hic
~~so that we~~Can

d to   let it be
convertEnjoy the chaos/~~that~~ you are./
stet

— John Cage (1912–1992)

NOTES ON CONTRIBUTORS

JOHN ADAMS is one of America's foremost contemporary composers. His works — including the operas *Nixon in China* and *The Death of Klinghoffer* — are recorded on Nonesuch, New Albion and Phillips labels.

ADONIS is the pen name of Ali Ahmed Said, who was born in Syria in 1931. He has published a dozen volumes of poetry and has been translated into many languages. His latest book of prose is *Introduction to Arab Poetics* (Texas University Press, 1990). He lives in Paris.

ESTHER ALLEN has two translations coming out this fall: Blaise Cendrars' *Modernities and Other Writings* (University of Nebraska Press) and Octavio Paz's *Villaurrutia: Hieroglyphs of Desire* (to be published along with Eliot Weinberger's translation of Villaurrutia's *Nostalgia for Death*, Copper Canyon Press).

DAVID ANTIN's *Selected Poems 1963–73* was published last year by Sun & Moon Press. New Directions is bringing out his third book of talk pieces, *What It Means to be Avant-Garde*, in the Spring of 1993.

JOHN ASHBERY's most recent books of poetry are *Flow Chart* (Knopf, 1991) and *Hotel Lautréamont* (Knopf, 1992). He is currently Charles P. Stevenson, Jr., Professor of Languages and Literature at Bard College.

DONALD BAECHLER is an artist living in New York. He has shown at the Tony Shafrazi and Paul Kasmin galleries in New York and most recently had an exhibition of large-scale works on paper at the Sperone Gallery in Rome.

JOHN BARTH's most recent novel is *The Last Voyage of Somebody the Sailor*, published by Little, Brown in 1991.

Composer, poet and essayist JOHN CAGE died this summer just before his eightieth birthday. The poem presented on the final page of this issue is from his book: *X: Writings '79–'82* and is reprinted with the permission of Wesleyan University Press.

PAT CALIFIA is the author of a book of short stories, *Macho Sluts* (Alyson Publications, 1988). "Fix Me Up" is from a forthcoming collection, *Melting Point*.

TOM CLARK's most recent books are *Charles Olson: The Allegory of a Poet's Life* (Norton) and *Sleepwalker's Fate* (Black Sparrow).

Novelist, theologian, art and literary critic, editor and publisher, ARTHUR A. COHEN (1928–1986) was among the most important figures in American Jewish intellectual life in the last half of this century. The two essays published here have never before been printed.

PETER COLE is working on a book of translations from medieval Hebrew poetry. His book of poems, *Rift*, was published by Station Hill Press in 1989.

WILLIAM CORBETT's book on Philip Guston will appear from Zoland Books in the Fall of 1992. He is at work on the Faber guide to literary New England.

CID CORMAN is the author of many books of poems, essays and translation, including *Of* (Lapis Press, 1990). He lives in Kyoto, Japan.

MARTIN EARL teaches at the University of Coimbra, in Portugal.

BARBARA EINZIG lives in Manhattan. The title work of her book *Life Moves Outside* (Burning Deck) received a 1989 Pushcart Prize.

ELAINE EQUI's most recent book is *Surface Tension* from Coffee House Press. She lives in New York City.

FORREST GANDER's most recent books include *Eggplants and Lotus Root* (Burning Deck) and *Lynchburg* (forthcoming from University of Pittsburgh Press). He is also the editor of *Mouth to Mouth: Poems by 12 Contemporary Mexican Women* (Milkweed Editions).

ALEXANDER GELLEY, professor of comparative literature at the University of California, Irvine, is preparing a book-length selection of Novalis fragments. His translation of Novalis' "Pollen" was published in *New Literary History* 22 (1991). Gelley is also the author of *Narrative Crossings: Theory and Pragmatics of Prose Fiction* (Johns Hopkins University Press, 1987).

ELI GOTTLIEB's critical prose has appeared in a variety of journals, including *Elle* and the *Voice Literary Supplement*. He is currently working on a novel.

HENRY GREEN is the pen name of Henry Vincent Yorke (1905–1973). His novels, including *Living* (1929), *Party Going* (1939), *Loving* (1945), *Nothing* (1950) and *Doting* (1952), are all available in Penguin paperback editions. "Impenetrability" is taken from the forthcoming *Surviving: The Uncollected Writings of Henry Green*, to be published by Viking Press in February 1993.

BARBARA GUEST recently published *The Altos* in collaboration with the artist Richard Tuttle. Her new book, *Defensive Rapture*, will be published in January by Sun & Moon.

THOM GUNN's most recent book is *The Man With Night Sweats* (Farrar, Straus & Giroux).

FRIEDRICH HÖLDERLIN (1770–1843) was one of the first great modern poets of Europe. A new translation of his *Essays and Letters* is available from S.U.N.Y. Press.

FANNY HOWE's most recent books of poems are *Quietist* (O Books) and *The End* (Littoral Press). Her novel *Saving History* is due out this winter from Sun & Moon Press.

AARON JAY KERNIS is a composer living in New York City. Two CDs of his music will be released this fall: *Symphony in Waves* and *String Quartet (musica celestis)* from Argo/Decca, and three vocal works on CRI. He is currently composing works for the New York Philharmonic and the San Francisco Symphony.

EWA KURYLUK is a Polish writer, artist and art historian who settled in New York City and switched to English in 1982. Since then she has published *Salome and Judas in the Cave of Sex* (Northwestern University Press, 1987), *The Fabric of Memory* (Formations, 1987) and *Veronica and Her Cloth* (Basil Blackwell, 1991). "Conrad and Lowry in Mexico" is an excerpt from *Century 21*, her first novel, to be published by Dalkey Archive Press in December 1992.

JAMES LAUGHLIN's *Collected Poems* will be published by Moyer Bell in November. His novella, *Angelica*, is being published by Grenfell Press (New York).

PHILLIP LOPATE, a novelist, essayist and poet, is the author of *Bachelorhood, The Rug Merchant* and *Against Joie de Vivre*. He teaches at Bennington College.

CHRISTOPHER MIDDLETON, an English poet and translator, teaches German and comparative literature at the University of Texas, Austin. He is the author of *Selected Writings* (Carcanet and Grafton Paladin, 1989), *The Balcony Tree* and *Andalusian Poems* (Godine, 1992).

NOVALIS (Friedrich von Hardenberg, 1772–1801) was, together with Friedrich Schlegel, the most original practitioner of the "fragment," a term that denotes not merely incompletion but an authentic genre in the tradition of German Romanticism. He is also the author of the novel Heinrich von Ofterdingen and the cycle of poems *Hymnen an die Nacht*.

MICHAEL PALMER's most recent book is *Sun* (North Point Press, 1988). He is completing a new collection of poetry and has translated Emmanuel Hocquard's *Theory of Tables*, which is forthcoming from *o·blēk*.

ALEKSEI PARSHCHIKOV was born in 1954 and is one of the most influential poets of his generation in Russia. English translation of his work can be found in *Third Wave: The New Russian Poetry* (eds. Kent Johnson and Stephen M. Ashby, University of Michigan Press), and in a forthcoming volume from Avec Press.

JIM POWELL's collection of poems, *It Was Fever That Made The World*, is available from University of Chicago Press. Next year Farrar, Straus & Giroux will publish his translation, *Sappho: A Garland*.

JAMES PURDY's new book *Out With The Stars* has just been published by Peter Owen Ltd. in London. His book of plays published in English in the Netherlands is titled *In the Night of Time and Four Other Plays* (Polak and Van Gennep).

CARL RAKOSI is one of the Objectivists. His *Collected Poems* and *Collected Prose* were issued by the National Poetry Foundation, which later this year is bringing out *Carl Rakosi: Man and Poet*, edited by Michael Heller.

PETER READING is an English poet born in 1946. His latest books of poetry are *3 in 1* (which reprints three earlier collections) and *Evagatory*, both published by Chatto & Windus. This is his first appearance in print in this country.

DARLENE REDDAWAY is a graduate student in Slavic studies at Stanford. She will be co-editing a new magazine of Russian literature and cultural studies with Aleksei Parshchikov.

DAVID SHAPIRO has published many books of poetry and art criticism, most recently *House (Blown Apart)* (Overlook, 1988). A new collection of poems, *After a Lost Original*, is forthcoming.

RICHARD SIEBURTH is the editor of Ezra Pound's *Walking Tour in Southern France* (New Directions, Fall 1992). His translation of Hölderlin's *Hymns & Fragments* is available from Princeton University Press.

DENNIS SILK lives in Jerusalem. He has published three books of poems with Viking: *Punished Land* (1980), *Hold Fast* (1986) and *Catwalk and Overpass* (1992).

IAIN SINCLAIR's novel *Downriver*, published by Paladin in 1991, received the James Tait Black Memorial Prize and the Encore Award for the Best Second Novel of that year. An American edition will be brought out next year by Random House.

A selection of work from CHARLES STEIN's *theforestforthetrees* is in preparation from Station Hill Press.

ADAM THORPE was born in Paris in 1956, and brought up in India, Cameroon and England. "Friends: 1689" is excerpted from his forthcoming novel *Ulverton*, to be published in November by Farrar, Straus & Giroux.

MELISSA TOWNSEND is an artist and writer living in New York City. Her writing has appeared in *Central Park* and *Story Quarterly*.

LEWIS WARSH's most recent book is *A Free Man* (Sun & Moon, 1991). He is publisher of United Artists Books and editor of *The World*.

ELIOT WEINBERGER's essays are collected in *Works on Paper* and, most recently, *Outside Stories* (both New Directions). Among his translations are the *Collected Poems of Octavio Paz* (New Directions), Vicente Huidabro's *Altazor* (Graywolf) and Xavier Villaurrutia's *Nostalgia for Death* (Copper Canyon).

MARJORIE WELISH's most recent book of poems, *Casting Sequences*, will be published in Spring 1993 by the University of Georgia Press.

JOHN WIENERS' books include *The Hotel Wentley Poems* (1958), *Ace of Pentacles* (1964), *Asylum Poems* (1969) and *Behind the State Capitol* (1975). *Selected Poems* (1986) and *Cultural Affairs in Boston* (1988) are available from Black Sparrow Press.

Issues That Matter

CONJUNCTIONS: 14

THE NEW GOTHIC
with contributions from Kathy
Acker, John Edgar Wideman,
Peter Straub, Robert Coover,
Lynne Tillmann, Patrick
McGrath, William T. Vollmann,
Mary Caponegro, and others

THE POETRY ISSUE
with contributions from Susan
Howe, John Ashbery, Barbara
Einzig, Leslie Scalapino, Charles
Bernstein, Ronald Johnson,
Norma Cole, Michael Palmer,
and others

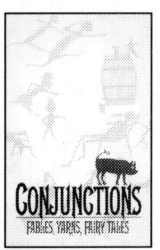

THE MUSIC ISSUE
with contributions from Albert
Goldman, Paul West, Barbara
Guest, Amiri Baraka, Quincy
Troupe, Lukas Foss, Seth
Morgan, Gerald Early, John
Abercrombie and David Starobin
interview

**FABLES, YARNS,
FAIRY TALES**
over 80 tales worldwide with
contributions from Rosario
Ferre, Can Xue, Norman Manea,
Grozdana Olujic, Kurt
Schwitters, Robert Antoni, Paola
Capriolo, and others

ED RUSCHA

"Anchor In Sand"
Two color lithograph
21" × 32"
edition 100
signed and numbered
1991

Anuszkiewicz • Christo • Chryssa • Clemente • Crash
d'Arcangelo • Paul Davis • deKooning • Dine
Jimmy Ernst • Janet Fish • Frankenthaler
Freilicher • Haring • Hockney • Indiana
Krushenick • Katz • Kelly • Kushner
Lewitt • Lindner • Lichtenstein • MacConnel
Marca-Relli • Marisol • Motherwell • Nevelson
Oldenburg • Rauschenberg • Rivers • Rosenquist
Ruscha • Salle • Saroyan • Shahn • Stamos
Steinberg • Sultan • Summers • Trova • Vicente
Warhol • Winters • Youngerman

Galleries and dealers contact Joan Krawczyk,
The Paris Review, 541 E. 72nd St., New York, NY 10021.

George Robert Minkoff, Inc.

RARE BOOKS

20th Century First Editions, Fine Press Books,
Letters, Manuscripts & Important Archival
Material Bought & Sold
Catalogues issued

Rowe Road, RFD, Box 147
Great Barrington, MA 02130
[413] 528 - 4575

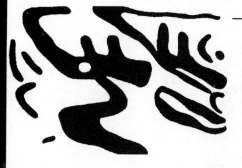

Lannan Literary Series

Some of the world's finest writers are profiled in these acclaimed videotapes. Each program features one writer reading before an audience and discussing the origins of his or her poetry, history, and writing process with an interviewer. The poets and writers in the series are:

Yehuda Amichai
Amiri Baraka
Kay Boyle
Ernesto Cardenal
Lucille Clifton
Robert Creeley
Victor Hernandez Cruz
Carolyn Forché
Carlos Fuentes

Allen Ginsberg
Louise Gluck
Joy Harjo
Larry Heinemann
Galway Kinnell
Philip Levine
W. S. Merwin
Czeslaw Milosz
Sharon Olds

Octavio Paz
Ishmael Reed
Sonia Sanchez
Gary Snyder
Andrei Voznesensky
Anne Waldman
Alice Walker
Richard Wilbur
Yevgeny Yevtushenko

Lannan

These hour-long videotapes (VHS) in the *Lannan Literary Series* can be leased for $15.00 or purchased for $29.95 through The Poetry Center/American Poetry Archives at San Francisco State University, 1600 Holloway Avenue, San Francisco, California 94132, (415) 338-1056.

NEW FICTION # LOST ROADS

by **Frank Stanford**
CONDITIONS UNCERTAIN AND LIKELY TO PASS AWAY $10.95
by **Sharon Doubiago**
EL NINO   (2nd printing) $9.95

NEW POETRY

by **Keith Waldrop**
THE OPPOSITE OF LETTING THE MIND WANDER
   Selected Poems and a Few Songs $8.95
by **Arthur Sze**
RIVER RIVER   (2nd printing) $7.95

POETRY FORTHCOMING

by **John Taggart**
STANDING WAVE $10.95
by **Donald Berger**
QUALITY HILL $9.95

WRITE OR CALL
SPD   1814 San Pablo Av   Berkeley, CA 94702 (510)549-3336
   LRP   PO Box 5848   Providence, Rhode Island 02903